National Dreams

National Dreams

The Remaking of Fairy Tales in Nineteenth-Century England

Jennifer Schacker

PENN

University of Pennsylvania Press
Philadelphia

10   9   8   7   6   5   4   3   2   1

Published by
University of Pennsylvania Press
Philadelphia, Pennsylvania 19104–4011

Library of Congress Cataloging-in-Publication Data

Schacker, Jennifer.
    National dreams : the remaking of fairy tales in nineteenth-century England / Jennifer Schacker.
        p.   cm.
    Includes bibliographical references and index.
    ISBN 0-8122-3697-1 (acid-free paper)
    1. Fairy tales—England—History and criticism. 2. Fantasy fiction, English—History and criti-
cism. 3. Children's stories, English—History and criticism. 4. Popular literature—England—History
and criticism. 5. Books and reading—England—History—19th century. 6. English fiction—19th
century—History and criticism. I. Title.
PR868.F27 S33 2003
398.2'0942'09034—dc21

                                                                                    2002032345

Contents

Chapter 1
Introduction

> *There exists, at present, a very large and increasing class of readers, for whom the scattered fragments of olden time, as preserved in popular and traditionary tales, possess a powerful attraction. The taste for this species of literature has particularly manifested itself of late; the stories which had gone out of fashion during the prevalence of the prudery and artificial taste of the last century, began, at its close, to re-assert every where their ancient empire over the mind.[1]*
>
> —Edgar Taylor, 1821

A large readership still exists for what were once known as "popular and traditionary tales"—what we might today call fairy tales, folktales, wonder tales, or *Märchen*. From the early Victorian period to the present, written versions of such tales have been mainstays of popular and children's literature. Celebrated as imaginatively liberating, psychologically therapeutic, or as windows onto particular cultures, fairy tales are generally embraced as products of something larger than an individual consciousness, older than the medium—writing—in which we experience the stories. But we have inherited more than a taste for "popular tales" from our nineteenth-century predecessors: We have also inherited a set of ideologically charged textual practices and interpretive frameworks that reveal as much about Victorian literary culture as they do about oral folk cultures.

National Dreams is about the emergence of the popular tale collection as a form of popular reading material in England, during a crucial period: the 1820s through the 1850s. Specifically, this study addresses the resonance of four representative collections as literature for children and common readers—what was, in Victorian parlance, referred to as "class literature."[2] The wondrous stories found in the popular tale collections from this period certainly have inherent imaginative appeal, which has contributed to their readability and ongoing popularity. But my objective here is to uncover the allure of the larger stories of cross-cultural encounter—from field collection and translation, to reading itself—in which these books were embedded and which shaped their contents.

The works I study in detail—Edgar Taylor's *German Popular Stories* (1823), T. Crofton Croker's *Fairy Legends and Traditions of the South of Ireland* (1825), Edward Lane's *Arabian Nights* (1839–41), and George Webbe Dasent's *Popular Tales from the Norse* (1857)—unified a diverse and rapidly expanding readership in their enjoyment of imported tales. As translators, editors, or tale collectors, Taylor, Croker, Lane, and Dasent developed strategies for rendering imported narrative traditions readable, interpretable, entertaining and, most of all, relevant to the interests of their audience. The reading of popular tales—transcribed, translated, transnationalized—emerged as a form of cultural and historical adventure, a space in which to encounter and then reflect upon national identities and differences.

At the same time that "Folk-lore" was emerging as a distinct cognitive category, a subject of widespread interest, and a scholarly pursuit, publishers' conceptions of the English reading public were shifting to embrace an increasing number of literate working- and middle-class consumers. The commodification and objectification of folklore forms as reading material offered a privileged perspective to English readers of various classes and ages. The interpretive frameworks developed for imported tale collections and the very act of reading such material marked a transformation of popular literary culture, asserting geographic, mental, and cultural distance between English readers and the bearers of the narrative traditions about which they read. As traditional culture was made a textualized spectacle available in relatively affordable editions, a form of bourgeois subjectivity became the birthright of every English person—or at least every literate English person.

The roots of folklore study have generally been traced to the quest for national identity and cultural purity that began in the late eighteenth century, as nationalist movements, particularly in Europe, were fueled by the " 'discovery' of popular culture" by "intellectuals . . . from the upper classes."[3] The model for this endeavor was the work of Jacob and Wilhelm Grimm:[4] Motivated by German romantic nationalism, the brothers sought a narrative tradition untouched by foreign influence, representative of German *Volksgeist*. The Grimms' *Kinder- und Hausmärchen* [Children's and Household Tales], first published in 1812, was warmly received outside Germany, where it introduced a new research methodology and the powerful rhetoric of field-based authenticity.[5] Nationalistically motivated folklore enthusiasts in

Norway, Switzerland, Russia, and many other European nations followed the Grimms' lead, creating tale collections modeled after the *Kinder- und Hausmärchen*.[6]

The efforts of the Grimms and their followers to locate, record, and publish nationally distinctive *Märchen* within their respective homelands were only partially mirrored in England. The 1813 publication of John Brand's *Observations on Popular Antiquities*, edited by Henry Ellis, represents one strand of English antiquarianism, focused not on narratives but on customary practices thought to have their roots in pre-Christian ritual and belief. From the publication of Thomas Percy's *Reliques of Early English Poetry* in 1765 to Harvard professor Francis James Child's mammoth collection of *English and Scottish Popular Ballads*, published between 1882 and 1898, the ballad took center stage in English folklore studies. But until folk music collectors like Cecil Sharpe and Ralph Vaughan-Williams applied fieldwork techniques to the traditions of the English countryside in the 1890s, it had been assumed that England had no traditional music. Regional collections of tales were made in the 1860s—such as Robert Hunt's two-volume collection *Popular Romances from the West of England* (1865), or William Henderson's *Notes on the Folk-Lore of the Northern Counties of England and the Borders* (1866)—but none was embraced as an index of Englishness.

It is now accepted as truth that "the English have never used folklore to assert their patriotic identity,"[7] and they certainly did not do so in the way many of their European neighbors did. The search within national borders for narrative, material, or musical traditions that can be celebrated as characteristic and distinctive has played a large part in folklore's history; studies of the nationalist uses and abuses of folklore in modern Greece, Finland, and Nazi Germany[8] demonstrate the durability of the connection between national folklore and nation-building. But the construction of "identity" is always a fundamentally contrastive process. For instance, in Germany the nationalistic turn to vernacular language and narrative was accompanied by scholarly attention to classical and "oriental" texts and the advocacy of what Antoine Berman has coined a "foreignizing" translation style.[9] National identities are formed through the delineation of boundaries (geographical, cultural, social, moral), as Peter Sahlins, Linda Colley, and others have demonstrated. This process is more often the result of encounter with or reaction to "an obviously alien 'Them' " than it is the product of "cultural consensus at home."[10] Folklore books, specifically collections of popular tales, provided many such encounters.

Nationalistically motivated folklore research has, from very early on, yielded some unexpected results. The traditions documented by the participants in the philological revolution of the late eighteenth and early nineteenth centuries served as the bases for published works that often crossed the boundaries of class, language, and nation. The nationalizing and "internationalizing" of folklore, as Richard Bauman suggests, often occurred side by side.[11] The development of Folklore as a written discourse was shaped by the need for, and then sustained by the existence of, a sufficiently large audience. In the early nineteenth century, England emerged as the center of folklore publishing.

From the 1820s onward, dozens of folklore books were issued by London publishers, making available to English readers the epics, ballads, folksongs, myths, legends, and other "traditionary tales" that were being collected, transcribed, published, and translated by these new classes of scholars. The vast majority of these publications were intended for an audience of nonspecialists and were imported: selective translations of books published abroad or, especially later in the century, collections made by those English people who "governed colonies, planted missions, and travelled the globe, diligently [amassing] folk traditions and customs."[12] The publishing houses involved in the burgeoning enterprise of folklore publication were not limited to those, like Alfred Nutt, which were willing to take a loss on such endeavors.[13] They also included Charles Baldwyn, John Murray, and Charles Knight, for whom the folklore book, frequently illustrated, proved immensely profitable.

As reading material for an emergent mass audience, these imported collections took on new, *trans*national resonance: transnational not because the national frame of reference had been transcended or surpassed but because the books' status as displaced, representative now of both foreign orality and domestic literacy, gave them a new depth of meaning. Like other forms of print culture, such as novels, periodicals, and travel narratives, folklore books served to consolidate and define the English "reading public"[14] as it addressed them. If, as Benedict Anderson has suggested, "the development of print-as-commodity is the key to the generation of wholly new ideas of simultaneity" fundamental to the imagining of a national community,[15] the fact of mass literacy takes on a heightened resonance when the subject of reading is oral tradition.

One long-term effect of the widespread fame of the Grimms' *Kinder- und Hausmärchen* was that *Märchen*—understood in England as the popular tale, nursery tale, or fairy tale—eventually emerged as a privileged genre, sought in cultural contexts as diverse as those of the Ukraine, South Africa, and Japan.[16] Compared with contemporary genre definitions, the nineteenth-century category of popular tale was remarkably elastic: Although all four works considered in the following chapters were once regarded as of a kind, they represent not only *Märchen* (orally told tales framed as fiction/fantasy) but also legends (orally told tales framed as fact) and a medieval literary tradition (in which oral narration is a literary device). While the particularities of cultural origin and indexicality were of the utmost concern to English translators, editors, reviewers, and other commentators, as we will see, this generic diversity was elided and erased. But English writers developed their own very powerful and enduring "tales," as they narrativized the social, cultural, and economic transformations that seemed to separate modern England from the "peasant" cultures of other nations—and from its own past, constructed as preindustrial and oral.

By the early nineteenth century, mass literacy and technological change had been cast as the enemies of English oral tradition for over one hundred years. For instance, in the late seventeenth century, John Aubrey paid homage to popular traditions lost with specific reference to the invention of the printing press:

Before Printing, Old-wives tales were ingeniose: and since Printing came into fashion, till a little before the civil-Warres, the ordinary sort of People were not taught to read: now-a-dayes Bookes are common, and most of the poor people understand letters: and the many good Bookes, and variety of Turnes of Affaires, have put all the old Fables out of dores: and the divine art of Printing, and Gunpowder have frighted away Robin-good-fellow and the Fayries.[17]

While the printing press was undoubtedly an "agent of change,"[18] what is remarkable is that subsequent social and technological developments were credited with similar effects.

Thus, a century later, Francis Grose reflected that "formerly, in countries remote from the metropolis, or which had no immediate intercourse with it, and made every ploughman and thresher a politician and freethinker, ghosts, fairies, and witches, with bloody murders, committed by tinkers, formed a principal part of rural conversation."[19] For Grose, the threats to traditional English culture lay in mass transportation, mass publishing, and urban life. The historiography of Folklore in England, which extends back to the antiquarianism of figures like Aubrey and Grose, is punctuated by eulogies to English narrative traditions, with literacy and technology repeatedly cast as folklore's executioners.

In his 1957 study of the English common reader, Richard D. Altick echoes his antiquarian predecessors, casting industrialization as tradition's nemesis and reading as the usurper of customary forms of entertainment. "Under the conditions of industrial life," he writes,

the ability to read was acquiring an importance it had never had before. The popular cultural tradition, which had brought amusement and emotional outlets to previous generations, had largely been erased. . . . the regimentation of industrial society, with its consequent crushing of individuality, made it imperative that the English millions should have some new way of escape and relaxation.[20]

Altick makes no mention of folklore books, which would seem to negotiate these dramatic socioeconomic and cultural changes by incorporating "popular tradition" into new forms of amusement. Not only were popular publications, in general, regarded as appropriate substitutes for oral traditional forms of entertainment, but English common readers were offered collections of foreign oral traditions to include in their home libraries.

The long-standing association of orality and literacy with particular social formations and belief systems can still be seen at work in late twentieth-century scholarship, despite critiques of such dualities. Ruth Finnegan has highlighted the resilience of the assumptions that underlie the "dichotomizing framework" in which orality and literacy are approached as "two opposing types":

the one, the characteristic setting for oral tradition, typified as small-scale and face to face, rural and non-industrial, communal and conformist rather than individualist, and dominated by ascribed kinship, religion and revered traditions; the other—the locale for written transmission—typically industrial, urban and bureaucratic, characterized by a respect for rationality, individual achievement and impersonal norms, heterogeneous and secular.[21]

As Finnegan suggests, the power of such a framework resides not only in the romantic appeal of the oral Other but also in its apparent correspondence with "the actual course of historical development" in early modern Europe[22]—all this despite the fact that ethnographic investigation has revealed that orality and literacy are not autonomous domains.[23]

While oral traditions were considered extinct, or in the process of disappearing from England, the new field-based tale collections from abroad were demonstrating that oral traditions still thrived elsewhere. These translations of story texts across cultures were thus also understood as translations across time, useful to understanding the domestic past as well as the foreign present. If history could be approached as a "cross-cultural discourse,"[24] literary and cultural differences could be theorized in progressive and chronological terms. Within an emergent evolutionary framework—which would come to shape midcentury thought about language, culture, and race—modern-day "savages," "primitives," or peasants offered glimpses into the prehistory of "civilization."[25] In the formative decades of the early nineteenth century, the terms "popular antiquities" and "popular literature"—not replaced by "Folk-Lore" until 1846—reflected the classically evolutionary bent of reigning literary historical models and situated traditional narratives as junior forms of written literature.

And for the curious reader of the early nineteenth century, available texts would have supported such characterizations. Many of the literary fairy tales of the previous century, especially those imported from France, had been progressively infantilized, stripped of subtext and innuendo until they indeed appeared to be the "artificial" and empty extravagances of Edgar Taylor's description. In late seventeenth-century France, the literary fairy tale had been fashionable but marginalized, and it was precisely this marginal status that gave it its power. For a generation of French aristocrats, mostly women, the *conte de fées* served as a space in which to refine rhetorical skills and in which subversive ideas and indirect criticisms of Louis XIV could be safely articulated. The genre was associated with the peasantry, servants, women, children. These associations were encouraged in illustration, as the "source" of these tales of times past was imagined and depicted as an elderly peasant woman,[26] far removed from concerns of the court.

In English translation, the original tales of Mme. d'Aulnoy—great favorites from the early eighteenth century to the late nineteenth century, both in chapbook form and onstage—lost their status as encoded statements about education, justice, courtship, marriage, and so forth, and were reframed as simply fanciful and romantic. Even d'Aulnoy's authorship was erased, as the tales became commonly known as the tales of "Mother Bunch." While Charles Perrault's renditions of traditional tales were first translated in their entirety in 1729, the rhyming morals he had appended to each story—which warned readers against sweet-talking, lascivious suitors (Little Red Riding Hood), addressed the balance of power in a marriage (Blue Beard), or highlighted the importance of mentorship to a debutante (Cinderella)—were rarely included in English versions thereafter. What was left? Perrault's relatively straightforward, deceptively childlike renditions in the style this prominent aristocrat called *au bas peuple*, now known as the tales of "Mother Goose."

As literacy rates among the English working classes increased in the late eighteenth and early nineteenth centuries, the content of accessible reading material was a matter of great concern.[27] When compared with the popularity of political pamphlets, epitomized by the unprecedented sales of cheap editions of Thomas Paine's *Rights of Man* (1791–92),[28] chapbook versions of traditional narratives—especially when emptied of storytellers' potentially subversive messages—posed little threat to existing power structures.[29]

In the early nineteenth century, as chapbooks lost favor among common readers, traditional narratives were mourned once again. For instance, from the vantage point of 1819, Francis Cohen reflected:

Scarcely any of the *chap books* which were formerly sold to the country people at fairs and markets have been able to maintain their ancient popularity; and we have almost witnessed the extinction of this branch of our national literature. Spruce modern novels, and degenerate modern Gothic romances, romances only in name, have expelled the ancient "histories" even from their last retreats.[30]

Like Aubrey and Grose, Cohen links the status of the traditional tale to the reading habits of common people. Moreover, as suggested by Aubrey's pairing of printing and gunpowder and Grose's image of the politicized ploughman, the social change associated with mass literacy inspired ambivalence; George Craik was later to remind his working-class readers, "Knowledge is power."[31]

One of the earliest systematic observers of folktale publication in England, Charlotte Yonge, reflected in 1869 that "the first real good fairy book that had found its way to England since 'Puss in Boots' and Co."—that is, since the fairy tales of d'Aulnoy and Perrault entered the English literary marketplace—was none other than Edgar Taylor's translation of the Grimms' fairy tales, entitled *German Popular Stories* (1823).[32] The lineage Yonge traces from this now conventional starting point is striking and corresponds with the path my own project takes. Next in Yonge's history is T. Crofton Croker's *Fairy Legends and Traditions of the South of Ireland* (1825), which "though not professedly intended for children, were soon heartily loved," and George Webbe Dasent's *Popular Tales from the Norse* (1858), which Yonge deemed "nearly as good, in its way, as 'German Popular Tales,' and infinitely better in style."[33] Into this heritage I have placed Edward Lane's annotated and illustrated translation of the *Arabian Nights*, which was similarly positioned in contrast to eighteenth-century fairy-tale books and was shaped by the commercial and philanthropic agendas of the mass publishing movement.

The international popularity of the Grimms' *Kinder- und Hausmärchen* can be understood as a transformative phenomenon in children's literature or linked to the birth of serious folklore research, but the generic continuity

of *German Popular Stories*, as a form of publication, with the works of Croker, Lane, and Dasent, so readily apparent in 1869, has generally eluded modern observers. Some recent accounts of the history of English literature for
children identify Croker's *Fairy Legends* as next in a line that would seem to
lead directly to the literary fairy tales of Hans Christian Andersen and the
"golden age" of imaginative children's literature in the late nineteenth and
early twentieth centuries.[34] Addressing the "assumed connection between
children and fairy tales" more directly than most, Jacqueline Rose has recognized the "problematic . . . link between the interest in the fairy tale and a
preoccupation with cultural infancy and national heritage,"[35] although she
takes a very late example, Andrew Lang's *Blue Fairy Book* (1899), to demonstrate the point. The cross-cultural processes by which international folktale
collections first became canonical English literature for children are frequently overlooked; the transformation of English children's literature was
not, after all, enacted by the fairies and elves.

Since the 1980s, there has been a move to historicize the fairy tale and to
reveal the ideological underpinnings of particular texts. The work of Cristina
Bacchilega, Ruth Bottigheimer, Maria Tatar, Marina Warner, Jack Zipes, and
others has exploded assumptions about the genre's timelessness and uni-
versality, situating it squarely within a politics of culture.[36] In recent years,
there has been increasing attention to folklore in the transnational sphere,
both past and present—problematizing issues of cultural ownership and cultural authenticity, and foregrounding the processes of translation and "cultural
adaptation."[37] *National Dreams* combines and extends these lines of inquiry,
focusing on the translation of narrative traditions across semiotic, linguistic,
cultural, and national boundaries, which occurred with increasing frequency
and commercial success in nineteenth-century England.

Richard Dorson's *British Folklorists* (1968) has stood for more than
thirty years as the authoritative history of Victorian folkloristics across the
disciplines. As chair of the newly founded Folklore Institute at Indiana University, Dorson's primary interest was the professionalization of Folklore,
demonstrating that Folklore was, had been, and could continue to be a field
of serious intellectual inquiry. Despite Dorson's stated interest in "the stir-
ring debates . . . that had once kept all Victorian England in thrall,"[38] the focus of his work did not extend to the general interest in folklore topics that
characterized the nineteenth century nor to the more popular forms of folkloristic publication. Although Taylor, Croker, Lane, and Dasent earn mention
in *The British Folklorists*, Dorson was most enthusiastic about midcentury
figures like John Francis Campbell, an independently wealthy amateur

whose *Popular Tales of the West Highlands, Orally Collected* (1860) is strikingly modern. Campbell assembled a team of fieldworkers and instructed them to transcribe stories word for word and to record information about the narrator (age, occupation, residence, and so forth). The result was a collection of highly idiosyncratic, relatively inaccessible texts—an impressive work of scholarship that likely earned its author and publisher very little money. *Popular Tales of the West Highlands* stands in marked contrast to the book that apparently inspired it, Dasent's *Popular Tales from the Norse*, and, in fact, to all other tale collections of the century.[39]

The state of academic folklore study is rather different in 2003 from what it was in 1968. The issue is no longer legitimization of the discipline through disavowal of its intersection with popular discourses (what was, for Dorson, "fakelore").[40] Over the past ten years, increasing attention has been paid to the processes by which the academic has been divorced from the popular and applied uses of folklore, to critical reflection on folklorists' "construction of the dominant's quintessential 'other,' " and to the future of a discipline now decentered.[41] It is a particularly interesting moment at which to examine the roots of folklore discourse in the realm of popular print culture. This issue acquires symbolic depth in early to mid-nineteenth-century England: Interest in such matters as "manners and customs" and "national character" was expressed in popular publications, which were in and of themselves considered markers of English modernity.[42]

That folklore study is entrenched in the very processes posited as tradition's enemies—writing, publication, transnationalization—is an oft-noted paradox.[43] Nonetheless, the lives of the symbolic constructions of folklorists past and present as material, textual objects—designed to cross geographical, temporal, social, and cultural boundaries—have yet to be charted. Scholars have directed their attention toward dimensions of folklore's "textuality" and the intersemiotic transformation of folklore from the performed to the printed before this,[44] but far less attention has been paid to the role of popular printed texts in the diffusion of and theories about folklore.

From the standpoint of the interdisciplinary field of inquiry known as the history of books, Robert Darnton has delineated a "communications circuit" that includes authors, publishers, printers, shippers, booksellers, and readers. In its strivings for a socially situated understanding of particular forms of communication, Darnton's communications circuit extends from a similar impulse as performance-oriented approaches to folklore. As a working model for the contextualization of books as cultural artifacts, this circuit need not be regarded mechanistically but as a dynamic exchange that shapes the form books take and the ways they are used and rendered meaningful to various readers.[45] In the chapters that follow, I have highlighted ways in which popular tale collections are shaped by the communicative circuits in which they were situated, adapting Darnton's model to include informants (oral storytellers) and tale collectors, where applicable.

The folklore book emerges as a performance of sorts, shaped by emergent notions of the genre and its audiences, negotiated by a number of players—from storytellers to translators to illustrators to publishers to readers and reviewers—and responsive to its context of reception. During this formative period in the history of folklore, as a discourse and as a form of reading material, the dynamic exchange between informants, collectors, translators, editors, publishers, and readers was especially important in establishing how popular tales were to be published, for whom, and why.

Like much of the popular publishing of the period, these folktale collections were framed not as mollifying trifles but as both entertaining and instructive. The objectives of amusement and instruction are often regarded—through our contemporary lens—as a dichotomy and one that is paralleled by child versus adult. Alan Richardson has pointed out that placing these categories in opposition to one another may serve to obfuscate the implicit mores and political motivations of "entertaining" forms and the pleasurable aspects of "improving" ones.[46] As popular literacy and mass publishing movements make clear, the two categories could be conceived of as not only compatible but also complementary.

The particular challenge facing Taylor, Croker, Lane, and Dasent was how to represent imported narrative traditions on paper—a problem of defining and then maintaining cultural and textual accuracy—and how to render those representations readable and meaningful. On the one hand, foreign popular tales had to survive semiotic, linguistic, and cultural translation and remain accessible to general readers. On the other hand, each of the writers considered in the following chapters seems to have felt compelled to address the "usefulness" of his work to English readers. Most often, popular tales were cast as sources of insight to the national character of their respective places of origin, drawing on the rhetoric and ideology of Romantic nationalism, social evolutionism, and comparative philology. These "national dreams," to borrow Dasent's evocative phraseology, were regarded as offering insight to foreign minds, hearts, and history. This orientation toward cultural indexicality shaped not only arguments made about the tales' meaning and significance but also choices made in the formal and stylistic presentation of the tales—from the selection and editing of stories, to the representation of narrative voice.

The following case studies aim at both close attention to text—written and sometimes pictorial—and exploration of the context in which the tale collections were created, published, and read. From a twentieth-first-century standpoint these writers can appear naive, even foolish in their attempts to represent complex tale traditions as neatly segregated, stylistically homogeneous narrative units, sometimes featuring such English-sounding heroes as Tom or Boots, making sweeping cultural generalizations in their editorial commentaries, digressing horrendously in annotation. Close attention to the various prefaces, introductory essays, popular tales, annotations, and illustrations of the books themselves reveals how contextual factors ramify on the page; it also illuminates the imaginative and intellectual appeal of traditional and editorial narratives. As popular reading material for an expanding audience, tale collections offered opportunities for reflection on the oral Other, but also on the modern self, on the transformation of popular culture, on the nature of "Englishness" in the midst of rapid social, cultural, and technological change.

Popular English editions of foreign popular tales contain a form of reflexivity, of modernity constructing and reflecting on itself in print while presenting and representing oral narratives.[47] As we watch these writers experiment with modes of textual presentation and interpretive frameworks, we can catch glimpses of the images they drew of themselves and of their projected readership. Against a background of orality, superstition, and rustic simplicity emerges a portrait of modern, literate, cosmopolitan Englishness. This portrait is as imaginative, as powerful, and as enticing as any fairy tale.

The Household Tales in the Household Library: Edgar Taylor's German Popular Stories

In rhetoric that is nothing short of revolutionary, Grimms' fairy tales have been described as a "landmark" both in writing and illustration for children,[1] ending "the fairy tale war" in England and marking the moment when fairy tales "emerged unassailable" as reading for children,[2] ushering "a new era of imagination into English juvenile literature,"[3] acting as "a challenge to the anti–fairy tale movement in Britain," or even instigating "the revolt of the fairies and elves."[4] In fact, such descriptions refer not to Jacob and Wilhelm Grimm's own *Kinder- und Hausmärchen* [Children's and Household Tales] but to the first English version of their work: *German Popular Stories*, translated, edited, and adapted by Edgar Taylor and illustrated by George Cruikshank.

By the time this little volume appeared in 1823, English readers with established amateur interest in "popular tales" were aware of the Grimms' research in Germany; those who read German were likely to have read the Grimms' *Kinder- und Hausmärchen*, in either its first edition (1812–14) or the second (1819). For the majority of English readers, however, publisher Charles Baldwyn's *German Popular Stories* was an introduction to what would come to be known as "Grimms' fairy tales."

Jacob and Wilhelm Grimm had hoped that the tales they collected in the early nineteenth century, first published in 1812 as *Kinder- und Hausmärchen*, would have some popular appeal; they frequently had this end in mind as they experimented with content and style in successive editions of the collection, as we will see. But it is Taylor and Cruikshank's *German Popular Stories* that fully transformed the tales into a popular and commercially viable form of reading material—influencing the publishing history of the Grimms' tales in German, their legacy as "classics" of international children's literature, and the genre of the popular tale collection.

German Popular Stories, translated from the Kinder und Haus-Marchen [*sic*] *Collected by M.M. Grimm, from Oral Tradition* is a collection of thirty-one tales that begins with a short preface and concludes with twenty-one pages of notes, commenting on characters, motifs, literary and folkloristic parallels, and the process of translation. In both word and picture, *German Popular Stories* offered the curious reader of the early 1820s odd and other-worldly occurrences situated in a pleasant, almost pastoral locale—as much in harmony with English romanticizations of the preindustrial past as with romantic accounts of European peasant life.

Taylor was attracted to the tales for their imaginative appeal "as works of fiction," but he also assigned them a "literary value as bearing on ancient mythos and superstition,"[5] linking the tales to English social and literary histories and echoing the German philological underpinnings of the Grimms' work. To a certain degree, *German Popular Stories* adopted both the analytic framework and the general format of the *Kinder- und Hausmärchen*—a collection of discrete, titled, cohesive narrative units with claims to oral traditional authenticity, sandwiched by critical writings that feature a comparativist perspective. Even Taylor's most extreme revisions, as exemplified by the second edition of *German Popular Stories*, known as *Gammer Grethel*, drew creative inspiration from the scholarly processes of field encounter, transcription, and analysis to which it is often assumed Taylor was insensitive.

Like much art and literature of the period, this first English treatment of Grimms' fairy tales was shaped by the early nineteenth-century impulse to visualize and artistically represent the "vulgar" within a "decorous aesthetic."[6] With a focus on humor, justice, and romance, this little book encapsulates the themes and worldview that have since come to be associated with the genre of the fairy tale. Indeed, no one has done more to shape contemporary conceptions of the fairy tale—its content, tone, function, origin, and intended audience—than English solicitor and amateur folklorist Edgar Taylor, primary author of *German Popular Stories*.

Taylor was born in Norfolk in 1793, studied Classics, and was fluent in German, Italian, Spanish, and French. He moved to London in 1814 and opened what was to be a successful law practice.[7] Taylor's interest in and reflections on the subject of "popular and traditionary literature" were first expressed in a series of articles in *New Monthly Magazine and Literary Journal* (1821–22).[8] On June 6, 1823, Jacob and Wilhelm Grimm received a letter from this young English lawyer, introducing himself and an enclosed manuscript:

Not knowing the precise address of either of you I trust the accompanying packet to a friendly hand hoping it may reach you in safety.

It contains a copy of a little work consisting of translations (made by my friend Mr. Jardine and myself) from your volumes of *Kinder und Hausmärchen,* and we beg your acceptance of it as a small tribute of gratitude for the information and amusement afforded us by your entertaining work as well as by your valuable productions.[9]

Edgar Taylor's most enduring legacy is not his legal writing, his annotated collection of German lyric poetry, *Lays of the Minnesingers . . . with Historical and Critical Notices* (1825), nor his edition of the New Testament (1840),[10] but the work to which he refers in the letter above: begun in collaboration with David Jardine but published anonymously,[11] illustrated by popular caricaturist George Cruikshank.

While *German Popular Stories* has been personified and cast as a war hero of sorts, marking the triumph of fairy tales and nursery rhymes over the attacking moralists and didacts, Edgar Taylor himself has remained a marginalized (if not forgotten) figure in the histories of both children's literature and Folklore. To a certain extent, Taylor rendered himself "invisible" from the start by downplaying his own work, giving credit to the Grimms but not to himself on the title page, and employing a highly fluent and readable translation style in the stories themselves.

General readers and scholars have their reasons for keeping Taylor invisible. For the casual reader of Grimms' fairy tales, there may be little interest in bibliographic and editorial processes. In fact, to recognize the "power and privilege" of a translator or an editor (a figure generally overlooked, as Vincent Crapanzano has noted)[12] destabilizes the notion of "the true unadulterated fairy tale,"[13] which still holds sway in the minds of many general readers. For academic folklorists, on the other hand, Taylor represents the kind of hack scholarship from which we have made pains to disassociate ourselves. As early as the 1830s, scholars of the popular tale complained that Taylor's translation of the *Kinder- und Hausmärchen* was "too free," an insufficient resource for their comparative studies.[14] While it has become almost commonplace to trace the blossoming of modern folklore study, English and otherwise, to the initial publication of the two volumes of the Grimms' *KHM* in 1812 and 1814,[15] Taylor's role in the popularization of the tales and the genre is considered insignificant, best forgotten.

German Popular Stories was reprinted in 1824 and 1825. Taylor published a second volume in 1826 and a revised edition in 1839, and the work was reissued with impressive frequency in the decades to follow, both in England and the United States.[16] Thus, when in 1868 John Ruskin recalls with fondness "the good old book" of his childhood, he is invoking Taylor's widely available and well-known re/vision of the wonder tale, not that of the Grimms. Likewise, when readers of the early twenty-first century express affection for Grimms' fairy tales, many if not most are thinking of a playful, romantic, lighthearted canon of wonder tales far removed from the *Kinder- und Hausmärchen*. Taylor's treatment of these tales, accompanied by Cruikshank's now famous illustrations, injects the frequently dark and punitive world of the German *Märchen* with the levity and kindness that English readers presumably craved and continue to enjoy.[17]

Inspired by German Romantic nationalism, Jacob and Wilhelm Grimm had sought a nationally distinctive narrative tradition, untouched and unspoiled by foreign influence. Taylor reframed this tradition as a new source of amusement and pleasure for the English common reader, but also as a source of cultural and historical insight. The illustrated tale collection was presented simultaneously as a key to English people's understanding of German national character and a key to readers' understandings of England's own history—reflecting a picturesque vision of England's preindustrial, peasant past, which held considerable sway over the English imagination. The traces the tales retained of their journey from the German spoken word to the English printed word were framed as indicators of the foreignness of the source culture, as well as indices of England's own social, cultural, and literary evolution. Imported, displaced, the power of the nationally distinctive German *Märchen* now resided in their *trans*national status.

Visions of the Past

As Jacob and Wilhelm Grimm began to amass a collection of folktales in the early years of the nineteenth century, they grew excited about the "rich and delightful book" their researches might produce, and Jacob expressed his hope that it might "make up for the injustice these tales have suffered by being overlooked for so long."[18] Even before the resulting collection had been translated, it was received warmly in England. In both national contexts, German *Märchen* were regarded as not only entertaining but also instructive, offering ideologically charged forms of historical insight.

At first glance, early Victorian interest in the Grimms' work appears to be little more than a manifestation of antiquarian curiosity. Amid reflections about the transformation of nursery and popular reading, united under the aegis of "class literature,"[19] and calls for reexamination of the significance of these "humble" forms, English reviewers alternately deemed the Grimms' German texts "the most important addition to nursery literature" of the age and exemplary documentation of oral narratives.[20] Francis Cohen, for example, contrasted the tales collected by the Grimms with similar ones available in print:

Under the title of "Kinder und Hausmärchen," [the Grimms] have published a collection of German popular stories, singular in its kind for extent and variety, and from which we have acquired much information. In this collection we recognize a host of English and French and Italian stories of the same genus and species, and extant in printed books; but the greater part of the German popular or nursery stories are stated by the editors to be traditionary, some local, others more widely known.[21]

The genre and tale types represented by the *Kinder- und Hausmärchen* may have been familiar to an international readership, but the novelty of a "traditionary" collection—a corpus of tales taken from oral tradition—was quickly embraced. True to such early assessments, the influence of the *KHM* extended beyond Germany's borders in the decades that followed, and the work inspired such figures as T. Crofton Croker, Peter Asbjørnsen and Jørgen Moe, and John Francis Campbell to collect folk narratives of their respective homelands.

Although the *KHM* drew international attention and acclaim, it originally reflected localized concerns. Inheriting a Herderian opposition between *Naturpoesie* and *Kunstpoesie*, the Grimms sought narrative traditions untouched by foreign influence, "suffused with the same purity that makes children appear so wondrous."[22] The brothers regarded *Märchen* as the remains of "the riches of German poetry from olden times," preserved by particular segments of society: peasants, women, and children. Spontaneously recited, unpolished, innocent, these tales were envisioned as growing wild in the cultural margins, the "places by the stove, the hearth in the kitchen, attic stairs."[23]

The degenerative model of Herderian romanticism that shaped the Grimms' thinking would seem to contrast with the evolutionary framework that dominated histories of English poetry: Where the Grimms saw *Märchen* as the vestiges of a golden age of German poetry, English scholars routinely cast "popular tales" as embryonic forms of literature, the "childhood of fiction."[24] Children and the masses could be seen as logical components of the audience for "traditionary literature" within either paradigm or in a blending of the two, which occurred more frequently than one might expect. "The mythology of one period," Cohen quotes Walter Scott, "would . . . appear to pass into the romance of the next century, and that into the nursery tale of the subsequent ages" (92), until the works of primitive genius become "the fitting source of pastime to the untutored peasant and the listening child" (93). In this odd but not unusual pairing of social evolution and literary devolution, "creations embodied by the vivid imagination of man in the childhood of his race" (94) were not simply curiosities to be pondered by idle armchair scholars. They were eventually to be cast as appropriate reading material for children and literate workers in the modern age.

Reflecting on the relevance of the *KHM* to English concerns, Cohen extended his assessment of the significance of the Grimms' collection from the domain of a strictly German literary history to a more broadly Teutonic one, embracing both Scotland and England. "Since the people of England and the Scottish Lowlands are undoubtedly offsets and grafts from the Teutonic stock," he writes, "it is probable that our popular fables also are chiefly of Teutonic origin." He continues,

These idle stories boast a higher antiquity than romances and poems of much greater pretensions. . . . even the knights of the romances of the Round Table in their present form are mere striplings when compared to the acquaintance of our early childhood, who troop along by the side of the go-cart and help to rock the cradle. Jack, commonly called the Giant Killer, and Thomas Thumb landed in England from the very same keels and warships which conveyed Hengist and Horsa, and Ebba the Saxon. (97)

The Grimms' researches, thus interpreted, imply a reordering of the English antiquarian's priorities, situating the newly imported *Märchen* at the center of English inquiry, and elevating the household tale—German and English—to a literary stature of greater historical significance than Arthurian romance.

Edgar Taylor found the Grimms' devolutionary theory to be "overstrained,"[25] and described the value of popular tales, particularly those of Germany, in more strictly evolutionary terms than had his contemporary, Francis Cohen. "No countries in Europe," Taylor wrote in 1821, "are so rich as the Teutonic tribes of Germany in characteristic records of the various stages of society and literature, from the first putting-forth of the bud of promise, to the full development of the luxuriant flower."[26] Among the nationally distinctive literary traditions of Germany are "the abundant stores of popular legends and traditions, which often preserve most curious illustrations of heathen mythology, and still more frequently exhibit it in a most incongruous combination with the Christian faith," and it is under this heading that Taylor places the Grimms' "beautiful collection of Nursery Literature" (148).

In the early 1820s, Taylor identified at least two modes of adult appreciation for German *Märchen*: "Though we have long left our nurseries," he writes, "we retain our best relish for these tales, and hardly know whether to admire most their interest as works of fiction, or their literary value as bearing on ancient mythos and superstition" (148). For Taylor, the matter is not simply one of alternate modes of appreciation but of hierarchically ordered ones:

The originality and simplicity of these tales recommend them strongly to our notice, but we are inclined to go further, and to assign to many of them a *higher* literary value, as almost the only records of ancient manners and opinions, and as furnishing very often important historic information. (151; emphasis added)

So while Taylor values the content of tales, he implies that form and style are also in some way related to their origins in an "ancient" way of life. Appreciating the tales as good stories, nicely told, becomes, in and of itself, a cross-cultural and historical exercise.

For Edgar Taylor, the German source of these household tales *was* significant, not because he believed the narratives reflected a literary history that was distinctively or uniquely German, as did the Grimms, but because he regarded the tales as particularly valuable evidence in a philological quest to trace social, cultural, and literary development. Taken together, Teutonic mythology, German "Nursery Literature," and medieval lyric poetry exhibit "a complete cyclus of ancient indigenous literature, singularly various and characteristic of the progress of a people through all its stages of civilization" (149).

In his preface to *German Popular Stories*, Taylor revisits some of his earlier statements as he asserts the value of the German tales to an intergenerational and international audience of readers. He explains that the translators "were first induced to compile this little work by the eager relish with which a few of the tales were received by the young friends to whom they were narrated." But they are not strictly for the young: Taylor suggests that the translated tale collection parallels established forms of English popular entertainment in terms of both content and audience. The reader is reminded that wonder tales are, "like the Christmas Pantomine, *ostensibly* brought forth to tickle the palette of the young, but are often received with as keen an appetite by those of graver years."[27]

Taylor establishes the collection as a source of pleasure for both children and adults, but is quick to note that "the amusement of the hour was not the translators' only object." He proposes that the tales are valuable "from a literary point of view, as affording a new proof of the wide and early diffusion of these gay creations of the imagination" (iv). They have specific relevance to an English readership:

The collection from which the following Tales are taken is one of great extent, obtained for the most part from the mouths of German peasants by the indefatigable exertions of John and William Grimm [*sic*], brothers in kindred and taste.—The result of their labours ought to be peculiarly interesting to English readers, inasmuch as many of their national tales are proved to be of the highest Northern antiquity, and common to parallel classes of society in countries whose populations have been long and widely disjoined. (v–vi)

In all of these statements, Taylor conceives of "literary value," and hence the value of the *KHM*, in historical terms. More specifically, Taylor's arguments are guided by a progressive, evolutionary model of social and literary history in which stages of civilization/social formations correspond with certain literary forms. Within such a paradigm, a work's "literary value" is measured in terms of its capacity to illuminate these evolutionary processes.

Taylor echoes Cohen's assertion that English and German popular tales stem from one source. In addition, Taylor suggests that the reading of *German Popular Stories* may offer English readers insight to their social and literary history that would be unavailable otherwise. In contrast to Germany, England would appear to provide little in the way of oral traditions to satisfy the burgeoning interests of readers and scholars. Taylor continues:

In England, the repeated changes in population and dynastics—the irruptions of conquering tribes, and the consequent adoption or amalgamation of foreign languages, traditions, and customs, have broken much of the continuity of its literature, and rendered its stores very incomplete, except in romance, which unfortunately was in all countries compounded of very similar materials, and is, therefore, little distinctive or characteristic of national peculiarities.[28]

As opposed to the vibrant *Märchen* traditions of Germany, Taylor argues, distinctively *English* oral literature is nonexistent. Of course, Taylor would be disingenuous if he suggested that his reader should regard this vision of England—as a nation long engaged in dynamic interaction with other peoples—as simply unfortunate. This self-image could quite easily be credited as the basis of England's increasing political and colonial power, and it could also serve as the basis for claims of critical authority. So while Taylor states that distinctive oral traditions evaporated in the face of war, trade, and emigration, his own words upon the page carry symbolic weight, indicating that in the absence of such folklore something else has taken its place: scholarship and the folklore book.

Deeply rooted in German Romantic Nationalism, the Grimms' vision of *Märchen* had invoked a number of dichotomies: local and foreign, natural and cultivated, oral and written, peasant and bourgeois, child and adult. Self-proclaimed saviors of a threatened literary heritage, the Grimms glorified the former terms in each of these pairings by mobilizing the latter: as educated, bourgeois, adult researchers, their researches were instrumental in introducing a broad-based readership to the German *Märchen* in written form. In the name of preservation, the Grimms were complicit in the processes they had identified as tradition's enemies. In fact, by the century's close, S. O. Addy would lament the "deluge of cheap literature [that] has fallen upon us since the days when the brothers Grimm made their famous German collection, and the memory, assisted by books, is apt to forget the unwritten lore."[29] This deluge was primarily a phenomenon of the nineteenth-century English publishing industry. But as Addy was aware, it can be traced to the appearance of the Grimms' *KHM* in Germany.

Audience and Form

Eighteenth-century antiquarian research and popular literature, including adaptations of literary fairy tales from Old Regime France, primed reading publics for the tale collections of the nineteenth century. This was as true in Germany as it was in England. As early as 1710, translations of Antoine Galland's *Contes Arabes*, the first European treatment of *Alf Layla wa Layla* [1001 Nights], began to appear in Germany; German versions of the literary fairy tales of Charles Perrault and Mme. d'Aulnoy were available by the 1760s; the use of fairy-tale themes and structures was rampant in German Romantic literature; and retellings of folktales specifically aimed at German children began to be published in the late eighteenth century.[30] If general interest in *Märchen* or "popular tales" was established in both England and Germany by 1812, the form the Grimms' research should take in print and the audience to which the material should principally be directed were, and remain, more contentious matters.

The Grimms were well aware of the various forms this developing market had produced, but they distinguished their own efforts with the emphatic claim that "no details have been added or embellished or changed" in their tales. "A collection of this kind," they wrote, "has never existed in Germany."[31] In fact, this is a very shaky foundation on which to build claims of distinctiveness: As twentieth-century scholars have documented, the Grimms' successive editions of the *KHM* were themselves the results of extensive rewritings, abridgments, and formal experimentation.[32] Nonetheless, such statements were central to the "romantic rhetoric of authenticity" employed so powerfully by the Grimms.[33] More than ever before, the concept of the (oral, folk) narrator signified in the written tale text, not as a literary author's adopted persona but as the "actual" and "authentic" source of the story. While the Grimms "freely admit their own editorial work,"[34] the power of *the idea* of the unmediated folk voice was undiminished, undeniable.

Attempts to categorize the *Kinder- und Hausmärchen* as either serious scholarship or light entertainment span the entire publishing history of the work, from 1812 to the present. The Grimms clearly regarded their researches as a serious endeavor, guided by "scholarly principles," which has led Maria Tatar to conclude that "they therefore implied that they were writing largely for academic colleagues."[35] Yet the romantic nationalist underpinnings of the *KHM* are expressed not only in the brothers' search for remains of a purely German literary heritage but also in their wish to make their collection available to a mass German readership—to establish a place for the *Hausmärchen* in the German household library. As the brothers searched for a publisher for the work in 1811, they expressed their hope that the proposed book would both contribute to scholarship and be found entertaining by a broader audience.[36]

In its initial published form, the *KHM* was "weighed down by a ponderous introduction and by extensive annotations."[37] But readers were *not* compelled to sift through pages of annotation and critical dissertation to locate the "small morsels of poetry."[38] The Grimms' critical writings were relegated to the introduction and appendix, and while they may have encumbered the holding of the book, they did not interfere with the reading of the tales.[39] In the preface to volume 2 of the first edition (1814), the Grimms address this matter directly and indicate that they anticipated a dual readership: "We have published variant forms, along with relevant notes, in the appendix; those who feel indifferent to such things will find it easier to skip over them than we would have found it to omit them; they belong to the book, since it is a contribution to the history of German folk poetry."[40] From very early on, the Grimms arranged their scholarly writings in such a way that they might

easily be *ignored*. In addition, and despite the Grimms' numerous claims regarding the oral authenticity of the tales, as printed matter the contents of
the *KHM* resemble literary fairy tales more than they do transcriptions of
field collection. Each of the 156 tales in the first edition is a titled, cohesive
narrative, readily decontextualizable for reading aloud.[41]

   Surprisingly for Jacob and Wilhelm, some of their colleagues wished to
see the scholarly ambitions of the project downgraded, the critical writing
further marginalized. The Grimms' friends August Wilhelm and Friedrich
Schlegel shared their interest in *Naturpoesie*, and yet seemed more willing
to acknowledge the value of the tale collection as entertainment than as
scholarship:

As far as *Ammenmärchen* [nursery tales] are concerned, we do not wish to underesti-
mate their value too much, but we believe that excellent qualities are just as rare in
this genre of literature as in all other ones. Every good nurse shall entertain children,
or at least calm them down and put them to sleep. If she manages to accomplish this
through her stories, we can't expect more of her. Yet to clean out the entire attic
stuffed with well-intended nonsense while insisting that every piece of junk be hon-
ored in the name of an age-old legend, this is indeed asking too much of an educated
person.[42]

While the Schlegels objected to the Grimms' particular content selections
as subject matter for educated readers, Clemens Brentano and Achim von
Arnim—the editors of the folksong collection *Des Knaben Wunderhorn* who
had encouraged the Grimms to collect *Märchen*[43]—were bothered by the
style and form of the *KHM*.

   Like the Schlegels, Brentano's disdain was articulated in gendered and
generational terms: the association of *Märchen* with children, nursemaids,
and old women—which provided rhetorical and creative inspiration to the
Grimms, Taylor, and many of their followers—is invoked here in dismissal of
the collection's value. Early in 1813, Brentano wrote to Arnim:

I bought Grimms' *Märchen* a few days ago. The preface contains fine words, and many
Märchen have been got together; but the whole gives me less pleasure than I expected.
I find the narration on account of its fidelity exceedingly negligent and slovenly, and
in many places for that reason very tiresome. . . . If the pious editors wanted to satisfy
themselves they should have preceded every story by a psychological biography of the
child or the old woman who at all events related it badly. . . . The learned notes are dis-
connected, and too much is assumed in the reader, which he neither knows nor can
learn from these notes. A dissertation on the *Märchen* in general, a physiology of the
Märchen, would have been more useful, if there had to be any learning.[44]

For his part, Arnim found the preface and the appendix of notes inappropriate to such a collection, suggesting that they should be published in a learned periodical rather than alongside the tales[45] and that the Grimms' youngest brother, Ludwig, should provide some illustrations.[46]

Friends and colleagues may have offered criticisms of the *KHM*, but there was one audience apparently undaunted by the supposed mediocrity of the specimens and the tomelike appearance of the book: children. Letters from Joseph von Görres indicate that his daughter loved the collection, as apparently did the Savigny children.[47] In fact, the dual appeal of the *KHM* was increasingly to be cast not in terms of scholars and general readers, nor instruction and pleasure, but in terms of adults and children; likewise, calls for the modification of the form, style, and content of the *KHM* were increasingly made on behalf of child readers.

Following the publication of the first volume of the collection, Jacob Grimm argued strongly against editing the *KHM* for children, suggesting that the limits of young readers' understandings provided them with sufficient protection.[48] The "aim of our collection," the Grimms write in the preface to volume 2, "was not just to serve the cause of the history of poetry: it was also our intention that the poetry living in it be effective, bring pleasure wherever it could, and that it therefore become a manual of manners."[49] The Grimms thus envisioned their renderings of the tales not only as documentary evidence of German literary heritage but also as exemplars of cultural norms and values—and sources of pleasure.

The Grimms seem to have resisted the dichotomization of entertainment and instruction, of literature for children and that for adults, but the pressures to amend the *KHM* remained. In the preface to the second edition of *KHM* (1819), the Grimms reiterated their views, refined their characterization of the *Märchen* as "innocent" and yet noted that "in this new edition, we have carefully eliminated every phrase not appropriate for children."[50] In the second edition, the tales were given without notes, which instead were published as a separate third volume (1822). Ludwig Grimm provided ornamental title pages and illustrations for the frontispieces. While Ludwig's contributions must have added to the visual appeal of the *KHM*, it is important to note that it was not the supernatural population of fairyland he depicted in the second edition but the Hessian storyteller, Dorothea Viehmann, from whom his brothers had collected a number of their tales.[51] To a certain extent, the criticisms of the collection had been heeded, and the romantic, imaginative appeal of the storyteller, the *Märchenfrau*, had been privileged over that of the story, the *Märchen*.

The fact was that the first edition of the *KHM* sold reasonably well, but it certainly was not a best-seller. Correspondence from the Grimms' publisher indicates that by the time the second edition was scheduled for release in 1819, 350 of the 1,000 copies of volume 2 of the first edition were still in stock.[52] The second edition fared no better: It took twenty years for the 1,500 copies to sell out.[53] In striking contrast, the English version of the Grimms' collection was turning an impressive profit.

The Grimms wanted recognition from the German intelligentsia, but they also hoped their work would prove successful. Unlike the Grimms, Edgar Taylor was not part of a literary circle, did not seek academic support for his project, and was not in financial straits. Taylor was a successful solicitor, educated but not an academic. There is no indication that Taylor and Jardine approached this project with anything but earnest amateur interest; their publisher, on the other hand, was in desperate need of commercial success.[54]

Taylor and Jardine met Charles Baldwyn through Richard Taylor, Edgar's cousin and Baldwyn's printer. Baldwyn himself was a former bookseller who had turned to publishing around 1821, when he took over the *Retrospective Review* and the *London Chronicle*. Henry Southern, editor of the *Retrospective Review*, was collecting humorous tales for possible publication by Baldwyn, and around this same time Taylor proposed the project of translating the Grimms' collection.

As Francis Cohen had noted in 1819, the Grimms' tales were "of the same genus and species" as "English and French and Italian stories . . . extant in printed books,"[55] and this similarity was not lost on Baldwyn. Chapbook versions of folk tales and the juvenile adaptations of tales from Perrault, d'Aulnoy, and the *Arabian Nights*, which had proliferated in the eighteenth century, were visually attractive. In 1823 Baldwyn hired George Cruikshank to illustrate Southern's *Points of Humour* as well as Taylor and Jardine's *German Popular Stories*. Initially priced at 12s., at the time that the price of new works of fiction had reached a high of 31s. 6d, visually appealing works like *German Popular Stories* hardly took the place of the chapbook, but were far more affordable than newly published novels.[56] Cruikshank's illustrations contributed greatly to the appeal of *German Popular Stories* and helped to establish Cruikshank as the foremost illustrator of his generation.

While these projects were under way, the publisher's professional and personal life was in a shambles. Baldwyn had been shaken by the death of his wife and brother during a single week in 1822, and complications in the settlement of the family estate placed Baldwyn near financial ruin.[57] By early

1824, Baldwyn's financial situation had improved somewhat, a second printing of *German Popular Stories* was scheduled,[58] and an inheritance was soon to be released to the publisher. Baldwyn died before the estate could be settled; his demise was attributed to exhaustion, melancholia, and insanity.[59] Unfortunately, Baldwyn saw little of *German Popular Stories'* tremendous commercial success: In all, the book was reported to have turned a profit of £15,000.[60]

Inspired by reports from England, Wilhelm Grimm proposed a different tactic to his publisher in 1824:

In London a translation of the *Kindermärchen* has appeared under the title of *German Popular Stories*. . . . It has found such a popular response that already now, after only three quarters of a year has passed since its publication, they are preparing a second edition of the work. Now I, too, wish we could bring out a *small German edition* which, like the English edition, would contain only a selection of stories in a *single volume*.[61]

In 1825, the 1,500 copies of the first "Small Edition" of the *Kinder- und Hausmärchen* were printed, more fancifully illustrated by Ludwig, at the low price of 1 Taler.[62] True to Wilhelm's suggestions, the Small Edition was a single volume of fifty tales, and it did improve on the sales records of the second volume of the first and second editions. Whether the Small Edition's average yearly sales of 187 copies constitutes "full-scale popular success" is highly questionable.[63] The true publishing success of the *KHM* in Germany occurred only in the 1890s and the twentieth century—long after the *international* popularity of Grimms' fairy tales had been established.[64] Nine additional printings of the Small Edition were published during the Grimms' lifetimes, but they never garnered profits comparable to the English treatment of the collection that had inspired them.

Mediation and Deviation

More than 150 years after the publication of *German Popular Stories*, English-language readers may now choose from several "complete" editions of Grimms' fairy tales—often strikingly dissimilar from one another in content and style—and innumerable literary, cinematic, and theatrical reworkings of individual tales.[65] Readers of more than one hundred other languages likewise have access to these narratives, but very few read anything close to a literal translation of the *Kinder- und Hausmärchen*. So while millions feel they "know" Grimms' fairy tales, relatively few experience an accurate translation of what is known as the "final version" of the *KHM* (1857).[66] Those who venture into the terrain of the Grimms' *earlier* editions—"Grimms' grimmest," as they were recently dubbed[67]—are often surprised or even shocked by what they find. How does one account for this phenomenon?

What we have come to know as Grimms' fairy tales are texts mediated by the brothers and their informants, as well as the various editors, translators, and publishers who almost always come between the late twentieth-century reader and the *KHM*, as they did for the average nineteenth-century English reader. To begin with, Wilhelm and Jacob Grimm adapted their renderings to meet standards of bourgeois propriety and contemporary reading tastes, producing successive—and markedly different—editions not only in 1819 but also in 1837, 1840, 1843, 1850, and 1857, as well as an independent volume of notes in 1856 and the first of many abridged editions in 1825.[68] The versions collected in both oral and epistolary form by the Grimms had themselves been shaped by relationship of teller (generally members of middle-class German families) and audience (Wilhelm and Jacob) to the projected originators of the narratives (the German peasantry). The degree to which the Grimms could lay claim to a uniquely German and orally collected corpus is itself the subject of debate.[69] Nevertheless, it is safe to say that the various English editions of the *KHM* cannot be seen as unmediated records of nineteenth-century oral tradition; instead, they are the results of complex processes of semiotic, cultural, and linguistic translation.

Smoothly composed, neatly organized, and easily read, *German Popular Stories* is, in fact, a highly selective and inexact translation.[70] For example, the extensive notes that characterize the *KHM* were reduced to a compact twenty-one pages; of the 161 *Märchen* and nine legends in the 1819 edition of the *KHM*, only thirty-one selected for the first volume of *German Popular Stories*, an additional twenty-six for the second.[71] Taylor combined a number of tales from the *KHM* to produce those he titled "Chanticleer and Partlet," "The Young Giant and the Tailor," "Hans and His Wife," and "Roland and Maybird"; and tales such as "Snow-drop" and "Hansel and Grettel" were shortened to render them less "diffuse" in style and form.[72]

Some of the most notable changes were made in the content of tales, including elimination or mellowing of episodes of gory retribution, dangerous villains, premarital sex, and even references to the Devil.[73] Thus, Snow-drop's evil stepmother is spared "the truly Northern punishment of being obliged to dance in red-hot slippers,"[74] and instead she "choked with passion, and fell ill and died" (139). The princess in "The Frog-Prince" awakes to view "a handsome prince gazing on her with the most beautiful eyes that ever were seen." Unlike the German text, Taylor's version presents the Prince not as the heroine's bedmate but as standing decorously "at the head of her bed" (209). In order "to avoid offense" (236) in "Der Teufel mit den drei Goldnen Haaren," the Devil becomes a giant in translation and Hell is a cave (221).[75] In the last story of volume 1, Taylor transforms violent rage into slapstick comedy: Rumpelstiltskin's fury at being outwitted, which caused him to drive his foot into the ground and then tear his own body apart in the German text, becomes a comic display when "the little man dashed his right foot in a rage so deep into the floor that he was forced to lay hold of it with both hands to pull it out." In a lighthearted addendum to this loose translation of "Rumpel-stilts-kin," Taylor writes, "Then he made the best of his way off, while every body laughed for having had all his trouble for nothing" (217).

To conclude the second volume of *German Popular Stories* on an upbeat presented Taylor with a more formidable challenge. "The Juniper Tree" centers around a second wife's jealousy of the first wife's child. This stepmother is driven to murder her stepson, to trick her daughter into believing herself the murderess, and then to feed the boy's stewed body to his father. The stepmother's crimes are revealed in the songs of a magical bird, the spirit of the murdered stepson which lives on the juniper tree growing from the first wife's grave. Given the upbeat and generally comical tone of *German Popular Stories*, it is a wonder that Taylor selected "The Juniper Tree" for inclusion at all.

In Taylor's hands, the story remains unsettling, but the source of discomfort is sometimes difficult to pinpoint. For instance, a dinner of "black soup" stands, euphemistically, for the cannibalistic meal enthusiastically consumed by the murdered boy's father. The dinner scene maintains its mood of eerie foreboding, without any direct reference to the taboo act in which the father is engaged. Likewise, Taylor alters the bird's song, which appears five times in the tale, so that it loses its original function—to expose the stepmother's wrongdoings. The reader who is vigilant enough to read Taylor's notes to the tale will discover a literal translation of the German original:

My mother me slew;
My father me ate;
My sister Margery
Gather'd all my bones,
And bound them up in a silken shroud,
And laid them under the juniper tree.
Kywit! Kywit! Ah, what a fine bird am I![76]

In Taylor's treatment of the story, however, the bird offers a less horrific account of events:

My mother slew her little son;
My father thought me lost and gone:
But pretty Margery pitied me,
And laid me under the juniper tree;
And now I rove so merrily,
As over the hills and dales I fly:
O what a fine bird am I! (305)

Although the stepmother is still troubled by this song, attention has shifted away from criminal acts (murder, cannibalism) and corporeal imagery (the flesh which is eaten, the bones which remain), and the soul of the murdered son actually appears to find some joy in his supernatural state, flying "merrily" around the town and over his former home. Taylor's editing of "The Juniper Tree" is dramatic, completely altering the reader's experience of the tale.

In a generous spirit, David Blamires notes that Taylor never "attempted to camouflage what he was doing in adapting, combining and expurgating his originals—on the contrary, he signalled his changes very frankly in the notes he appended to the tales."[77] Indeed, from the time of his first correspondence with the Grimms, Taylor addressed the motivations for the project and its perceived difference from the *Kinder- und Hausmärchen*: "In compiling our little volume we had the amusement of some young friends principally in view and were therefore compelled sometimes to conciliate local feelings and deviate a little from strict translation; but we believe that all these variations are recorded in the Notes which were hastily drawn with a view to show that our book had some little pretensions to literary consideration though deep research was out of plan."[78]

Taking a different but equally sympathetic approach, Brian Alderson recasts Taylor's "cavalier" translation as an effort "to respond naturally to the language of the stories and make them sound as though they had originated in English rather than in German"[79]—an example of what Lawrence Venuti identifies as the "familiarizing" mode of translation.[80] But the acknowledgment of continuities between Taylor's efforts and the tradition of "domesticating translation" tells us little, in and of itself. As Venuti points out, domesticating or familiarizing modes of translation can have political implications: By "producing the effect of transparency, the illusion that this is not a translation, but the foreign text, in fact, the living thoughts of the foreign author," such translation strategies conceal "the cultural and social conditions of the translation—the aesthetic, class, and national ideologies" that produce a work like *German Popular Stories*.[81]

Taylor may indicate his editing choices in the notes, but his production of a cohesive, highly readable, inoffensive set of story texts makes it all too easy to ignore such notes. In fact, the notes appear in few later editions of *German Popular Stories*, including the one still in print. The seamlessness of the translated tales not only made for an easier reading experience; it also allowed for interpretation of these written versions of German popular tales as unclouded windows onto cultural difference and earlier points in social and literary development. This style of translation and editing could also give the impression that the written narratives represented the unmediated utterances of the German *Märchenfrau*—a possibility that Taylor exploited in the revised edition of *German Popular Stories*, as I will discuss shortly.

In fact, familiarization is only part of the story. Closer examination suggests that Edgar Taylor's editorial choices reflect another impulse, one more oriented toward *defamiliarization* or exoticization. While undoubtedly an heir to English translation strategies, Taylor also demonstrates some indebtedness to the "foreignizing" approach, which had recently emerged in Germany. Like his German counterparts, Taylor seems to use his translation of the imported text "not so much to introduce the foreign" to English readers but to "use the foreign to confirm and develop sameness, a process of fashioning an ideal cultural self on the basis of an other."[82] That English readers should even be interested in engaging with translations of foreign narratives does fashioning work in and of itself. As André Lefevere comments, foreignizing translation "makes sense and is of value only to a nation that has the definite inclination to appropriate what is foreign."[83] Such translinguistic, transcultural curiosity emerges as a defining characteristic of Englishness.

The preface to *German Popular Stories* reiterates the translators' hope that the tales would prove of interest to both "the curious reader" and those seeking amusement, and it details what were felt to be necessary conciliations to English sensibilities:

With a view to variety, [the translators] have wished rather to avoid than to select those, the leading incidents of which are already familiar to the English reader, and have therefore deprived themselves of the interest which comparison would afford. There were also many stories of great merit, and tending highly to the elucidation of ancient mythology, customs, and opinions, which the scrupulous fastidiousness of modern taste, especially in works likely to attract the attention of youth, warned them to pass by.[84]

Maintaining that the *Märchen* bear similarities to and share historical origins with English narrative traditions, Taylor softened the content of tales and passed over those too difficult to adapt to "modern taste." But he also purposefully excluded tales with which English readers were likely to be familiar. Taylor's conflation of stories from the *KHM* that resembled one another and his avoidance of those that had well-known English cognates stands in direct contrast to the practices of the Grimms, who regarded the publication of variants as a key contribution to the history of German poetry and evidence of the tales' authenticity. No less significant, Taylor's production of unified and unique narratives provided English readers with a vision of their own collective identity—as a readership that craved "variety" and moral fastidiousness, that was capable of comparative critique and historical inquiry.

Tamed and made into reading material for the English household, the German *Märchen* were "domesticated" in the fullest sense of the word. Like the domestic animal, the foreign tale collection is welcomed into the home and taught the rules of the house, but its place and role are always defined by its otherness. In Taylor's hands, the otherness of this narrative tradition was maintained and, through editing and selection, *accentuated*. Taylor's modification of tales' form and content rendered them distinctly but comfortably foreign.

To cast Taylor's *German Popular Stories* as the popularization of a strictly scholarly text is to do injustice to both works. While *KHM* has been deemed revolutionary for making folktales "the object of serious inquiry,"[85] it was truly a departure in that it made folktales *at* once the object of serious inquiry and a source of entertainment. As Donald Ward notes, had the Grimms, especially Wilhelm, not "revised" the *Märchen*, "no one other than a handful of philologists and narrative researchers would have heard of them today."[86] *German Popular Stories* is a highly selective translation and a significant departure from the narrative tone and worldview of the early editions of the *Kinder- und Hausmärchen*, but its status as a popular book and its claims to oral authenticity continue and extend the particular processes of entextualization and commodification of "popular tales" established in the German collection. By the end of the period examined here, English critics could look back at *German Popular Stories* and deem *it* "the first real good fairy book that had found its way to England."[87]

Picturesque Fictions

Like the written text of *German Popular Stories*, George Cruikshank's illustrations balance the familiar and foreign, the ordinary and the odd. As much as Taylor's increasingly creative textual practices, these illustrations shaped popular conceptions of the fairy tale and the social context out of which it is thought to emerge. Both Taylor and Cruikshank drew creative inspiration from the idea of the field encounter, from the act of storytelling and the personage of the storyteller.

These etchings made Cruikshank famous. When published in 1823, Cruikshank was already established as a caricaturist, specializing in the "satirical[ly] grotesque" rendering of political figures and scenes of "contemporary London low life."[88] But he was soon after associated with the more picturesque world of rustic beauty and magic he created for *German Popular Stories*.[89]

On one level, Cruikshank provides pictorial reinforcement for Taylor's mollifying efforts, diffusing the terrifying potential of the supernatural, and infusing some of the more disturbing of the Grimms' tales with hearty laughter or merry singing. The title-page of the first volume is, tellingly, illustrated by a scene of uproarious laughter as a book is read aloud (figure 1), giving readers a fair sense of what is to come. In fact, none of the supernatural characters illustrated by Cruikshank—be they fairies, elves, or giants—is depicted as particularly threatening. For example, the fairy with the power to transform, entrap, and forever separate the young lovers in "Jorinda and Jorindel" is depicted precisely at the moment that she is overcome by the hero (figure 2). Similarly, Cruikshank depicted Rumpelstiltskin not as a threat to the royal family but with his foot stuck in the throne-room floor (figure 3). The elves in "The Elves and the Shoemaker" are of a helpful variety, and Cruikshank provides an illustration of the scene in which they gleefully discover the little clothes left for them by the grateful shoemaker and his wife (figure 4). Cruikshank chose not to illustrate the dangerous title character of "The Giant with the Three Golden Hairs," opting instead for the nurturing giant of "The Young Giant and the Tailor," who stands in the middle of a half-plowed field, holding his minuscule adopted son gingerly in his enormous hand (figure 5).

Cruikshank is known for his rendering of figures such as these—for expression and movement—but his placement of these human and supernatural characters is no less notable. Perhaps most significant of all is the fact that so many of these supernatural beings and occurrences are situated in relatively humble surroundings: in the countryside, on a farm, in a work-

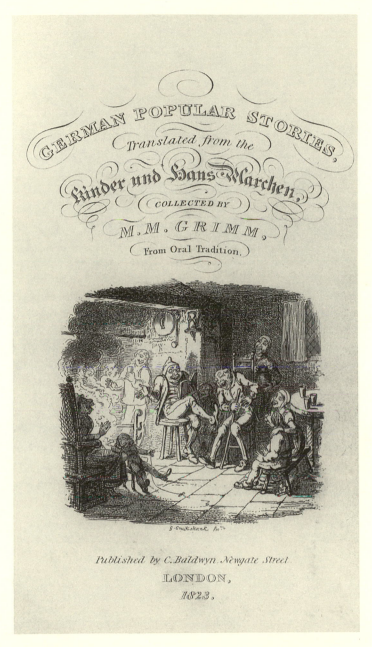

GERMAN POPULAR STORIES,

Translated from the

Kinder und Haus Marchen,

COLLECTED BY

M. M. GRIMM,

From Oral Tradition.

G. Cruikshank fecit.

Published by C. Baldwyn, Newgate Street.

LONDON,

1823.

1. George Cruikshank, title page for Edgar Taylor's *German Popular Stories* (1823). Courtesy, The Lilly Library, Indiana University, Bloomington.

2. George Cruikshank, "Jorinda and Jorindel," Taylor's *German Popular Stories* (1823). Courtesy, The Lilly Library, Indiana University, Bloomington.

3. George Cruikshank, "Rumpel-stilts-kin," Taylor's *German Popular Stories* (1823). Courtesy, The Lilly Library, Indiana University, Bloomington.

shop. Even Cruikshank's royal palaces, peopled with vaguely Elizabethan-style courtiers, have a relative intimacy of scale. These settings are remote, pastoral, and/or outdated. To English readers in the 1820s, they must have seemed vaguely familiar and yet in distinct contrast with contemporary English life. Like the "picturesque" tradition emerging in English landscape

4. George Cruikshank, "The Elves and the Shoemaker," Taylor's *German Popular Stories* (1823). Courtesy, The Lilly Library, Indiana University, Bloomington.

painting in the early nineteenth century, Cruikshank's interpretations evoke romanticized images of preindustrial English society, celebrating a rural culture that seemed to be disappearing rapidly.

Cruikshank's playful rendering of the odd, the ugly, and the imperfect is closely aligned with the aesthetic appreciation of "roughness, irregularity,

5. George Cruikshank, "The Young Giant and the Tailor," Taylor's *German Popular Stories*, vol. 2 (1826). Courtesy, The Lilly Library, Indiana University, Bloomington.

and variousness" which had come to dominate the English art world of the early nineteenth century.[90] The popular aestheticizing stance known as "the picturesque" was applied not only to places and things but also to certain classes of people. The picturesque thus became closely associated with "wandering tribes of gypsies," "beggars," and other human equivalencies to "the old mills, hovels and other inanimate objects" that drew painters' eyes.[91]

The picturesque was founded on, drew its energy from, the ambivalent stance of the viewer. For instance, the subjects of painter William Henry Pyne's 1803 work entitled "Rustics" were described as "peculiarly pleasing in imitation," no matter how "disagreeable the manners of rustics may be in real life."[92] Picturesque beauty was thought to be characteristic of a particular point in the *devolution* of people or objects. As Ann Bermingham summarizes, "With time, all things become picturesque," shabby, disheveled, and "with more time, picturesque things become 'deformed' "(69). It is thus always a short step from this form of aesthetic appreciation to disgust; from, for instance, Cruikshank's picturesque renderings of German folk magic to his grotesque depictions of London street life.

For nineteenth-century theorist Uvedale Price, the double-edged nature of the picturesque was best represented by the figure of the old country woman, found visually charming but not desirable, admired but with ambivalence. Drawing on oral tradition, Price uses the "picturesque old woman" to demonstrate that the eye and imagination are drawn, in art, to precisely those figures with which one would not desire actual contact. "I have read, indeed, in some fairy tale," Price wrote in 1842, "of a country, where age and wrinkles were loved and caressed, and youth and freshness neglected; but in real life, I fancy, the most picturesque old woman, however her admirer may ogle her on that account, is perfectly safe from his caresses."[93] It was just such a figure that came to represent German popular stories in England.

Among the most frequently reproduced of Cruikshank's illustrations for *German Popular Stories* are the frontispieces of volumes 1 and 2, which lure readers to the books not with fairies or giants but with images of storytelling events. The illustration which opens volume 1 presents a comical-looking man reading to a group, primarily adults, at a large hearthside (figure 1). The image fits nicely with the collection's epigraph, which Taylor drew from "History of Tom Thumb the Little": "Now you must imagine me to sit by a good fire, amongst a companye of good fellowes, over a well spiced bowle of Christmas ale, telling of these merrie tales which hereafter followe." It is, as the epigraph suggests, easy to imagine Cruikshank's droll and antiquated reader as Taylor himself, in fancy dress.

Both volumes of *German Popular Stories* indicate an oral source of the tales in their subtitles—"Translated from the Kinder und Haus-Marchen, Collected by M.M. Grimm, from Oral Tradition"[94]—but Cruikshank's opening illustration for volume 2 did much to reinforce this image, drawing on an established pictorial tradition. Thus, on the 1826 title page, the mirthful adults with drinks in their hands have vanished. The scene is now darker, more intimate, as an elderly woman, spinning wheel and cats nearby, narrates to a group of attentive children (figure 6).

By the mid 1820s, the elderly spinster/storyteller had already played a significant role in the history of fairy-tale illustration, the most famous and widely circulated image being the title page illustration of Charles Perrault's *Histoires, ou Contes du Temps Passé* (1697), reproduced in Robert Samber's 1729 English translation. The iconography was evocative: an elderly peasant woman seated at hearthside, flanked by cats, drop spindle, and an audience of young aristocrats. Although in Cruikshank's picture a spinning wheel has replaced the drop spindle of Perrault's *mère l'oye* ("Mother Goose"), and the old woman's audience has become much younger, the iconography has remained remarkably constant.[95]

What gives such images their power? Recently, this iconography has been interpreted symbolically, as representing women's sexual or social identities. Tracing the root of "fairy" to the fates of Greek and Roman mythology, Karen Rowe suggests, "compel[s] us to see the origin of fairy as closely related to the female acts of birthing, nursing, prophesying, and spinning." The depiction of the fairy-tale teller as an old (wise) woman at a spinning wheel thus taps into a host of deeply rooted associations between women and spinning, storytelling, soothsaying, procreation, birthing and dying, creation and destruction, as Rowe and others have revealed.[96]

But in a social evolutionary framework, and in the context of picturesque representations of English country life, this imagery acquired an additional layer of resonance and meaning. Spinning presented itself as a powerful image not only because it could symbolize female powers of creation and reproduction but also because the craft and its materials could function iconically. By the early nineteenth century, former handcrafts had become mechanized and steam-powered, and after nearly 1,500 years the export of wool and woolen textiles ceased to be the basis of England's economic strength.[97] Despite the "special place of wool in English history," by the nineteenth century the material had come to represent only the past. This was an age of iron and coal, industrialists argued, for "wool has long ceased to be the staple commodity of England."[98] As England moved from

GERMAN POPULAR STORIES,

Translated from the

Kinder und Haus-Märchen,

COLLECTED BY

M. M. GRIMM,

From Oral Tradition.

VOL. II.

G. Cruikshank fect.

JAMES ROBINS & C?. LONDON.

AND

JOSEPH ROBINS JUN? & C?. DUBLIN.

MDCCCXXVI.

6. George Cruikshank, title page for Taylor's *German Popular Stories*, vol. 2 (1826). Courtesy, The Lilly Library, Indiana University, Bloomington.

one economic base to another, from one mode of production to another, the spinner of wool was coming to signify a world quickly disappearing.

The image can also be "read" in terms of another fantasy, one not historical but cross-cultural, not ancient but newly emergent: the fieldwork encounter.[99] In a revised edition of *German Popular Stories*, Edgar Taylor put a name to the face of Cruikshank's storyteller: She was to be imagined as Dorothea Viehmann, the Grimms' highly romanticized informant. The revised edition of *German Popular Stories* shifted attention from tale to teller.

Gammer Grethel; or, German Fairy Tales and Popular Stories was first published in 1839, shortly before Taylor's death[100]—with some striking differences. For this edition, Taylor selected forty-two tales from his two volumes of *German Popular Stories* and arranged them in twelve groups of three to four stories each, entitled "Evening the First," "Evening the Second," and so on. In the preface to *Gammer Grethel*, Taylor explains the new title:

Gammer Grethel, the supposed narrator of the stories, in fact lived, though under a different name. She was the Frau Viehmännin, the wife of a peasant in the neighbourhood of Hesse-Cassel, and from her mouth a great portion of the stories were written down by MM. Grimm. (vii)

This is certainly the most direct of Taylor's references to the Grimms' collection process—mythologized and inaccurate though it may be, given that Dorothea Viehmann was neither a peasant nor as elderly as the woman depicted by Cruikshank.[101] But "Gammer Grethel," the "supposed" oral source of the tales, is not Taylor's only creation in this edition. He also fictionalizes the identity of the collector.

The revised collection begins with a copy of Cruikshank's title page illustration from volume 2, the elderly woman storyteller, placed under the heading of "Gammer Grethel: Who she was and what she did" (figure 7). Using this image as his point of departure, Taylor proceeds to construct a framing narrative for the twelve nights of tale-telling. The collection thus begins with a new story, authored by—and featuring—Edgar Taylor:

Gammer Grethel was an honest, good-humoured farmer's wife, who, a while ago, lived far off in Germany.

She knew all the good stories that were told in that country; and every evening about Christmas time the boys and girls of the neighbourhood gathered round to hear her tell them some of her budget of strange stories.

One Christmas, being in that part of the world, I joined the party; and begged

GAMMER GRETHEL.

WHO SHE WAS AND WHAT SHE DID.

7. Cruikshank's title page illustration for Taylor's *German Popular Stories,* vol. 2 (1826), from *Gammer Grethel,* or *German Fairy Tales and Popular Stories* (1839). Courtesy, the Lilly Library, Indiana University, Bloomington.

her to let me write down what I heard, for the benefit of my young friends in England. And so, for twelve merry evenings, beginning with Christmas eve, we met and listened to her budget.

Many a time have my acquaintances, of both sexes, called for a chapter out of my Tale-book: as I have reason to think that there may be a great many more—not only of boys and girls, but of men and women too—than I know, or should like the trouble of reading to, who would be glad to have been of Gammer Grethel's party, or at least would like to know how it was that she so much amused her friends, I at last resolved to print the collection, for the benefit of all those who may wish to read it. (xi–xii)

In this new frame, the book itself seems closely connected to Gammer Grethel's evening performances. Only Taylor mediates between our reading and her narration. In his preface, Taylor had made an appeal to the oral authenticity of the tales, as rooted in a German peasant culture and collected from the mouth of Frau Viehmänn by the Brothers Grimm. On the following page, he now fictionalizes the processes of collection, transcription, *and* publishing—drawing on the imaginative appeal of these scholarly activities and creating a frame story in which Taylor himself is star and authority. The genesis of this edition—from the researches of the Grimms, through their entextualization and publishing of tales in various forms, to Taylor and Jardine's translations, to Taylor's revision for *Gammer Grethel*—is erased.

* * *

In 1868, Hotten published a reprint of *German Popular Stories*, with the two original volumes combined, etchings based on those of Ludwig Grimm as well as Cruikshank's originals,[102] and a new introduction by John Ruskin. Ruskin conveys an affection for "the good old book,"[103] despite his privately expressed frustration with Taylor's work[104] and some qualifying words in the introductory essay:

I do not bring forth the text or the etchings in this volume as examples of what either ought to be in works of this kind: they are in many respects common, imperfect, vulgar; but their vulgarity is of a wholesome and harmless kind. (xi)

The imperfection of which Ruskin writes was not, as one might expect, a matter of faulty or liberal translation on Taylor's part; instead, Ruskin attributes these qualities to the particular social conditions in which the household tales arose. He continues:

[I]n genuine forms of minor tradition, a rude and more or less illiterate tone will always be discernible; for all the best fairy tales have owed their birth, and the greater part of their power, to narrowness of circumstances; they belong properly to districts in which walled cities are surrounded by bright and unblemished country, and in

which a healthy and bustling town life, not highly refined, is relieved by, and contrasted with, the calm enchantment of pastoral and woodland scenery, either under
humble cultivation by peasant masters, or left in its natural solitude. (xii)

Around the popular tale Ruskin builds a setting. The picture he constructs
is of active but isolated social life, in harmony with its natural surroundings. The "imperfect" quality of *German Popular Stories* is here linked to its
rootedness in these "narrow" circumstances and positioned as evidence of
the tales' status as "genuine forms" of German oral tradition. Echoing aesthetic theories of the picturesque, Ruskin suggests that the power of the
"best" fairy tales results from precisely those conditions which may appear
vulgar to the modern English reader and which serve to distance readers
from the projected originators of the tales.

These social conditions are seen to produce a particular mode of narrative creativity and to give fairy tales a set of characteristic qualities:

Under conditions of this kind the imagination is enough excited to invent instinc-
tively, (and rejoice in the invention of) spiritual forms of wildness and beauty, while
yet it is restrained and made cheerful by the familiar accidents and relations of town
life, mingling always in its fancy humorous and vulgar circumstances with pathetic
ones, and never so much impressed with its supernatural phantasies as to be in danger of retaining them as any part of its religious faith. (xii)

Ruskin thus presents a highly idealized vision of the social formation believed to give rise to *Märchen*. His is a vision of humble, illiterate peasants
who from instinct, not inspiration, produce tales of crudeness, but not cru-
elty; of calm enchantment, not dangerous magic; of wildness that knows its
limits.

Ruskin's characterization of *Märchen* may be applicable to the stories as
they appeared in the original and revised editions of *German Popular Stories*,
but the layers of editorial intervention that separate this English publication
from a German oral tradition are considerable. In order to produce a collection of discrete, coherent narratives which met bourgeois standards of propriety, Taylor—like the Grimms before him—selected, combined, edited,
inserted. Nonetheless, Ruskin's introduction makes clear that what were in
1823 regarded by Taylor as adaptations to local (English) feeling, by 1869
could be interpreted by English readers as the defining characteristics of authentic (German) folk tradition.

Writing just one year later, Charlotte Yonge celebrated *German Popular
Stories* as representative of "the true unadulterated fairy tale."[105] Yonge finds

this edition to be distinguished at once by its authenticity and the skill of the editor: she declares it "much safer and better-weeded" than other available editions, which also lack "Mr. Taylor's excellent notes" (306). For better or for worse, the form, style, and spirit of *German Popular Stories*—altogether a gentler and more picturesque world of fantasy—influenced later editions of Grimms' fairy tales, from the "Small Edition" of the *Kinder- und Hausmärchen* through contemporary English versions of the tales directed at children, as well as conceptions of the "true" nature of the traditional fairy tale.

Chapter 3

Everything Is in the Telling:
T. Crofton Croker's Fairy Legends and
Traditions of the South of Ireland

I make no pretensions to originality, and avow at once, that there is no story in my book that has not been told by half the old women of the district in which the scene is laid. I give them as I found them—as indications of a particular superstition in the minds of a part—and an important part of my countrymen—the peasantry.[1]

—*T. Crofton Croker, 1826*

[I]t is exceedingly pleasant to meet with something which we can believe to be Irish. We believe it to be so, as we often feel assured that a portrait is a likeness, although we are unacquainted with the person whom it was designed to represent. Such, in both cases, is the effect of individuality and consistence of features.[2]

—*Anonymous reviewer for the* Quarterly Review, *1825*

In *German Popular Stories*, Edgar Taylor and George Cruikshank discovered that field-based folklore research, pioneered by the brothers Grimm, had inherent imaginative appeal. Oral narratives "collected" and transformed into reading material were engaging and artistically inspiring, and the figure of the storyteller—imagined as an elderly peasant woman—provided the basis for a new fantasy of cross-cultural encounter. Within two years of the initial appearance of *German Popular Stories*, a new field-based tale collection was published in London: Thomas Crofton Croker's *Fairy Legends and Traditions of the South of Ireland* (1825).

The text Croker produced bears a formal resemblance to *German Popular Stories*. Like its successful predecessor, it was initially published in a small, relatively inexpensive, fancifully illustrated, anonymously authored form.

Fairy Legends was regarded as valuable to a wide range of readers and able to serve a number of potential functions. Mused a reviewer,

Popular tales recommend themselves to the antiquary by illustrating the origin or connection of different races of men; to the philosopher, as being usually the vehicle of some physical or moral truth, sometimes of some mystery; and to the general reader, as exhibiting specimens of national manners, and affording innocent and not irrational entertainment. On all these grounds, and more especially upon the two last, the little work which is under our review has claim upon our attention.[3]

Looking back at the initial appearance of *Fairy Legends*, Thomas Wright similarly concluded that the value of the work was that it "taught people the real importance of the legends themselves, and their interest [was] taken, not only philosophically, but in a historical and ethnological point of view."[4] These perspectives were regarded as mutually illuminating, so that the experience of reading *Fairy Legends* was imagined at once as entertainment, an opportunity for meditation upon human belief systems, a source of insight to the history of this neighboring nation, and a process of cultural discovery.

By the 1860s, *Fairy Legends* had been canonized as a foundational work of children's literature. In her survey of important works of "class literature," Charlotte Yonge followed her recommendation of Taylor's translation with praise of Croker's "genuine" fairy tales. For Yonge, these tales represent a world of "lovely princes and princesses, the dreamy groves and glittering palaces, that childish imagination ought to revel in."[5] The imaginative terrain Yonge describes was firmly entrenched in fairy-tale discourse, thanks in part to the verbal and visual interpretations of *Märchen* in *German Popular Stories*. But while W. H. Brooke's early illustrations of the Irish fairy legends are "lovely," "dreamy," and sometimes "glittering," the legends themselves rarely are.

Croker's collection may not have achieved the prominence of Grimms' fairy tales in international publishing, but it continues to be resuscitated in adaptations for children.[6] Neil C. Hultin and Warren U. Ober acknowledge Croker's place in this historiography, but argue against the positioning of *Fairy Legends* as literature for children. Like Yonge, they base their argument on the content of the tales:

Croker's tales are not as suitable for children [as Grimms' fairy tales], for they concern the theft of children, abduction of marriageable girls, sudden and violent attacks of the phooka which leave one deformed, and the horror of the banshee's screams. . . .

These are tales for adults with adult problems, however much those adults live in a world which is coterminous with a supernatural world.[7]

However, to suggest that the presence of horror and danger in these Irish legends precludes their classification as literature for children is to ignore what was by 1825 already a long tradition of uncheerful writing for young readers, from the English Puritanical writings of James Janeway through the efforts of the Grimms themselves. More compelling than the question of whether the legends are *appropriate* for children, what sort of cultural work was achieved by categorizing these narratives as "class literature"?

The cultural and national boundaries broached by Croker held a significantly different political charge than those addressed in *German Popular Stories*. The Grimms had worked within a nationalist discourse to illuminate their native literary heritage and national character for a domestic reading audience; in this context, the association of *Märchen* with child readers reinforced the idea that the narratives were culturally and morally "pure." Taylor, on the other hand, tapped into romantic and picturesque visions of preindustrial peasant life as he adapted German tales to English tastes, presenting his readers with a corpus of tales that could be experienced as comfortably foreign or sweetly nostalgic—distinctly Other and distinctly unthreatening. As "class literature," *Fairy Legends and Traditions of the South of Ireland* served a different function, drawing the young and poor alike into a dominant discourse and bourgeois subject position. The character and present state of the Irish peasantry were matters at the heart of English debates concerning the "Irish question," particularly issues of land ownership and Catholic emancipation: Any attempt at representing the Irish peasantry to an English readership in the 1820s would be read through this lens. Croker claimed political neutrality, and his tale collection is characterized by ambiguity, as I will explore throughout this chapter; nevertheless, in key passages Croker invokes an established colonialist rhetoric that places the reader—whether adult or child, upper-class or working-class—squarely in a position of critical authority and cultural superiority.

In contemporary scholarship, Croker is most often remembered for his methodology, not his politics. Croker's claim to "give them as I found them" resonates with claims made by the Brothers Grimm—and has earned Croker honorable, if not frequent, mention in the historiography of folklore study. *Fairy Legends* stands as "the first field collection to be made in Great Britain."[8] If Croker can claim a place in the history of field-based folklore research, he also had to contend with fieldwork's attendant problems—which Taylor, as

translator and editor, did not. How does one go about collecting oral traditions and representing them on paper? More specifically, how does one
maintain both readability and authenticity? Thinking about folklore before
the term had even been coined, Croker and his contemporaries lacked any
clear model for the methodology, genre distinctions, interpretive frameworks, readership, and textual presentation appropriate to such work. As the
reviewer cited earlier observed upon the publication of *Fairy Legends* by John
Murray in 1825, the work's anonymous author was all the more commend-
able, since he "must be guided rather by his own tact than by any fixed rules;
must steer by the light of his own star rather than by the assistance of a compass."[9] It was in his textual and editorial experiments that Croker managed
to depart from the conventional colonialist stance of his day and quietly sub-
vert it.

With the benefit of retrospect, Croker appears in many ways to have
been ahead of his time. As we will see, he takes interest not only in story
themes and motifs but also in storytelling events and the artistry of oral
performance—anticipating the mid-twentieth-century turn in academic
Folklore away from the study of oral "texts" as artifacts and toward the study
of oral performance as process.[10] However, some of Croker's judgment calls
have fallen out of favor: most notably, his unacknowledged inclusion of legends collected or recollected by fellow antiquarians, discussed later, and what
some critics have seen as the overly "literary" style of *Fairy Legends*.[11] Nevertheless, in 1825 this tale collection was praised specifically for "the species of
style . . . judiciously adopted by the author" and the authenticity it conveyed:

Never indelicate, it is easy, and yet is precise, enough for its purposes—colloquial
without being coarse, and pleasing from the coherence of its parts and the natural
transition of its colours. Add to this a provinciality of idiom, which, without obscur-
ing the meaning, seems to stamp a certain authenticity upon the narrative.[12]

In such a context "authenticity" was construed to be something constructed
and artistically shaped, rather than a quality intrinsic to a certain class of
narratives or method of field collection. Praise of Croker's style was thus
characterized by this awareness that the fairy legends were, like a portrait, an
artistic representation of the real.

Croker's enduring legacy may be primarily as a field collector, but his
collection of fairy legends was embraced by English readers not for its origins in fieldwork, and certainly not for the originality of the tales, but primarily for its careful balancing of the authentic and the readable, a "true

Hibernicism of tone and manner" that all could understand. As another of Croker's reviewers commented, "Everything . . . is in the telling."[13]

The Implied Narrator and the Implied Reader

Fairy Legends and Traditions of the South of Ireland is prefaced by a short but evocative statement of purpose, in which Croker delineates his field of study and its value to English readers:

The following Tales are written in the style in which they are generally related by those who believe in them; and it is the object of the Compiler to illustrate, by their means, the Superstitions of the Irish Peasantry—Superstitions which the most casual observer cannot fail to remark powerfully influence their conduct and manner of thinking.[14]

Although many of Croker's subjects were neither poverty-stricken nor uneducated, as current usage of the term "peasant" might suggest,[15] the "object of the Compiler" rests on an implied distinction between the Irish peasantry (credulous and superstitious) and the reader (a critical observer of such phenomena). Moreover, Croker suggests that this fundamental difference in "conduct and manner of thinking" is indexed stylistically.

It was Croker, and not the Irish peasant storytellers from whom he had collected the legends, who was commended for the "telling" of the tales in this collection. For example, an anonymous writer for *Blackwood's Magazine* focused readers' attention on "the description of the peculiar costume in which these stories appear, in the particular country from which the *narrator* has drawn his immediate subject; in both of which main branches of art, our present *story-teller* has most admirably succeeded."[16] This apparent confusion of the Compiler's voice with that of the Irish peasant is striking, especially in the context of a work that purports to represent a particular style of storytelling in order to shed light on a foreign worldview.

It is not (solely) out of disregard for the artistry of oral narrators that reviewers of *Fairy Legends* conflated the role of tale collector with that of storyteller. When it comes to traditional arts—narrative, musical, or material— issues of authorship and intellectual property are notoriously difficult to resolve, as recently demonstrated by thirty years of work by UNESCO and the World Intellectual Property Organization to develop standards and mechanisms for the legal protection of folklore at the regional, national, and international levels.[17] The idea of "the author" can itself be historicized and denaturalized: it emerged and was codified in the eighteenth century, it "constitutes a privileged moment of individualization in the history of ideas,"[18] and, one can add, it stands in direct opposition to the Romantic construction of the folk and their lore—echoed by Croker in the quotation with which we began—as collective and wholly unoriginal.[19] This contrast has had profound implications for the professionalization of the humanities and social sciences, as scholars could lay claim to such "discoveries" as their own.

So, at one level, we can read the Blackwood reviewer's blurring of the distinction between compiler and storyteller as a reflection of the authorship problem inherent to the folklore book: All written representations of oral discourse may be seen as double-voiced, and only one of those voices fits well with the modern, proprietorial concept of the Author. Verbatim transcription—the ideal sought and, more recently, problematized by twentieth-century folklorists and ethnographers—seeks to "capture" the voice of a speaker. But, of course, transcription also "speaks" the concerns of the transcriber. Like Bakhtin's category of literary heteroglossia, transcriptions are composed of "*another's speech in another's language*" and serve "to express authorial intentions [of the fieldworker] but in a refracted way." Like heteroglossia in novelistic discourse, transcription can be said to serve "two speakers at the same time" and express "simultaneously two different intentions: the direct intention of the character [or storyteller/consultant] who is speaking, and the refracted intention of the author [or fieldworker]."[20] Even if a written representation of oral performance were left unaccompanied by written commentary—an event so rare as to be hypothetical—one could read a second "voice" in the transcriptional choices made: what has been transcribed, how, and why. It is this (English) voice which is given priority and commendation by Croker's nineteenth-century reviewers.

In the folktale collections of nineteenth-century England, storytelling is wed to interpretive framing, the intentions of collectors/translators/editors are addressed in introductory essays, annotations and the like, and double-voicing is, it would seem, readily apparent and somewhat self-reflexive. Nonetheless, in the case of T. Crofton Croker's *Fairy Legends and Traditions of the South of Ireland*, the issue of voicing—who speaks and how that voice should be received—is both highly charged and highly ambiguous.

Fairy Legends represented Irish national character for an English readership, defining cultural and national boundaries as it crossed them. To serve this function, individual storytelling voices in the collection would seem to signify in their representativeness (of the district's "old women," of the peasantry, of the Irish), while the interpretive, editorializing voice gains its authority from scientific disinterestedness (the ability "to give them as I found them"). This particular form of double-voicing was to become deeply entrenched in anthropological and folkloristic discourse over the next 150 years, but as Clifford Geertz points out, the clarity of these constructions functions more powerfully as rhetoric (statements about what one is up to) than as practice (ethnographic writing itself). Geertz's work suggests that ethnography is more akin to literary discourse than its authors may care to acknowledge,[21] and as with any literary text, readers must be wary of unreliable narrators. Indeed, the simple story Croker tells about his own enterprise belies the complexity of his work. The ambiguities of voicing that characterize this text would seem to speak different concerns and perspectives than those presented in the work's brief preface.

One of the most striking dimensions of the style of *Fairy Legends* is the use of first-person narration. The first tale in the collection, "The Legend of Knocksheogowna," opens with a colorful setting of scene by an unidentified narrator:

In Tipperary is one of the most singularly shaped hills in the world. It has got a peak at the top like a conical nightcap thrown carelessly over your head as you awake in the morning. On the very point is built a sort of lodge, where in the summer the lady who built it and her friends used to go on parties of pleasure; but that was long after the days of the fairies, and it is, I believe, now deserted. (3)

The mise-en-scène with which this legend begins appears to be provided by a local and to be intended for an audience unacquainted with the locale. It offers readers a privileged, "insider's" perspective but is very much oriented toward an "outsider's" sensibility and frame of reference.

Fairy Legends is rife with passages that make rhetorical assumptions of familiarity while simultaneously providing readers with background information about people and places. For example, the narrator of "The Priest's Supper" manages to introduce the legend's main character while stating that he needs no introduction: "I need not say that Father Horrigan was a welcome guest wherever he went, for no man was more pious or better beloved in the country" (39). "The Haunted Cellar" begins with a comparable rhetorical maneuver:

There are few people who have not heard of the Mac Carthies—one of the real old Irish families, with the true Milesian blood running in their veins as thick as buttermilk. Many were the clans of this family in the south; as the Mac Carthy-more—and the Mac Carthy-reagh—and the Mac Carthy of Muskerry; and all of them were noted for their hospitality to strangers, gentle and simple. (149)

The completeness of information given by the narrator ensures that those "few people" who have not heard of the Mac Carthies, should they be among the readers of *Fairy Legends*, would not be at a disadvantage. Such passages as these accommodate and tacitly acknowledge the transnational, cross-cultural status of the book. At the same time, the leap into first-person narration creates a compelling tone of authenticity and immediacy, especially when used metanarratologically. "I should be all day about it were I to tell you all," comments the narrator of "Knocksheogowna" (4). The use of the first person and such elements of addressivity leave the reader to wonder: Who is doing the telling here? Who is the "I" of these tales?

The content of the preface and the format of the book would seem to reinforce a distinction between the storytelling voices of the Irish peasantry and the critical voice of a single collector, with whom the reader is encouraged to align him- or herself. The twenty-seven tales included in the 1825 edition are arranged into five sections, based on the type of fairy encounter featured. Each is a titled and complete narrative, followed by notes that explain relevant aspects of Irish beliefs and practices, provide background information when necessary, and reflect on the style and accuracy of narration. Nevertheless, the use of the first person in the tales themselves does not, as one might expect, consistently indicate the voice of a "folk" narrator, nor does it invariably denote the voice of the anonymous compiler (Croker). Closer reading of the work reveals that the distinction between the voices of the storytelling Irish peasantry and the voice of the Compiler is neither clear nor consistent.

The narration of many tales is framed, editorially, as exemplary of Irish storytelling. For example, in the notes that follow "The Legend of Knocksheogowna," Croker comments that although the use of imagery in this telling may strike readers as "perhaps rather too absurd . . . it has been judged best to give the legend as received, particularly as it affords a fair specimen of the very extravagant imagery in which the Irish are so fond of indulging" (11). Croker implies that the tale text represents a storytelling event—the way a tale was told, presumably by a specific person and on a specific occasion. It is to be taken as representative of both that event and a characteristic style of narration.

Croker thus invokes a rhetoric of field-based authenticity and alludes to the act of field collection in the notes to "Knockshegowna," without detailing the conditions under which he "received" the tale or revealing the identity of the Irish narrator. Croker does identify a source for "The Brewery of Eggshells," a story about a mother's attempts to slay the fairy baby that has replaced her own. In the notes that follow this legend, Croker comments: "The writer regrets that he is unable to retain the rich vein of comic interest in the foregoing tale, as related to him by Mrs. Philipps, to whose manner of narration it may perhaps be ascribed" (71). But this gesture toward acknowledgment does little to clarify the mode of narration and representation being employed here. This story begins with literary references: "It may be considered impertinent," the narrator begins, "were I to explain what is meant by a changeling; both Shakespeare and Spenser have already done so" (65). The implied narrator is clearly familiar with canonical English literature. Is it Mrs. Philipps who speaks here, who narrates Mrs. Sullivan's desperate attempts to banish the fairy changeling from the cradle, and describes her joy at recovering her natural baby? Or is it Croker himself? Even as he provides editorial commentary within the tale text, is Croker emulating, or perhaps mimicking, the humorous style of his informant?[22]

Such ambiguity also characterizes "The Confessions of Tom Bourke." Tom's appearance and character are described at length by the narrator: "Tom Bourke lives in a low long farm-house, resembling in outward appearance a large barn, placed at the bottom of the hill. . . . He is of a class of persons who are a sort of black swans in Ireland: he is a wealthy farmer [etc.]" (105). The narrator proceeds to refer to conditions "in Ireland" (105), sets "the good people" in quotation marks (106), and makes reference to such phenomena as "an Irish beggar's appetite" and "an Irish peasant's heart" (110). Obviously, such phrases are directed toward a non-Irish audience and indicate the perspective of one who does not speak often of fairies or count himself among the beggars and peasants of Ireland.

There are clues to be found in "The Confessions of Tom Bourke" and its accompanying notes that Bourke is not a person Croker only heard about but a man encountered in "the field" by an outsider. This may be a tale of fieldwork; certainly it re-creates a storytelling event, in which traditional tales are narrated. For instance, before any of Tom's tales are told, the narrator describes the context in which the storytelling took place:

The accommodation took place after dinner at Mr. Martin's house, and he invited Tom to walk into the parlour, and take of a glass of punch, made of some excellent *potteen*, which was on the table: he had long wished to draw out his highly-endowed neighbour on the subject of his supernatural powers, and as Mrs. Martin, who was in the room, was rather a favourite of Tom's, this seemed a good opportunity. (114)

In the notes that follow this tale, Croker claims that the "character of Tom Bourke is accurately copied from nature, and it has been thought better to preserve the scene entire" (133). These concluding notes would seem to imply that the narrator of "Confessions" is Croker himself. But in actuality it remains unclear whether Croker was a participant in/observer of this event, or whether he is reporting an event as it was described ("copied from nature") by a third party.

John Mulligan is described as knowing "more fairy stories than would make, if properly printed in a rivulet of print running down a meadow of margin, two thick quartos for Mr. John Murray, of Albermarle-street; all of which he used to tell on all occasions that he could find listeners" (137). If engaged in the communications circuit of print culture, Mulligan could easily fill a book of his own—for Croker's own publisher, no less. But the voice that narrates "Fairies or No Fairies" again appears to be that of the collector addressing readers, not that of "the fine old fellow" Mulligan addressing his listeners.

The narrator again draws on an English literary frame of reference to make humorous comment on his own abilities and on the genre in which he is engaged: "If I were a poet like Mr. Wordsworth," he reflects,

I should tell you how the beautiful light was broken into a thousand different fragments—and how it filled the entire tree with a glorious flood, bathing every particular leaf, and showing forth every particular bough; but, as I am not a poet, I shall go on with my story. (140–41)

In "Fairies or No Fairies," the narrator is humorously self-deprecating and self-reflexive, drawing attention to his role in the production of the folklore book, to his writing style and shortcomings. But like "The Confessions of Tom Bourke," this is a story *about* an Irish storyteller, and that storyteller is clearly *not* our narrator.

In fact, no storytelling event is detailed in "Fairies or No Fairies." Instead, the narrator generalizes about the dynamics of John Mulligan's performances and problematizes the Compiler's earlier characterization of the Irish peasantry as "believers." "Many believed [John's] stories," the narrator comments, and "many more did not believe them—but nobody, in process of time, used to contradict the old gentleman, for it was a pity to vex him" (137–38).

If commentary on the attitudes of John Mulligan's listeners undermines their status as "true believers" in supernatural lore, attention to the performance and reception of stories in "The Crookened Back" offers a performer's perspective on the manipulation of audience response. As in "The Confessions of Tom Bourke," the narrator begins by introducing an individual whose "powers of conversation are highly extolled" (296): in this case, Peggy Barrett. The narrator then reflects on Peggy's skill at adapting her story-telling to particular contexts:

Peggy, like all experienced story-tellers, suited her tales, both in length and subject, to the audience and the occasion. She knew that, in broad daylight, when the sun shines brightly, and the trees are budding, and the birds are singing around us, when men and women, *like ourselves,* are moving and speaking, employed in business or amusement; she knew, in short (although certainly without knowing or much caring wherefore), that when we are engaged about the realities of life and nature, we want that spirit of credulity, without which tales of the deepest interest will lose their power. At such times Peggy was brief, very particular as to facts, and never dealt in the marvellous. (296–97; emphasis added)

Peggy is thus portrayed as an Irish peasant storyteller with a keen sense of genre and context, fully capable of narrating straightforward and factual stories. Furthermore, the narrator suggests that the daily lives of Peggy and her audience are akin to those of English readers.

Peggy Barrett may have a wide and diverse repertoire of stories, but the performance that is highlighted in *Fairy Legends* is neither straightforward nor factual. It is, rather, a tale of suspense and supernatural encounter quoted at length, uninterrupted by audience or editorial commentary. Peggy selects an appropriate time to tell such a story as "The Crookened Back":

[R]ound the blazing hearth of a Christmas evening, when infidelity is banished from all companies, at least in low and simple life, as a quality, to say the least of it, out of season; when the winds of "dark December" whistled bleakly round the walls, and almost through the doors of the little mansion, reminding its inmates, that as the world is so vexed by elements superior to human power, so it may be visited by beings of a superior nature;—at such times would Peggy Barrett give full scope to her memory, or her imagination, or both; and upon one of these occasions, she gave the following circumstantial account of "the crookening of her back." (297)

This prologue to Peggy's narration situates her storytelling and encourages readers to reflect on the connection between genres of narrative and the conditions in which they are narrated. In the collected tales and notes, Croker has blurred the distinction—which had initially seemed so clear—between oral and literary storytellers, listeners and readers, reflecting on the art of storytelling and the complexity of "belief."

Fairy Legends concludes with a statement that harks back to the preface and asserts a significant divide between the English reader and the Irish peasant. The "Shefro, the Banshee, and the other creatures of imagination who bear them company . . . take their farewell of the reader," not because Croker has exhausted his material, nor because it is bedtime, but because critical reading of the collection forces such creatures of superstition to disappear. "As knowledge advances," these creatures "recede and vanish, and mists of the valley melt into the air beneath the beams of the morning sun." As the book concludes, Croker projects a future in which superstition is diminished in Ireland itself, and the two nations are equalized by education, particularly literacy:

When rational education shall be diffused among the misguided peasantry of Ireland, the belief in such supernatural beings must disappear in that country, as it has done in England, and these "shadowy tribes" will live only in books. The Compiler is therefore not without hope that his little Volume, which delivers the legends faithfully as they have been collected from the mouths of the peasantry, may be regarded with feelings of interest. (362–63)

Croker identifies the medium of the book—that is, the very communicative process in which his readers have been engaging with the supernatural—as an icon of rational modernity. Echoing his contemporary Edgar Taylor and their philosophic forefather John Aubrey, Croker casts the written entextualization of supernatural narratives as the death knell of oral tradition, the harbinger of progress, and England stands as the agent and prime example of this seemingly inevitable process.

The comparative perspective that characterizes Croker's work on Ireland allows him to address explicitly his intended readership's own frame of reference, as English people. Such statements do more than generalize about the Other; they also posit a level of skepticism on the part of Croker's adult and child readership, who may or may not have completed the requisite education identified as key to the dismantling of superstition. Croker's concluding statements invite English readers, regardless of education, class, or age, to direct a critical and patronizing gaze on their Irish objects; it is this process which unifies and defines them. The reader is encouraged to think himself or herself into the dominant culture; if the reader happens to be a child, she is invited to imagine herself beyond childhood. The gap between author and reader, adult and child—that rupture identified by Jacqueline Rose as a defining characteristic of literature for children—is thus minimized.[23] The true child here, in need of education and guidance, is the Irish peasant.

Within the emergent evolutionary model of culture, the English child or working-class adult *as reader* is positioned one rung above the oral story-tellers about whom he reads.

Yet the differentiation of English readers from Irish storytellers—based on technologies of communication (the written versus the oral) and world-views (the rational versus the superstitious)—is somewhat murkier than it first appears. Croker's inclusion of contextual detail and metanarrative commentary problematizes the impulse to approach the legends as transparent windows onto "misguided" belief. Instead, these distinctive dimensions of Croker's collection offer glimpses of a perspective on Irish oral tradition as artistic, playful, and ironic. Narrational ambiguity in the fairy legends themselves is the product of the strategy of mimicry that Homi K. Bhabha has identified as characteristic of colonialist discourse. But as it is often unclear who speaks, it is also unclear what is being mimicked. Croker may be speaking as the Other within the tale texts, but the interpretive framework (preface, notes) in which he places the tales may also be functioning as trompe-l'oeil, mimicking conventional representations of the Irish by the English.[24]

Placing Croker

Even the most cursory study of *Fairy Legends* reveals that Croker did not give the tales exactly as he had "found" them. Of course, it was not transcriptional but rather a form of cultural accuracy that Croker hoped to achieve and for which this work was immediately praised. Addressing an English readership of nonspecialists, Croker hoped to present his material in a way that was comprehensible and meaningful to general readers, but he lacked precedents for how to achieve these ends. Perhaps it is therefore unsurprising that *Fairy Legends* is characterized by a rather confusing narrative voice that continuously shifts perspective from insider to outsider, storyteller to commentator. These ambiguities of voicing are, in fact, paralleled by the ambiguities of Croker's relationship to his material. Croker was writing as a Londoner and for a rapidly changing English reading public, but he was raised in Cork as an Anglo-Irishman. Croker's subject position vis-à-vis his material can thus be regarded as a form of what Fiona Giles has called "enjambment," a location "between categories which are themselves in movement."[25]

Thomas Crofton Croker was born in Cork in the year of the unsuccessful Irish rebellion, 1798. As his obituary was at pains to make clear, the roots of the family—at least on the paternal side—were solidly English. Croker's father, Major Thomas Croker, was "descended from the ancient Devonshire family of that name, branches of which became settlers in the South of Ireland in the reign of Elizabeth, and under the Commonwealth."[26] The period during which Croker's ancestors emigrated from England to Ireland was important in the history of English-Irish relations.

In 1534, Henry VIII had ordered Gaelic Irish and Gaelicized English landholders alike to surrender their land to the Crown, and then regranted it. As Robert Kee has summarized, the result of these actions was that land was no longer held "according to ancient Gaelic law and tradition but by the English king's law and by the English king's goodwill, which required in return their good behaviour."[27] This requirement was enforced vigorously during the reign of Elizabeth I, and the customs and character of the Irish were scrutinized with politicized intensity throughout the Elizabethan wars in Ireland. A new and politically significant wave of English settlement in Ireland began as the queen replaced old Norman-English Irish lords and their Irish retainers with newly appointed lords and soldiers, freshly imported from England. By the mid-1590s, more than four thousand English people had been settled in the south of Ireland, as property was transferred from Irish to English ownership.[28]

If Gaelic assault against English settlers had been a constant fear and a recurrent reality, the English policies of the late sixteenth century deepened Irish resentment of the English presence further still.[29] Like generations of Anglo-Irish before him, Major Thomas Croker made a career of suppressing nationalistic uprisings in Ireland.

T. Crofton Croker downplayed this dimension of his family's heritage and did not follow in his father's footsteps.[30] Instead, he began an apprenticeship in a Cork mercantile firm in 1813. It was during this early period of his life that Croker also began to demonstrate an interest in the "antiquities" of his birthplace. Croker filled notebooks with narratives and songs he heard, peasant "character and manners" he observed, and sketches of sights he viewed during walking tours of the south of Ireland.[31]

Shortly after his father's death in 1818, Croker moved to London where he became a clerk in the Admiralty under John Wilson Croker (a family friend, unrelated). Croker was employed by the Admiralty until 1850, when he retired as clerk of the first class.

Following his move to London, Croker continued to visit the Irish countryside. In 1821, he was accompanied by the children of the painter Francis Nicholson—Croker's future wife, Marianne Nicholson, and her brother Alfred. The notes Croker made during this journey along with those from earlier excursions formed the basis for his first major published work, *Researches in the South of Ireland, Illustrative of the Scenery, Architectural Remains, and the Manners and Superstitions of the Peasantry with an Appendix, Containing a Private Narrative of the Rebellion of 1798* (1824).

Researches was "magnificently published in quarto" format[32] by John Murray and illustrated by the younger Nicholsons, Croker himself, and W. H. Brooke. Despite its impressive format, Croker indicates in his 1824 preface that the work was directed toward general interest:

The pretensions of this Volume are very humble, as it consists of little more than an arrangement of notes made during several excursions in the South of Ireland between the years 1812 and 1822.—These I have endeavoured to condense into a popular shape rather than extend by minute detail.

In this popular shape, Croker guided readers through description of the landscape, supernatural beliefs, manners and customs, architecture, natural resources, literature, and above all, the history of Ireland.

As Croker writes in the first chapter of *Researches*, this portrait of Ireland takes shape through an English lens, with past and present relations of the two nations a pervasive concern:

I have made use of the Journal of a Tour through some of the Southern Counties, as the most convenient means of combining and conveying information derived from various sources, with topographical remarks, and observations on the manners and superstitions of the peasantry. Taking the broad outline of rational and authentic history, since the connection of England with Ireland, my object has also been to illustrate the cause of existing distinctions between their respective children—a difference so strong and peculiar a nature as decidedly to separate those who should feel united in one common interest. (4)

Croker envisioned his reading audience to be primarily British and his mission to be the remedy of a general ignorance, on the part of the English, of Ireland and the Irish:

Intimately connected as are the Sister Islands of Great Britain and Ireland, it is an extraordinary fact that the latter country should be comparatively a terra incognita to the English in general, who, still notwithstanding their love of travel and usual spirit of inquiry, are still contented to remain very imperfectly acquainted with the actual state of so very near a portion of the British empire. (1)

If Ireland was indeed a terra incognita to most English readers in 1824, it was not for lack of commentary on the Irish. Considering the number of Irish immigrants (including Croker) newly settled in Britain—twelve times more Irish in Britain than British in Ireland by shortly after midcentury[33]—as well as the abundance of moralistic and politically charged portraits of the Irish in the English press, Ireland must have seemed extremely close-at-hand to the English reader of 1824. Croker's goal would therefore seem to be less the exploration of the unknown than a corrective to the accounts of Ireland and the Irish that then dominated English discourse.

Part of Croker's objective in *Researches* was to give readers pictorial and descriptive portraits of southern Ireland as a place, but his primary interest was in constructing a revised portrait of a people, especially as they compared and contrasted with the English. Croker's was an attempt to reveal the "actual state" of his birthplace and, most specifically, of the Irish peasantry: "for in the lower classes alone can national distinctions be traced" (2).

Contemporaneous assessments of the "Irish situation" were increasingly drawing a distinction between the peasantry and other classes in Ireland, with the result that the peasantry was identified not only as the most nationally distinct of classes but frequently as the most backward and corrupt. Complains one writer for *Blackwood's Magazine,*

Ireland is almost invariably spoken of as though the whole people were wretched and criminal; and almost every measure is declaimed against as useless, that is not calculated to bear upon every class alike. . . . which of the various classes of the people of Ireland needs relief and reformation? The peasantry alone.[34]

Croker obviously held the Irish peasantry in higher esteem than many of his contemporaries, but his outline of the "Irish character" similarly suggests a need for relief and reformation:

Hasty in forming opinions and projects, tardy in carrying them into effect. . . . An Irishman is the sport of his feelings; with passions the most violent and sensitive, he is alternately the child of despondency or of levity; his joy or his grief has no medium; he loves or he hates, and hurried away by the ardent stream of a heated fancy, and naturally enthusiastic, he is guilty of a thousand absurdities. . . . With a mind inexhaustible in expedient to defeat difficulties and act as a substitute for the conveniences of life which poverty denies, the peasant is lively in intellect, ardent in disposition, and robust in frame. . . . Such is an outline of the Irish character, in which there is more to call forth a momentary tribute of admiration, than to create a fixed and steady esteem. (12–13)

With the Irish peasantry as his primary study object, Croker sought to reveal the "national character" of the Irish, "the witty servility . . . mingled with occasional bursts of desperation and revenge—the devoted yet visionary patriotism—the romantic sense of honour, and improvident yet inalterable attachments" that he accepted as characteristic. Croker regarded these qualities as the products of historical circumstances, as "evidences of a conquest without system, an irregular government, and the remains of feudal clanship, the barbarous and arbitrary organization of a warlike people" (2).

Contemporaneous English characterizations of the Irish peasantry as "barbarous," "disaffected," and "rebellious"[35] echo in *Researches in the South of Ireland*, but Croker was equally critical of the English. Throughout the history of English commentary on Ireland, Croker writes,

the epithets "perfidious traitor" and "notorious rebel" are applied to every Irish chieftain—terms that almost silence further inquiry; but if the Irish were rebels and traitors, the English were at the same time plunderers and tyrants; their rapacity awakened by the hope of the spoil, and their ferocity increased by the view of that property, which violence alone could wrest from its original possessors. (6)

Researches was framed as instructive, oriented toward improvement of English understanding of the Irish as a people, and repeatedly grounded in the historical relations of Ireland to England. But Croker also invited critical reflection on an inherited historical discourse, reminding or informing his readers that this form of inquiry "presents few features that will gratify the pride of a native or the feelings of an Englishman" (4).

Despite such criticisms of British policy, and despite such thinly veiled commentaries on contemporary political issues (like property rights, for example), Croker argued that his work in *Researches* was apolitical: "Politics have been carefully avoided; whether this will be considered a recommendation, or a defect, I have yet to learn" (preface). Indeed, Croker makes no explicit references to the "actual state" of Irish-English politics circa 1824, such as renewed English fears of Irish rebellion or the movement for Catholic emancipation. Nonetheless, Croker's overarching concern with Irish national character and history, continuously placed in comparative relation to English national character and history, is in itself politically charged. At the nexus of Croker's interests in history, national character, and political relations is folklore.

Foreshadowing statements made at the outset and conclusion of *Fairy Legends*, Croker suggests in *Researches* that "the vulgar superstition—the traditionary tale—even the romantic legend—possess a relative value from the conclusions to which they lead." Such folklore forms have "claims on the attention" of English readers, "superior to those of mere curiosity." Antiquities, he asserts, are valuable "as they afford a means of forming a correct judgment of the civilization, knowledge and taste of the period to which they belong" (3). In the context of Croker's own writing, as well as in the broader context of English-Irish relations, judgments of Irish civilization, knowledge, and taste were not mere curiosities but politically resonant.

Despite Croker's claim of apoliticism, the political implications of *Researches in the South of Ireland* were clear to his contemporaries, some of whom drew more radical and derisive conclusions about Irish culture than Croker ever suggests. Wrote one reviewer:

In the South of Ireland, the fairy superstition is one of the forms in which entire ignorance disguises itself—one of the thousand creeds in which "the mystery of iniquity" is expressed, and exists actively operating;—though separable from Popery, it is not, and will not be, separated, except in argument, intended to deceive.[36]

Cast as the embodiment of Irish superstition and as a symptom of Irish ignorance, this living narrative tradition provided ready "proof" of the need for religious reformation.

In *Researches in the South of Ireland*, Croker emphasizes the "present state of Irish superstition," not "the traditionary tale" per se. Yet even in this context Croker indicates that folk narratives offer more than comparative and historical insight. Characterizing Irish conceptions of the supernatural as "an odd mixture of the ridiculous and the sublime" (78), Croker here points toward an appreciation of fairy legends on aesthetic grounds and because they may serve as indices of a distinct Irish national character. Issues of style and cultural indexicality would continue to shape Croker's study of such tales.

Although Croker's son, T. F. Dillon Croker, remembers *Researches in the South of Ireland* as "favourably received," it never achieved much popular success (v). It was not until the spring of 1825, when John Murray published the small, anonymous volume illustrated by W. H. Brooke and entitled *Fairy Legends and Traditions of the South of Ireland*, that Croker's work achieved great popularity.

Dillon Croker writes that he could discover little information in his father's papers "to throw any light on the history of his first collection of Irish legends" (v). It is known that Croker received an encouraging letter from Murray, in which the publisher stated his confidence that the "Fairy Tales deserve to be sold" and his belief that "they will sell well."[37] Certainly the fact that Croker's second work was published anonymously, in a more modest format, and garnered the author the relatively small sum of £80 would seem to suggest that Murray was, at least initially, more interested in maximizing profitability than in building Croker's reputation as a cultural expert.

Fairy Legends did prove popular, and a second edition was released within a year. In stark contrast to the initial volume, in which the collection of narratives was prefaced by just a short paragraph, the second edition of 1826 included not only the author's name but also an "Author's Preface," in which Croker emerges from the shadows of anonymity. Here, he expresses surprise at the success of the work: "When collecting the following stories I had no idea that I should be called upon for a preface to a second edition; the favour with which they have been received was completely unexpected by me" (xx). Croker promises readers that he means "to comply with the hint" that additional volumes were desired "so far as shortly to trouble the public with *one* more" (iv).

Within weeks of the initial publication of *Fairy Legends*, Croker had departed for Bristol, "with an intention of making a tour in the South of Ireland, for the purpose of gleaning, in the course of six weeks, the remainder of the fairy legends and traditions which Mr. Murray, of Albermarle Street, suspected were still to be found lurking among its glens—having satisfied himself as to the value of dealing in the publication of such fanciful articles."[38] It was Murray, not Croker, who "suspected" that there were yet more fairy legends "still to be found lurking" in the south of Ireland; it was primarily commercial, not scholarly, motivations that sent Croker back to the field and expanded *Fairy Legends* beyond its initial format. Fatigue and sickness delayed Croker's fieldwork somewhat, but he managed to publish the second and third volumes of *Fairy Legends* in 1827 and 1828, respectively.

The small, single volume was to prove to be the work's most enduring format. The three volumes were condensed into one and reissued in 1834 as number 47 of John Murray's "Family Library." As opposed to the work's original format, in which each and every tale was followed by Croker's notes, the Family Library edition substituted "a brief summary" at the close of each section. The process of selection utilized in the editing of the notes, the reader is assured, sacrificed "nothing which illustrates in the slightest degree the popular Fairy Creed of Ireland" (iv). The result is a more marginalized editorial voice and a set of notes more clearly and much more narrowly focused on Irish fairy beliefs.

The condensed version reduced the fifty tales of the original three volumes to forty. The exclusion of these ten tales, as the preface to the Family Library edition asserts provocatively, "will sufficiently answer doubts idly raised as to the question of authorship" (iv). That Croker's name did not appear on the title page of the initial volume of this work has generally been attributed to "its being in some measure a joint production," made necessary when Croker lost his manuscript and turned to fellow antiquarians for help in reconstructing the tales.[39] Thomas Keightley in particular had laid claim to "a fair proportion of the tales, and a very large proportion of the Notes in the first and second volumes," and had pointed to "no less than eight or ten other persons [who] contributed portions of fairy lore."[40] Although Croker alludes to several folk informants by name, he makes no mention of his fellow antiquarians as sources.

While it has been acknowledged that "the exact nature of the cooperative venture remains obscure,"[41] that *Fairy Legends* was in some way the product of collaboration has rarely been called into question. Hultin and Ober liken the writing of *Fairy Legends* to practices current among "nineteenth century collectors and . . . also a method much practised by the writers and editors of popular journals, whose essays were frequently the product of a number of writers" (xxv). But, as Keightley's complaint makes clear, authorial ambiguity did not always sit quite so comfortably, and the appropriateness of such a method to the publication of folktale collections was not universally accepted.

Considering the present historical status of the work as the first field-based collection in Britain, it is somewhat ironic that the Irish peasant narrators Croker ostensibly quotes figure nowhere in the debate over the authorship of *Fairy Legends and Traditions of the South of Ireland*. As we have seen, Croker does, on a few occasions, credit named individuals with the renditions of tales in his collection: for example, Mrs. Philipps of "The Brewery of Eggshells" (71) or Tom Bourke of "The Confessions of Tom Bourke" (133). Yet it was not so much a passion for individual creativity among the Irish that stimulated Croker's work as his interest in drawing an accurate portrait of the Irish peasantry as a whole. If, as he claimed, the legends had been "told by half of the old women of the district in which the scene is laid," then a figure such as Mrs. Philipps was, like the Grimms' informant Dorothea Viehmann, more significant as a representative of such a group than as a named individual.

Croker based *Fairy Legends* on the same research he used for chapter 5 of *Researches in the South of Ireland*, entitled "Fairies and Supernatural Agency,"[42] but his treatments of traditional narratives in the two works are distinguished in several important ways. In chapter 5 of *Researches*, Croker had integrated tales in paraphrased form or, in one case, embedded in a letter to his sister (88–90). The focus had been on the content of such narratives: types of fairies and categories of supernatural phenomena. No attempt is made in this earlier work to reproduce actual storytelling events or to evoke even a generalized Irish storytelling context. *Fairy Legends* is, by contrast, a tale collection: twenty-seven distinct, cohesive, titled narratives. Stories and storytellers take center stage, with most of the observations about the nature of Irish belief and customs relegated to the notes that follow each tale. Croker makes clear from the outset that style of narrative presentation signifies; that a particular mode of expression may index nationally distinctive modes of thought and behavior.

The different emphases of *Researches* and *Fairy Legends* are exemplified by Croker's quite different treatments of the same narratives in the two works. In *Researches*, for example, Croker refers to the legend of O'Donoghue, as the narrative had been "preserved" by other writers:

O'Donoghue, a chief of much celebrity, whose May-Day visit on a milk white horse, gliding over the lake of Killarney, to the sound of unearthly music, and attended by troops of spirits scattering delicious spring flowers, has been lyrically preserved by Mr. Moore, and is accurately recorded in a poem by Mr. Leslie on Killarney, and in Mr. Weld's account of that Lake, as also in Derrick's Letters, where some additional particulars may be found from the pen of Mr. Ockenden.—"There is a farmer now alive," says that gentleman, "who declares, as I am told, that riding one evening near the lower end of the Lake was overtaken by a gentleman, who seemed under thirty years of age, very handsome in his person, very sumptuous in his apparel, and very affable in conversation. (97–98)

The few details of the story Croker provides here arrive fourthhand: Croker's citation of Ockenden's quotation of an anonymous report of a farmer's declaration.

By contrast, "The Legend of O'Donoghue" stands as an independent, five-page story in *Fairy Legends*. So while in *Researches*, O'Donoghue had been described as simply "a chief of much celebrity," Croker's later version of the legend begins with significantly more flourish and a variation on "Once upon a time":

In an age so distant that the precise period is unknown, a chieftain named O'Donoghue ruled over the country which surrounds the romantic Lough Lean, now called the lake of Killarney. Wisdom, beneficence, and justice distinguished his reign, and the prosperity and happiness of his subjects were their natural results.

As opposed to Croker's earlier treatment, the legend itself unfolds in *Fairy Legends* in a narrative voice that tells the tale as true and with considerably more dramatic flare than previously:

Some years have elapsed since the last appearance of O'Donoghue. . . . The first beams of the rising sun were just gilding the lofty summit of Glenaa, when the waters near the eastern shore of the lake became suddenly and violently agitated, though all the rest of its surface lay smooth and still as a tomb of polished marble. The next moment a foaming wave darted forward, and, like a proud high-crested war-horse, exulting in his strength, rushed across the lake towards Toomies mountain. Behind this wave appeared a stately warrior fully armed, mounted upon a milk-white steed; his snowy plume waved gracefully from a helmet of polished steel, and at his back fluttered a light blue scarf. . . .
   The warrior was O'Donoghue; he was followed by numberless youths and maidens, who moved light and unconstrained over the watery plain, as the moonlight fairies glide through the fields of air; they were linked together by garlands of delicious spring flowers, and they timed their movements to strains of enchanting melody. (355–56)

Both the legend and O'Donoghue himself had previously been treated by Croker in a perfunctory way, of interest only as they were exemplary of certain classes of supernatural narratives and folk heroes. In *Fairy Legends*, on the other hand, both the narrative and its hero are ennobled by the use of a rather flowery style and the inclusion of elaborate detail.

   In the notes that follow "The Legend of O'Donoghue," Croker again makes reference to the narrative's appearance in a number of written sources. Yet he also implies that the legend is part of an ongoing oral tradition, stating that "Every person who has visited Killarney must be familiar with the Legend of O'Donoghue and his white horse" (357). Presumably, Croker is no exception, drawing his rendition from field rather than library research.

   This particular form of access to others' stories emerges, somewhat ironically, as the mark of both authenticity and authority: to deliver "the legends faithfully as they have been collected from the mouths of the peasantry" Croker at once gives "credit to the imagination of the Irish peasantry" (359) and defends his status as "author" and cultural expert. Such claims may further confuse the issue of voicing and deeper issues of oral tradition as intellectual property, but they also serve the important function of directing reader attention to Croker's overarching objective, which was to teach the English about the Irish.

It is to this point that we must return, for despite the marked differences between *Researches* and *Fairy Legends*, the two works share a central authorial goal: to represent Irish national character for a primarily English readership, as a means of reflection on the differences between the two. As Croker asserts in *Researches*, he believed that "closer study" of Ireland "would prove that in political feeling, in language, in manners, and almost every particular that stamps a national character, the two Islands differ essentially" (2). Despite differences, Croker casts the current state of the Irish as directly relevant to English readers' understanding of themselves: "On the whole," he writes, "from what may be collected, the present state of Irish superstition closely resembles that of England during the age of Elizabeth; a strong proof of the correct measurement of those who have stated a space of two centuries to exist between the relative degree of popular knowledge and civilization attained by the sister kingdom" (99).[43] Croker's positioning of these "essentially" different nations on the great ladder of cultural evolution reinforces English stereotypes about the Irish, and feeds English fantasies of cultural superiority, but in a backhanded way. These portraits of Irish manners and customs may strike the English reader as distinctly foreign, but Croker encourages his audience to engage in this reading self-reflexively.

Despite the dichotomies invoked in Croker's statements of purpose—English/Irish, subject/object, storyteller/reader, superstition/knowledge—Croker himself remains difficult to locate in such schemata. Croker exhibits a profound ambivalence regarding the object of his study, describing the "present Irish character" as a "compound of strange and apparent inconsistencies, where vices and virtues are so unhappily blended that it is difficult to distinguish or separate them" (12). It is evident from his writings that he admires and is fascinated by the Irish peasantry of the South, yet he repeatedly projects a (desirable) future in which education, "reform and relief" make them increasingly similar to English people. As a Protestant Irishman of English descent, living most of his life in London, working for the English Admiralty, and writing about the Irish Catholic peasantry for a primarily English readership, Croker's personal relation to both his subject matter and his readership was indeed ambiguous.

Picturing the Peasantry

Two discourses have been connected to Croker's *Fairy Legends*: On the one hand, there is the deceptively innocent discourse about the timeless and universal qualities of the imagination—perhaps best exemplified by Charlotte Yonge's comments in the 1860s; and on the other, there is the politically charged discourse about cultural identities and national character. These two discourses have pictorial equivalents in the illustrations. Mimicry, ambiguity, and irony leave interpretive possibilities open. Are Croker's Irish narrators to be admired and emulated, pitied and assisted, or despised and conquered? As Croker's illustrators shifted attention from fairy to peasant, from the romantic picturesque to the comic grotesque, they helped shape the way in which these legends were received by English readers.

As with *German Popular Stories*, illustration played a significant role in the commercial success of *Fairy Legends*. Croker may have remained anonymous in the first edition, but the book's illustrator did not: He was William Henry Brooke. Most of the engravings Brooke provided for the 1825 edition of *Fairy Legends* were not, strictly speaking, illustrations. The designs are not attached to particular events or characters, but positioned at the beginning and end of each of the five sections of the book: "The Shefro," "The Cluricaune," "The Banshee," "The Phooka," and "Thierna Na Oge."

Brooke's engravings offer images of the supernatural that are, like Cruikshank's, generally playful and distinctly unthreatening. At the opening of "The Shefro," graceful fairies frolic around a mushroom (figure 8); at the section's close, a fairy lounges gracefully under a mushroom while another tickles a butterfly with a cattail (figure 9). The "cluricaune" are represented by a humorous leprechaun perched upon a barrel and another who cobbles a little shoe. Brooke's work is clearly part of a tradition of fairy art, which gained momentum in the late nineteenth century.[44] More specifically, he inhabits that corner of fairy painting in which the "good people" appear charming, delicate, unthreatening, but his illustrations stand in contrast with the fairies as described in the narratives themselves.

In the stories Croker collected, fairies often appear as mischievous and often malicious beings. They hinder the ordinary Irishman's attempts to farm the land, herd his cattle, or fish the waters; they pose a distinct threat to young children, whom they snatch and replace with hideously malformed and ill-tempered changelings; they are often aggressive, capable of disfiguring human beings; and they possess superhuman strength. Nonetheless, even the subtle pictorial references to frightening incidents in the legends are

FAIRY LEGENDS.

THE SHEFRO.

——————————————————"Fairy Elves
Whose midnight revels, by a forest side
Or fountain, some belated peasant sees,
Or dreams he sees, while over-head the Moon
Sits arbitress, and nearer to the earth
Wheels her pale course."—

MILTON.

8. W. H. Brooke, frolicking fairies from T. Crofton Croker's *Fairy Legends and Traditions of the South of Ireland* (1825).

9. W. H. Brooke, fairies from Croker's *Fairy Legends and Traditions of the South of Ireland* (1825).

muted. For example, the drawings that decorate the section on "The Ban-shee" do bear some relation to the narratives: The title character of "The Bunworth Banshee" (figure 10) is described sitting "under a tree that was struck by the lightning" (224), but what Brooke does not depict is the terror, dread, and panic that the banshee's keening, screeching, howling, and win-dow scratching arouse in the Bunworth household.

Brooke's lovely and picturesque fairies are not the only beings to have decorated this tale collection. When the second edition of *Fairy Legends* was issued in 1826, it contained the original artwork as well as six new pictures. Although these 1826 engravings were credited to W. H. Brooke, the designs on which they were based are reputedly the work of Irish artist Daniel Maclise.[45] The new engravings were meant to depict precise moments in the narratives and faced relevant pages in the written text. In this second set of illustrations the fairy folk share the stage with Irish peasants.

The human characters drawn here are of a stock type, almost

10. W. H. Brooke, banshee from Croker's *Fairy Legends and Traditions of the South of Ireland* (1825).

indistinguishable from one another, uniformly grotesque in their facial features, frequently ridiculous in their behavior. For instance, this set of illustrations includes depictions of such human folly as Billy McDaniel's enslavement to a fairy who offers unlimited drink, from the story "Master and Man" (figure 11), and Pat Murphy and Jack Lynch's futile pursuit of a leprechaun (figure 12). When juxtaposed against elegantly drawn fairies, as in figure 13, the Irish peasant family looks all the more absurd. Unlike the "rustics" of English painting, these Irish peasants have ceased to be aesthetically pleasing and "picturesque"; they can be regarded with neither nostalgia nor complacence. In appearance, circumstance, and behavior, these peasants have become grotesque, in urgent need of reform.

* * *

As an attempt at cross-cultural representation, *Fairy Legends and Traditions of the South of Ireland* had a broader reach than Croker might have anticipated.

11. Daniel Maclise (attributed; signed by Brooke), "Master and Man," Croker's *Fairy Legends and Traditions of the South of Ireland*, 2d ed. (1826).

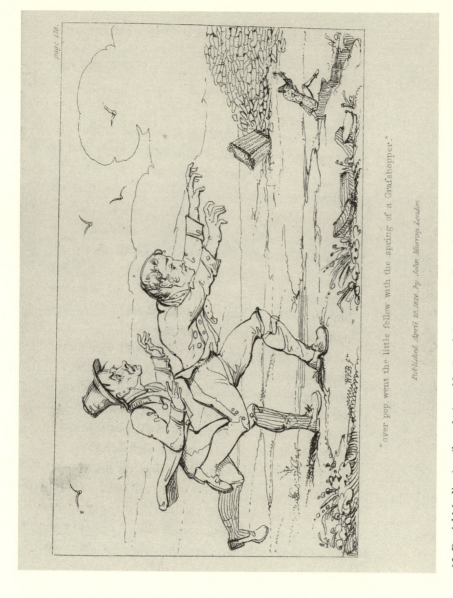

"over pop. went the little fellow with the spring of a Grasshopper."

Published April 12, 1826 by John Murray, London.

12. Daniel Maclise (attributed; signed by Brooke), Pat Murphy and Jack Lynch, Croker's *Fairy Legends and Traditions of the South of Ireland,* 2d ed. (1826).

"Look there! look there, mammy!"

Published April 10 1826 by John Murray, London.

13. Daniel Maclise (attributed; signed by Brooke), "Legend of Bottle Hill," Croker's *Fairy Legends and Traditions of the South of Ireland*, 2d ed. (1826).

Shortly after its anonymous publication, a very favorable and also anonymous review of the book appeared in the German periodical *Göttingische Gelehrte Anzeigen*. The author of that review was Wilhelm Grimm.[46] By the turn of 1826, Wilhelm had intimate familiarity with Croker's collection, having spent the previous summer translating the work into German with his brother Jacob.[47]

The Grimms' translation, entitled *Irische Elfenmärchen*, was published in February 1826. The resemblance of Croker's project to the Grimms' *Kinder- und Hausmärchen* has been evident to contemporary readers, as I mentioned earlier, but it was also evident to the tale collectors themselves.[48] The Grimms not only translated Croker's text; they added notes of their own, detailing parallels between their research and this Irish collection.[49]

The brothers valued Croker's *Fairy Legends* as more than a point of comparison. John Hennig suggests that "from the beginning of their acquaintance with the *Fairy Legends*, the Grimms had regarded them not only as a source of information on the folklore tradition of just another country in addition to the many others they had studied, but more especially as a means of acquiring some knowledge of Ireland" (49). Indeed, that the reading of such tales should serve to improve foreigners' understanding of the Irish was Croker's express goal, and resonates with the Grimms' view of their own collecting efforts as offering insight to authentic German national character.

Writing fifty years ago, Hennig complained that no one had explored the contact between and mutual influence of T. Crofton Croker and the Brothers Grimm. In fact, little has been said on the subject to this day. However, far less has been said about the parallels between *German Popular Stories* and *Fairy Legends*, published only two years apart and intended for a similar market of readers. One parallel lies in the fact that like the English versions of the Grimms' tales, Croker's legends are still read, whether anthologized or abridged, with the important difference that the name of Grimm has become inseparable from certain tales, while Taylor and Croker are all but forgotten. Despite Croker's reclaimed importance to the history of the study of folklore, he remains relatively unknown in the broader field of intellectual history, having "slipped into an obscurity so profound that even specialists in the nineteenth century do not recognize the name."[50]

Just two years before the initial publication of *Fairy Legends*, Edgar Taylor's translation of the Grimms' *Kinder- und Hausmärchen* had set a precedent for the publication in England of a folktale collection that was both critical and popular, instructive and entertaining. By the time the small, il-

lustrated, annotated, and anonymous volume of Irish traditional tales entitled *Fairy Legends and Traditions of the South of Ireland* was published in
1825, the commercial viability of such reading material had been demonstrated, and perceptions of its value for a wide readership had begun to take
shape. Croker's various experiments with the contextualization of oral traditional tales and the narrativization of his own field encounters resonate with
the intentions of later folklorists and provided an opportunity for a more
nuanced portrayal of the "superstitious" Irish than formerly available. Nonetheless, the matter of how best to provide an informed and informative rendering of traditional narratives in a format with mass appeal was far from
resolved.

To create a tale collection, Croker reshaped the fairy material he had
collected in the south of Ireland and published in *Researches,* and it was received differently by English readers. Instead of inspiring open attacks on
Catholicism, Irish fairy legends and beliefs were now *celebrated* as forms of
"innocent and not irrational entertainment," as "specimens of national manners," illustrations of "the origin or connection of different races of men," or
vehicles of "physical or moral truth."

Abstracted from the process of storytelling, Irish fairy belief had been
the politicized object of scorn. As a corpus of fairy tales, Croker's research
became linked to a transcendent vision of the oral traditional tale as timeless
and universal—rhetoric which would be mobilized with increasing frequency
by advocates of imaginative literature for children in the decades to come,
and which still echoes. But even as it was (re)constructed as ideologically
neutral, *Fairy Legends* retained its ambivalent political charge, as the reillus-
tration of the tales in 1826 demonstrates. As readers of imported tales, we are
never simply tapping into the realm of otherworldliness; we are also casting
our gaze, together, on the Other.

Chapter 4
Otherness and Otherworldliness: *Edward W. Lane's* Arabian Nights

The doubtful and obscure become truth and elucidation in his hands: we are improved, in spite of ourselves, and even by the very means we seek to avoid it; and customs, and manners, and habits of thought, become familiarized to us, even as amongst the chosen playthings of indolent recreation.[1]

—*Reviewer for the* Foreign Quarterly Review, *1838*

Edward William Lane's translation of *Alf Layla wa Layla*—known in English as *1001 Nights* or as the *Arabian Nights*—was commissioned by the Society for the Diffusion of Useful Knowledge (SDUK) and published by Charles Knight, first in thirty-two periodic installments (1838–40) and subsequently in three extensively annotated and illustrated volumes (1839–41). At 2s. an installment or 4s. 6d. a volume, Lane's treatment of the *Arabian Nights* was situated squarely in the midst of the philanthropically driven effort to bring literature to the masses. In these forms, the *Arabian Nights* was indeed the "chosen plaything" of many English readers in the late 1830s.

In each of its many manuscript forms, spanning six centuries,[2] *Alf Layla wa Layla* is infamously complex in its narrative structure and erotic in much of its content. The "frame story" establishes yet another woman as storyteller: Shahrazád, the vizier's daughter, who must narrate fascinating tales nightly to her husband in order to stave off her own execution.[3] The potentially destructive power of sexual desire is at the heart of the tales Shahrazád tells—as well as those told by characters in stories within her stories—and is central to her husband's own state of rage and distress. The unit of organization in *Alf Layla wa Layla* is not the self-enclosed "tale" but the "night," left purposely open-ended to hold the interest of the murderous King Shahriyár—and the reader.

Like both Taylor and Croker, Lane created a text comprised of distinct and coherent chapters, rendered "suitable" for family reading, and unified by a vision of foreign national character, constructed and reinforced in editorial commentary. In Lane's case, this required considerable manipulation of form and content. Selected tales were translated and grouped together into thirty chapters, accommodating the perceived tastes of a mass readership, the formal conventions of English literature, and the requirements of serial publication. Extensive annotation concluded each chapter, to "render it more intelligible and agreeable to the English reader."[4] The treatment that resulted was considered by many to be "the standard English version for general reading," from the publication of the first installment in 1838 until the early twentieth century.[5]

By the late 1830s, the *Nights* had long been regarded in England as appealingly fanciful, if slightly self-indulgent, reading material. Some forty years earlier, a letter to the editor of *Gentleman's Magazine* suggested that there "is perhaps no kind of reading better adapted to awake the mental faculties of childhood, and create the ardor of admiration, which is often succeeded in riper years, by superior energy of mind, and a thirst for more solid knowledge."[6] By creating a new translation that was entertaining and inoffensive, and by explicating the manners and customs of the source culture for the general English reader, Lane sought to offer an experience that would awaken both admiration and intellect, that would—like *German Popular Stories* and *Fairy Legends and Traditions of the South of Ireland*—be both diverting and improving. Although translations from later in the century, by John Payne (1882–84) and Richard Burton (1885–86),[7] proved to be influential, it was Edward William Lane who established rhetorical and editorial strategies that frame *Alf Layla wa Layla* as both ethnographically valuable and appropriate for a wide range of English readers, including children.[8]

Lane regarded his translation of the tales, his annotations, and, to a more limited extent, William Harvey's illustrations[9] to be mutually illuminating, intrinsically bound. The true "value" of the *Arabian Nights*, he proposed, resided in its "minute accuracy with respect to those peculiarities which distinguish the Arabs from every other nation, not only of the West, but also of the East." He regarded his mission to be the translation of both the narratives and the overall "character" of the text.[10] In order to understand the *Nights*, Lane believed that English readers must understand the culture in which the text originated and which he strongly held to be Egyptian.

The telling of stories provides the *Nights* with its master trope, shaping not only the frame story but also many of the tales Shahrazád "tells," as the characters in her stories-within-the-story are called upon to become narrators themselves. The pervasiveness of storytelling as a theme, its significance to the narrative structuring of the *Nights*, the anonymity of the scriptors, and the lack of a single authoritative text have combined to lead many critics, from the eighteenth century to the present day, to treat the *Nights* as if it were part of an oral rather than a popular literary tradition. Some have gone so far as to cast the fictional character of Shahrazád as master *raconteuse*, drawing on the established imaginative appeal of the female folk narrator and suggesting that it is she "who is the supreme storyteller in this text and the ventriloquist who manipulates the varied voices of the characters whose stories she tells."[11] As we will see, Lane himself repeatedly relates the fantastical stories of the *Nights* to the narrative habits of modern Egyptians, placing *Alf Layla wa Layla* within a broad oral discursive tradition, despite the fact that it is "generally viewed as a 'folk book,' normally not narrated."[12]

The role of storytelling within particular tale cycles and in the *Arabian Nights* as a whole has been examined from various angles elsewhere, and Lane has often been criticized in such contexts for his editorial insensitivity to the complex narrative structure of the work. But Lane's own interest in and treatment of such matters have been overlooked.[13] Critics have frequently characterized Lane's notes as sociological,[14] but the closer one looks, the more inadequate this designation seems. However erroneous Lane's underlying assumptions may be, the notes that accompany his translation are not only sociological but also ethnographic, philological, literary, and folkloristic. In particular, it is the seemingly incongruous combination of ethnographic detail and translated fantasy narratives or, as my title suggests, of "otherness" and "otherworldliness" that is of interest here.

In much recent scholarship, Lane's project of retranslation has been dismissed as "a pretext for a long sociological discourse on the East,"[15] and his approach has been characterized as "the imposition of a scholarly will on an untidy reality."[16] The *Nights* itself has been cast as a "frivolous text" used or manipulated by Europeans to support preconceived notions of Arab character.[17] But the status of the work as "fantasy" was not incidental to its emergence as popular English reading or as an accepted and frequently cited source of cultural insight. It was central to the orientalizing of the *Nights* and the popular tale in general. As Edward Said has revealed, the Orient of the nineteenth century was "less a place" than an imagined "*topos*, a set of references, a congeries of characteristics,"[18] or, in V. G. Kiernan's words, Europeans' "collective day-dream."[19] The Orient was central to the discursive construction of the West as dominant, civilized, and rational. The *Nights* could be used, as Rana Kabbani argues, "to express for the age the erotic longings that would have otherwise remained suppressed."[20] It also came to stand for irrationality, indolence, and the imagination itself.

The narrative genres that comprise *Alf Layla wa Layla* range, as Robert Irwin notes, from fable, "cosmological fantasy," and *Märchen* to bawdy stories and "pornography."[21] Despite this diversity, Lane drew special attention to tales of magic and the supernatural:

> I endeavour to shew, by extracts from esteemed Arabic histories and scientific and other writings . . . as well as by assertions and anecdotes that I have heard, and conduct that I have witnessed, during my intercourse with Arabs, that the most extravagant relations in this work are not in general regarded, even by the educated classes of that people, as of an incredible nature. This is a point which I deem of much importance to set the work in its proper light before my countrymen.[22]

In lengthy annotations as well as in his suggestions to Harvey, Lane sought to provide portraits of Arabian life based in large part on his firsthand experience of modern Egypt—from costume and architecture, to customs and morality, to the very acts of storytelling and interpretation. As we will see, Harvey's designs frequently present detailed depictions of architecture and costume, although a significant number focus instead on the fantastical dimensions of the tales, giving only the vaguest suggestion of Egyptian material culture. The imaginative qualities of the tales were constructed as a reflection of culture and of difference, as an ethnographic fact that distinguished Egypt from England.

The Tale of the Book

Alf Layla wa Layla has a history as long and as complicated as Shahrazád's tales, including multiple manuscripts, printed texts, translations, and correspondences with oral narrative traditions. Neither a static text nor a collection from oral tradition, the *Nights* may most accurately be regarded as a complex narrative phenomenon.[23] If the *Nights* weave a web of narrative structures and embedded authorial attributions, let us take our cue from the text and begin by paying special attention to the origins and history of Lane's own ethnographic, annotational narratives.

When Lane began work on the *Nights*, English readers were familiar with the work primarily through English translation and adaptations of Antoine Galland's *Les Mille et Une Nuits: Contes Arabes*, which had been published in French in the early eighteenth century.[24] Although the first seven volumes of *Contes Arabes* were based on a fourteenth-century Syrian manuscript, Galland's is anything but a literal translation of a single text. Because Galland had "exhausted his material" before exhausting his readers' interest,[25] his publisher "borrowed" from the work of another translator in the same publishing house, falsely linking these tales to the *Contes Arabes* in order to "furnish more 'copy.' "[26] The remainder of the tales in the collection were based on the repertoire of a Maronite scholar, Youhenna "Hanna" Diab, who met Galland while visiting Paris in or around 1709.[27] It is from this man, and not from manuscript translation, that many of the best-known tales—such as those of Aladdin and Ali Baba—were drawn.[28]

The demand for translations of Galland's *Contes Arabes* precipitated the appearance of versions in English, the first of which was available in 1706, if not earlier, with many others to follow in the decades to come.[29] By the turn of the nineteenth century, English editions of the *Arabian Nights' Entertainments*, as the work was then commonly known, numbered more than eighteen, and by midcentury the publication rate of new and reprinted editions had doubled.[30]

Not all English readers were satisfied with Galland's *Contes Arabes* as a model for editions of *Alf Layla wa Layla*. For example, the accuracy of the *Contes Arabes* became an issue of open debate in the correspondence section of *Gentleman's Magazine*. In September 1794, one reader of the magazine bemoaned the fact that available translations were incomplete. He pointed out that in "the Bodleian, there are many more of these fables in the original Arabick, which have not yet been introduced to the English reader, and which would probably form a valuable acquisition to the stock of innocent amusement in our language."[31] Four years later, "W.W." likewise called for a more complete edition of the *Nights*, although what this reader craved was not more innocent amusement but the inclusion of poetic and morally reflective passages:

The French translation, from which our English one is made, is generally supposed to be very defective. Would not a new translation, therefore, be gladly received by the publick; especially if it represented those fine poetical passages and moral reflexions with which, we are told, the original abounds, but of which scarce a vestige remains in the present translation.[32]

Complaint had begun to take the form of a cry for an edition that was both textually and culturally more accurate, truer to the manuscripts in content, form, and worldview.

The premise that the *Nights* was a potentially valuable source of information regarding Arab lifeways and attitudes was, in fact, well established by this time. As Leila Ahmed has detailed, such a notion was "proclaimed on the work's title-page almost since the *Arabian Nights'* first appearance in England: As early as 1713, the text had been presented as *Arabian Nights . . . containing a better account of the Customs, Manners, and Religion of the Eastern Nations, viz. Tartars, Persians, and Indians, than is to be met with any author hitherto published.*[33] When Henry Weber surveyed the mixed response with which eighteenth-century England had greeted the *Nights*, he proposed that the "true and striking picture of manners and customs" offered therein was the one aspect of the tales' value that had "never been called into question."[34] This dimension of the text was emphasized in other prefaces and introductory essays of the early nineteenth century, while the growing interest in textual accuracy inspired close analysis of Galland's translation and the various Arabic manuscripts.[35] It is in such a context that Lane, known to the English reading public as something of an expert on Egypt, was heralded as "absolutely the fittest of writers for the task" of translating the *Nights* anew.[36]

Born in 1801, Edward William Lane was a man of modest means who received little formal education. Although he planned to attend Cambridge, he never did so. Instead he followed the example of his brother Richard and apprenticed as an engraver in London.[37] After a bout of typhus fever and three years of self-teaching in Egyptian history and Arabic language, Lane left England for the Near East in 1825.[38] As Lane was later to be quoted, this voyage was undertaken with the intention to "throw myself entirely among strangers . . . to adopt their language, their customs, and their dress; and in order to make as much progress as possible in their literature, it was my intention to associate almost exclusively with the Muslim inhabitants."[39] Lane's interest in such matters as modern Egyptian language, custom, and dress and their relevance to the study of literature—the connection he implies between living as a native and reading as a native—would shape his approach to the *Arabian Nights*. However, the work he produced during this first voyage was even broader in its scope: Entitled *Description of Egypt*, the manuscript covered both ancient and modern times and included over a hundred of Lane's own sepia drawings.[40]

Description of Egypt was not published in Lane's lifetime, perhaps due to the expense of reproducing the illustrations.[41] As his grandnephew Stanley Lane-Poole writes, "Lane himself was never a rich man, and could not have issued the book at his own expense, and no publisher was sufficiently enterprising to risk the first outlay."[42] It was only when the material on ancient Egypt was dropped altogether, and the writings on contemporary Egyptian manners and customs were revised and expanded, that Lane found a publisher in Charles Knight. Lane's second voyage to Egypt was made with the express purpose of revising and expanding that section of his earlier work, and in 1836 the results were published as *Account of the Manners and Customs of the Modern Egyptians*. Years had passed since Lane's search for a publisher had begun, and the author's health and finances had suffered greatly in the meantime.[43]

The offer to publish a work on modern Egyptian culture came from the Society for the Diffusion of Useful Knowledge, an organization founded by Lord Brougham in 1826 and made up of "statesmen, lawyers, and philanthropists" with interests in mass publication and popular education.[44] In association with Knight,[45] the SDUK sought to make available in inexpensive editions works they deemed of value to a wide readership, serving "a blow aimed at the monopoly of literature [and] the opening of the flood-gates of knowledge."[46] Indeed, the joint efforts of Knight and the SDUK are generally given a place of prominence in the early nineteenth-century movement in which "the most expensive treasures of literature, the choicest garnerings of . . . knowledge, were placed at the disposal of the meagrest purse." As was to be the case with the initial printing of Lane's *Nights*, affordable publication was often enabled by the division of larger works into "small weekly or monthly parts, at an infinitesimal cost."[47]

Exactly how wide this "popular" readership was envisioned to be is clarified by Knight in an 1828 report for the SDUK. He writes:

We *all* want Popular Literature—we all want to get at real and substantial knowledge by the most compendious processes. . . . But we are all tasked, some by our worthless ambitions and engrossing pleasures—most by our necessary duties. . . . We are ashamed of our ignorance—we cannot remain in it; but we have not the time to attain any sound knowledge upon the ancient principle of reading doggedly through a miscellaneous library, even if we had the opportunity.[48]

Knight suggests that with the exception of those few people for "whom learning is the business of life," the entire reading public remained "all too ignorant" of certain subjects: "the wonders of Nature . . . the discoveries of Science and Philosophy . . . the real History of past ages—of the manners and political condition of the other members of the great human family" (69). The popular manners and customs of foreign cultures were conceived to be appropriate and even useful subject matter for English popular literature, and clearly it was to this latter category of knowledge that Lane's *Modern Egyptians* and his treatment of the *Arabian Nights* were seen to contribute.

In *Modern Egyptians*, Lane covered topics ranging from Muslim Egyptian costume and physical characteristics to festivals and funerary customs— all under the rubric of "manners and customs." The appeal of such material is evinced by the fact that the work was reissued in a "Cheaper Edition" within a year[49] and remains in print to the present day.

As Lane writes in the preface to *Modern Egyptians*, his early interest in Arabic as a language had been overtaken by determination to document aspects of Egyptian culture such as would be of general interest to the English reading public and of value in literary studies:

> During a former visit to this country, undertaken chiefly for the purpose of studying the Arabic language in its most famous school, I devoted much of my attention to the manners and customs of the Arab inhabitants; and in an intercourse of two years and a half with this people, soon found that all the information which I had previously been able to obtain respecting them was insufficient to be of much use to the student of Arabic literature, or to satisfy the curiosity of the general reader.[50]

Lane's interests in language, custom, and literature found expression throughout his career, as he turned his attention from *Modern Egyptians*, to the *Nights*, to translation and annotation of *Selections from the Kur-án* in 1843, and finally to the compilation of his *Arabic-English Lexicon* in 1863.[51] Lane's perception that such matters could speak both to students of literature and to a wider readership influenced his treatment and presentation of the *Arabian Nights*.

Lane began his work on *Arabian Nights* following the publication of *Modern Egyptians*, despite his ill health. Left relatively little time to complete each installment, he found himself under constant pressure, as passages from existing correspondence reveal. According to Ahmed, "In order that the numbers might appear promptly every month, Lane worked, he wrote, 'till my sight has become confused,' and towards the end of the month 'the printers suffer me to have no rest nor leisure.' "[52] The circumstances under which Lane was writing were far from ideal, with the pressures of constant deadlines and his sense of his own economic dependence on his publishers.[53] In addition, those aspects of the project most important to Lane and those seen to be of widest appeal by his publisher were not always in perfect harmony.

Lord Brougham said of Edward Lane, "I wonder if that man knows what his *forte* is?—Description."[54] From all indications, Lane did value this dimension of his work most highly. According to Lane-Poole, when Lane took on this project he was committed to providing the type of detailed description found in *Modern Egyptians* and "resolved to make his translation of 'The Thousand and One Nights' an encyclopaedia of Arab manners and customs" (93). Lane argued that what is "most valuable in the original work [is] . . . its minute accuracy with respect to those peculiarities which distinguish the Arabs,"[55] and it was this minute accuracy which he sought to make accessible to English readers in his notes.

In the preface to *Modern Egyptians* there is explicit foreshadowing of the approach Lane was soon to take to the *Nights*. Surveying the available literature on Egypt, he notes an apparent dearth of adequate information regarding "the Arabs," but he identifies an as-yet-unappreciated source of data.

There is one work, which presents most admirable pictures of the manners and customs of the Arabs, and particularly of those of the Egyptians; it is "The Thousand and One Nights; or, Arabian Nights' Entertainments": if the English reader had possessed a close translation of it with sufficient illustrative notes, I might almost have spared myself the labour of the present undertaking. (xxiv–xxv)

Lane echoes earlier claims about the *Nights'* ethnographic value and also, as Ahmed has pointed out, overturns the earlier assumption that the available editions were capable of revealing such dimensions of the text (128). But Lane's still tacit assumptions here regarding the nature of "close" translation and "sufficient" annotation deserve attention. In the essays with which Lane framed his translation of the *Nights*, his criteria for assessing quality of translation and commentary become more explicit.

Lane's clearest statement of purpose is offered in the preface. He understood that the very existence of his edition implied "an unfavourable opinion" of available versions of the *Nights*, and he strove to differentiate his approach from that of his French predecessor, Antoine Galland. Lane argues that the "chief faults" of English editions were "to be attributed" to Galland, and notes,

I am somewhat reluctant to make this remark, because several persons, and among them some of high and deserved reputation as Arabic scholars, have pronounced an opinion that his version is an *improvement* upon the original. That "The Thousand and One Nights" may be greatly improved I most readily admit; but as confidently do I assert, that Galland has excessively *perverted* the work. His acquaintance with Arab manners and customs was insufficient to preserve him always from errors of the grossest description, and by the *style* of his version he has given to the whole a false character. (1:viii)

Lane does not object in principle to Galland's manipulation of the text; he objects to Galland as translator, arguing that he lacked the cultural expertise required to make informed alterations to the content and style of the *Nights*. In so defining the falseness of Galland's edition, Lane implies that the "true" translation of the work was to be guided by knowledge of the manners and customs of the source culture. Like Lane, both Edgar Taylor and T. Crofton Croker had negotiated conceptions of cultural authenticity and a popular format. When Lane approached his project, there were precedents in place, not only for the presentation of the foreign "popular tale" but also for the translation and culturally based interpretation of Middle Eastern literature.

Translating Culture

In the 1760s, Johann Gottfried Herder had suggested a model for the translation of "oriental" works that corresponds with Lane's and addresses the issue of cross-cultural accessibility. Herder had suggested that ideally a translation of this kind would serve to "set apart the frontiers of foreign people from our own, no matter how convolutedly they may run; it makes us more familiar with the beauty and the genius of a nation that we had quite viewed askance and yet ought to have known face to face." To achieve such a goal, Herder argued that more than a shift in language was required:

The finest translator must be the finest explicator; should this sentence also be true in the reverse order, and should both be joined, we would soon be able to hope for a book entitled: "Poetic translation of the poems of the Morn in which they are explicated on the basis of the land, the history, the attitudes, the religious life, the condition, the customs, and the language of their nation, and transplanted into the genius of our day, our mentality, and our language.[56]

Herder's emphasis on both the translation of words and the explication of the "genius" behind them adds a significant dimension to the philologist's responsibilities and seems to foreshadow an approach such as Lane's. But Herder was neither the first nor the sole advocate of such a project.

In a series of lectures given in the 1740s at Oxford, published in 1753, and translated from Latin to English in 1787, Bishop Robert Lowth had proposed that textual criticism and interpretation of the Old Testament would best be served by a thorough appreciation of the time and place of its entextualization. It is "not enough," Lowth argued, "to be acquainted with the language of this people, their manners, discipline, rites and ceremonies; we must even investigate their innermost sentiments, the manner and connexion of their thoughts; in one word, we must see all things with their eyes, estimate all things by their opinions: we must endeavour as much as possible to read Hebrew as the Hebrews would have read it."[57] For Lowth, reading "as the Hebrews" entailed more than the mastery of facts: An adequate reading of the Scriptures required of the reader a total empathy of sentiment and mentality with the Old Testament Hebrews.

Lowth proposes that in expressing divine sentiment the Hebrew authors drew on the mundane, using "most freely that kind of imagery which was most familiar, and the application of which was most generally understood" (144–45). Images that at first seem "obscure" to the eighteenth-century English reader, Lowth suggests, do so because we "differ so materially from the Hebrews in our manners and customs." To overcome this barrier, Lowth argued that one must venture an imaginative leap, placing oneself in the intellectual, physical, and sensory world of the Old Testament (155–56). The process of reading was to take the form of an imaginative journey, providing increasingly revealing views of an otherwise inaccessible realm.[58]

Lowth proposed that "obsolete custom, or some forgotten circumstance opportunely adverted to, will sometimes restore its true perspicuity and credit to a very intricate passage" in the Old Testament (155–56); nearly fifty years later, this assertion was fully embraced with enthusiasm by the Reverend Samuel Burder of Cambridge. This quotation thus adorns the title page and provides the ideological foundation for Burder's 1802 work *Oriental Customs; or, An Illustration of the Sacred Scriptures, by an Explanatory Application of the Customs and Manners of the Eastern Nations, and Especially the Jews, Therein Alluded to, Collected from the Most Celebrated Travellers and the Most Eminent Critics.* Burder drew freely from ancient and contemporary sources, first- and secondhand accounts, scholars and amateurs, to complete his picture of Oriental customs and manners. He defends the lack of temporal and geographic specificity implied in his lengthy title, stating that "in the East the usages and habits of the people are invariable."[59] Quoting Sir J. Chardin, he asserts that in "the East they are constant in all things: the habits are at this day in the same manner as in the precedent ages; so that one may reasonably believe, that in that part of the world the exterior forms of things, (as their manners and customs) are the same now as they were two thousand years since" (1:xviii). Burder's eastern "Other" is thus sketched in what Johannes Fabian has identified as "allochronic" terms,[60] with the presumed durability of eastern material cultures indexing a general lack of cultural change, dynamism, or progress.

Lane similarly conflates the eastern past and present in his treatment of the *Nights*, albeit to a lesser degree—a matter of centuries rather than millennia. He draws on his firsthand experience of modern Egypt in order to illuminate a work which, he asserts, "was either composed or modernised at a late period, which I believe to have been shortly before or after the commencement of the sixteenth century" (3:739). Nonetheless, Lane is distinguished by his insistence regarding geographical and cultural specificity: He considered the type of traveler's account so freely drawn upon in Burder's annotation of Scriptures to be criminally "vague" in its account of manners and customs (1:viii). The "East" of the *Arabian Nights*, Lane argues, is not an uncertain locale nor is it all-inclusive. Rather, he proposes that "it is in Arabian countries, and especially in Egypt, that we see the people, the dresses, and the buildings, which [the *Nights*] describes in almost every case, even when the scene is laid in Persia, in India, or in China" (1:viii). This is reiterated in the "Review" essay that concludes volume 3, as Lane states,

All the complete copies (printed and manuscript) of which I have any knowledge describe Cairo more minutely and accurately than any other place; and the language, manners, customs, &c, which they exhibit agree most closely with those of Egypt. (3:740–41)[61]

One can certainly detect in Lane, as in Burder, an inheritance of Lowth's general proposition that detailed understanding of a place and its inhabitants may serve as a key to their literature. For Lane this understanding was to be gained not by means of an imaginative leap across cultural boundaries, as Lowth had suggested, but by means of a real one. Lane proposes that he is capable of the close translation and sufficiently explanatory annotation previously unavailable not because of expertise in literary translation or familiarity with Middle Eastern history but because he claims to have experienced Egypt as an Egyptian. Lane writes,

I consider myself possessed of the chief qualifications for the proper accomplishment of my present undertaking, from my having lived several years in Cairo, associating almost exclusively with Arabs, speaking their language, conforming to their general habits with the most scrupulous exactitude, and [having been] received into their society on terms of perfect equality. (1:ix)

Like Croker, Lane saw himself as situated within/between two cultures, fluent not only in the languages but also in the customs of both. It is this position, Lane proposed, that enabled him to achieve his goal of "presenting pictures of Arab life and manners" rendered "intelligible and agreeable to English readers" (1:xvii, xviii).

Lane took these twin objectives—intelligibility and agreeability—quite seriously, and was commended not only for his depiction and explication of Egyptian manners and customs but also for his selective editing of the text in which the "grossness . . . of Eastern manners is entirely avoided."[62] For instance, in Lane's version of the frame story, the brothers King Sháh Zemán and King Shahriyár are betrayed by their wives, as they are in the Arabic text.[63] But nowhere to be found is a wife in the arms of a "kitchen boy," or the wife who struts "like a dark-eyed deer . . . raising her legs" to the black slave who "went between her thighs and made love to her."[64] Instead, Lane presents slightly more ambiguous scenarios, in which the two kings are driven to "vexation and grief" (1:6) by a wife discovered "sleeping . . . attended by a male negro slave, who had fallen asleep by her side" (1:4), or by another overseen being "embraced" by black slaves and "revelling" until "the close of day" (1:6). When the brothers journey forth in search of a man similarly circumstanced, they meet a woman kept locked in a chest by a jealous and possessive djinn, just as in the original text; but rather than being raped by the lady as her powerful husband naps, Sháh Zemán and Shahriyár are "foolish" enough to engage in "conversation" with her (1:8). Lane offers no acknowledgment or explanation of these editorial choices.

In "The Porter and the Three Ladies of Baghdad," presented as chapter 3 of Lane's *Nights*, the debauchery of the title characters is similarly edited and modified. In the Arabic text, the three ladies of Baghdad seem to have a degree of true autonomy and power: They have the money to employ a porter and buy supplies for a lavish feast, and they live together without husbands, fathers, or brothers. It is these women who establish the ground rules by which the porter must abide if he is to join their poolside festivities, who get the porter drunk, who first peel off their clothes and dive into the pool.[65] In translating this tale, Lane notes that he has had to "pass over an extremely objectionable scene, which would convey a very erroneous idea of the manners of Arab ladies" (1:214). Lane modifies the drinking habits of the three ladies—he reduces the three cups consumed by the hostess in the Egyptian manuscript to one[66]—and transforms the sadomasochistic sex play that follows the drinking in the original text: "They threw off all restraint," Lane writes, "indulging their merriment with as much freedom as if no man had been present" (1:141).

Lane was careful to assure his readers that despite his omission of passages which were found to be "comparatively uninteresting or on any account objectionable" (1:xvii), he had drawn on his personal expertise so as to retain the original text's overall character. Moreover, Lane suggests that since the work can, at times, present "scandalous misrepresentations of Arab manners and customs" (1:215), it may be considered more accurate in its new form than the old.

Likewise, when Lane addresses the possibility of faulty translation, it is not textual or linguistic precision that he takes as his yardstick but a form of cultural accuracy:

No translator can always be certain that, from twenty or more significations which are borne by one Arabic word, he has selected that which his author intended to convey; but, circumstanced as I am, I have the satisfaction of feeling confident that I have never given, to a word or phrase in this work, a meaning which is inconsistent with its presenting faithful pictures of Arab life and manners. (1:xvii)

Translation as the accurate representation of cultural difference: In this fundamental way, Lane was an heir to the foreignizing translation strategies closely associated with orientalist scholarship, in both England and Germany. But in order to "diffuse knowledge," Lane had to engage in some domesticating strategies as well—adapting the form and content of tales for a readership of nonexperts who were to be sheltered from both dullness and immorality.

The Fascination of the Tongue

Lane did not intend his readers to comprehend Arab character through translation alone. He considered his edition distinctive because it offered a more accurate rendering of the text than previously available and because of the "faithful pictures" offered in the notes and illustrations that accompanied the stories. The notes, Lane writes, are intended to "give such illustrations as may satisfy the general reader, without obliging him to consult other works" (1:xviii)—to make readers more familiar with the manners, customs, and beliefs of the Arabs. The engraved illustrations by William Harvey serve the same purpose, Lane suggests, and may therefore "considerably assist to explain both the text and the notes" for the reader (1:xxi). Again, readers are assured that Lane has taken the utmost care to attend to accuracy of representation. Above all, Lane wanted to offer his English audience an illustrated translation guided by cultural expertise, as well as running ethnographic commentary.[67]

Lane's notes always take specific words or events in the narrative as points of departure. For instance, in the frame story Lane anticipates readers' discomfort with the portrayal of Shahriyar as a man both murderous and pious, but assures them that his engagement in "religious exercises, when about to give orders for the murder of his innocent wife, need not excite our surprise." To demonstrate that such behavior is "consistent with the character of many Muslims," Lane offers an anecdote. "In the year 1834," he writes, "when I was residing in Cairo, a General in the service of Mohammad 'Alee hired a large party of men to perform a recital of the Kur-án, in his house in that city, and then went up into his hareem, and strangled his wife in consequence of a report which accused her of incontinence" (1:41). Intended to illuminate the translated text, Lane composed many notes of this kind with such a thoroughness of description that they may be read and understood without reference to the ongoing narrative. They are short tales of their own.[68]

The organization of this edition facilitated not only its publication in short installments but also the reading of tales without reference to the notes—and vice versa. Positioned at the close of each of the thirty created "chapters," the notes are set apart, both typographically and spatially, from the narrative(s) they are intended to illuminate.[69] As the work progresses, a reader would have to be especially dedicated to follow the notes. In volumes 2 and 3 Lane's notes grow fewer and more concise, very often referring readers back to notes from the first volume. In fact, the lengthy annotations to which critics generally refer are actually typical only of the first volume. For example, when a male child is born in "The Story of Noor ed-Deen and His Son" of volume 1, Lane provides a six-page essay that details such topics as the relationship of Islamic teachings to childrearing practices; feasts, ritual sacrifice of animals, and other celebrations of birth; the naming of children; protection of children from the Evil Eye and other supernatural dangers; the hierarchy of power within the family; attitudes toward fertility; conceptions of appropriate behavior for children; circumcision; and the methods and content of Arab education. Few of these topics have any direct bearing on the tale to which this note is appended; rather, they are covered so that Lane may, as he writes, later "avoid an unnecessary multiplication of notes on the same or nearly the same subject, by availing myself of this occasion to insert . . . illustrations of numerous passages, in the preceding and subsequent tales."[70]

Some of Lane's contemporaries applauded his detailed annotations as the most distinctive and valuable feature of the edition. Ahmed, a late twentieth-century scholar, has suggested that the notes offered contemporary readers clarification of "the forms, images, manners and beliefs referred to in the *Arabian Nights* . . . binding it irrevocably with the Arabian world, and with reality," and that it was this distinctive feature of Lane's edition which profoundly altered "the experience of reading the *Arabian Nights* for the English reader."[71] But if one looks to the individual with the most significantly vested interest in this matter—Lane's publisher—the importance of the annotations to the general English reader is called into question.

According to Charles Knight's memoirs, Lane's general concern with faithful rendering of the text was occasionally in conflict with popular demand. Lane strove to differentiate his treatment of the tales from Galland's, and readers were likewise attuned to intertextual comparison. Knight suggests that Lane's introduction of transliterated Arabic words, a classic foreignizing translation strategy, "proved a stumbling block" for many readers, and "loud, too, was the complaint that Aladdin and his Lamp and the Forty Thieves [the most popular of Galland's additions] were no where to be found in these volumes." Particularly revealing is Knight's offhand reference to the annotations, which appear to have been of interest to only a fraction of the reading public. "However repellent to desultory readers might have been Mr. Lane's version," he continues, "it was soon discovered that no other 'Arabian Nights' would meet the wants of those who really desired to understand Oriental customs and forms of speech, and was worthy of the admiration of educated persons."[72] This sentiment is echoed by Lane-Poole, who claims that Lane's edition was "on all hands acknowledged to be the only translation that students of the East can refer to without fear of being misled. Every oriental scholar knows that the Notes are an essential part of his library."[73] Yet one must account for the possibility that while Lane's annotations may have provided the edition with an appealing "scholarly" tone—what Rana Kabbani has dubbed "the paraphernalia of academic discourse"[74]—they may have been infrequently consulted.[75] As Knight indicated, learned readers

(Lane-Poole's "students of the East" and "oriental scholars") did not constitute a significant portion of the publisher's desired market.[76]

Lane-Poole himself edited and recombined Lane's notes on "the main
characteristics of Mohammadan life,"[77] divorced from the text they were
originally intended to illuminate, and published them in 1883 as *Arabian Society in the Middle Ages: Studies from* The Thousand and One Nights. For this
work, Lane-Poole created eleven chapters and over 150 subheadings to en-
compass the scope of Lane's ethnographic notes,[78] and these could certainly
be further simplified. For example, entries on such matters as slavery, law,
childhood, and womanhood may be taken as indicative of Lane's interest in
social organization; those concerning play, festival, music, cooking, and
bathing, of his treatment of Egyptian customs. What I find to be most remarkable, however, is the predominance of entries centered around culturally specific belief systems—what in Croker's *Fairy Legends* would have been
called superstitions. Religion, astrology, magic, and dream interpretation are
only a few examples.[79]

As evident in the quotation with which this chapter began, Lane regarded one of the chief purposes of the annotations to be the explication of
differences between Arab and English mentalities, particularly in regard to
conceptions of "fact" and "fantasy." Lane's interest in Arab notions of credibility is made manifest in the lengthy annotations on such subjects as religious practice, the occult, festival, and funerary ritual. But perhaps most
salient are those that serve, either explicitly or implicitly, to comment on the
role of fantasy literature in Egyptian society. Lane's annotations may thus be
seen to provide a countertext to the *Nights* not only in terms of form (being
highly narrativized and coherently structured) but also in content, providing
a running metalevel commentary on the place of storytelling in the culture
that (presumably) produced the *Arabian Nights.*

One of the clearest instances of this is the lengthy note "On Magic"
(1:65–70), which is appended to "The Story of the First Sheykh and the
Gazelle" in chapter 1. In Lane's translation, a sheykh is in the midst of telling
an Efreet of previous misfortunes (a common occurrence in these tales). The
sheykh describes how his wife, concubine, and son came to be magically
transformed, explaining that his wife "had studied enchantment and divination from her early years" and had turned the other two into cattle during
the sheykh's absence (1:48). At this point, readers are referred to one of Lane's
notes, in which he describes such topics as the place of the occult in Egyptian
education, some of the practical uses of magic in everyday life, the various
classifications of magical power and practice as defined by Egyptians, meth-

ods and uses of astrology, types of divination, conceptions and indications of good and bad luck, and the careers of "celebrated magicians" (1:69). While the majority of these topics may appear irrelevant to the reader's understanding of "The First Sheykh and the Gazelle," their inclusion at this point in the text is not at all arbitrary. "The Arabs and other Mohammadans enjoy a remarkable advantage over *us* in the composition of works of fiction," the lengthy note begins, "in the invention of incidents which *we* should regard as absurd in the extreme, *they* cannot be accused by their countrymen of exceeding the bounds of probability" (1:65, emphasis in original). To support this claim, Lane draws on firsthand experience of modern Egypt and recounts a fantastical story he himself heard "related . . . as a fact, in Cairo," similar to that found in the *Nights* (1:65). Shahrazád's tale itself is not Lane's primary concern. Instead, he intends his annotational description of these related but diverse matters to contribute to the reader's comprehension of a more far-reaching notion: that the composition, oral narration, and reception of such tales must be understood as an ethnographic reality and a marker of cultural difference.

Only one page later in "The Story of the First Sheykh and the Gazelle," as morning comes and Shahrazád's storytelling is necessarily interrupted, Lane finds the opportunity to comment further on the art of fiction in Arab society and its relationship to notions of "probability." In his annotation entitled "On the Influence of Eloquence and Tales upon the Arabs" (1:72–76), Lane again links the Arab conception of "the probable" to the practice of storytelling in the culture as a whole:

The main incident upon which this work is founded, the triumph of the fascination of the tongue over a cruel and unjust determination which nothing else could annul, might be regarded, by persons unacquainted with the character and literature of the Arabs, as a contrivance too improbable in nature; but such is not the case. Perhaps there is no other people in the world who are such enthusiastic admirers of literature, and so excited by romantic tales, as those above named. (1:72)

The suspension of disbelief Lane requests of his readers is extended from tale to cultural context. Storytelling may take on an unusually powerful function in this text, but Lane urges his readers to allow their new appreciation of the "fascination of the tongue" to transform their reading experience.

As this entry continues, Lane elaborates on the uses of verbal artistry for entertainment, its relationship to religious belief and customs, and the role literature has played in Arab culture over time, drawing in this last instance upon studies of "the history and literature of early Arabs" (1:72–75). Lane's essay culminates with the argument that even in "the present declining age of Arabian learning . . . literary recreations still exert a magic influence upon the Arabs." In order to demonstrate the extent to which this is true, Lane describes public storytelling performances and the popularity of printed materials:

Compositions of a similar nature to the tales of a Thousand and One Nights (though regarded by the learned as idle stories unworthy of being classed with their literature) enable numbers of professional story-tellers to attract crowds of delighted listeners to the coffee-shops of the East; and now that the original of the present work is printed, and to be purchased at a moderate price, it will probably soon, in great measure, supersede the romances of Aboo Zeyd, Ez-Záhir, and 'Antar. (1:75)

The enduring popularity of the *Nights*—not only in the West but also in the East—becomes a way of linking the modern Egypt that Lane knew first-hand and the medieval work he was presenting to his readers. It also, perhaps unintentionally, links Lane's readers to the Arabs. If the Arabs were truly the world's most "enthusiastic" consumers of imaginative literature, surely the English came in a close second.

It is at this point in the text that Lane must defend one of the most significant omissions from the original: the recurrent passages that open each "night"—as Shahrazád's sister begs for continuation of the previous night's story—and close each night—as the sun rises, Shahrazád leaves the narration suspended at a particularly intriguing moment, and Shahriyár must decide, again and again, whether to execute this wife as he has the previous ones. Lane may not have had any control over the decision to eliminate this most distinctive feature of the *Arabian Nights:* From what is known of Knight's intended market, it seems likely that the publisher would have favored the restructuring of the text into a form more familiar to English readers. But whatever the case may have been, Lane felt compelled to explain the significance of these recurring passages and the reason for their omission both in his annotation and within the text itself. In the midst of "The First Sheykh," set apart by square brackets, Lane explains:

On the second and each succeeding night, Shahrazád continued so to interest King Shahriyár by her stories as to induce him to defer putting her to death, in expectation that her fund of amusing tales would soon be exhausted; and as this is expressed in the original work in nearly the same words at the close of every night, such repetitions will in the present translation be omitted. (1:49)

True to Knight's express concern with the time constraints of the general reader, Lane seeks a degree of brevity and simplicity in the midst of a thousand and one nights of tale-telling.

In the course of Lane's three volumes, redundancy emerges as only one of many reasons given for emendation of the original text. Particularly in the second and third volumes, a notion of "literary value" emerges as another criterion by which certain tales earn inclusion in the text, while others appear only in summary form at the close of chapters, and some are omitted completely. For example, following chapter 21, Lane provides a twenty-four-page "abstract," complete with illustrations, of "The Story of the King and His Son and the Damsel and the Seven Wezeers." While presumably of insufficient quality to be included in the chapter, Lane believes them "not entirely unworthy of being presented to the English reader" (3:158), and therefore includes such tales in this altered form.

Frequently, passages or entire tales disappear on the grounds of indecency, as is the case in "The Story of the Two Princes El-Amjad and El-As'ad," which is embedded in "The Story of the Prince Kamar Ez-Zemán and the Princess Budoor." When the "two ladies in the King's palace . . . became enamoured of the two princes" (2:150), readers are alerted to Lane's omission of "an explanation which is of a nature to disgust every person of good taste" (2:237). The object of disgust in this case is the transformation of stepmotherly affection into incestuous desire,[80] but it is never named. Instead, Lane turns to a discussion of obscenity in the tale-telling of Egyptians, placing the *Nights* in the context of oral narrative performance:

> He who is unacquainted with the original [of the *Nights*] should be informed that it contains many passages which seem as if they were introduced for the gratification of the lowest class of the auditors of a public reciter at a coffee-shop . . . It is highly probable that Haroon Er-Rasheed often exercised the wit of Aboo Nuwas by relating to him exaggerated or even fictitious accounts of occurrences in his own hareem; and, still more so, that the latter person, in his reciting his anecdotes to his friends, disregarded truth in a much greater degree. (2:237)

Once again, Lane characterizes his cultural subjects as great tellers of tales as he situates the "obscenity" of the *Nights* in a wider narrative tradition that includes public performance, conversational storytelling, and gossip.

Perhaps what is most remarkable about these entries is the ease with which Lane alternates between discussion of *Nights* and the multifarious uses of discourse in Arab culture. In these annotations, the *Nights* is portrayed as the product of a specific discursive tradition, deeply embedded in the belief system and narrative habits of a people. As Lane turns his attention from the practice of everyday life, to the material conditions of everyday life, to discourse about everyday life, the "character and the literature of the Arabs" (1:72) emerge as inherently related, mutually illuminating phenomena. Readily decontextualizable—and thus easily ignored—Lane's annotations offered readers the type of "explication" of manners and customs for which Herder had longed, detailing the foreign material and intellectual world that presumably produced the text, as Lowth had imagined. The notes also offered opportunities for justification of English interest in and enjoyment of the tales, asserting English decency and propriety, and casting readers' indulgence in eastern fantasy as an ethnographic and rational pursuit.

The Picturesque and the Picture

Despite the fact that Lane's annotations attracted only a select readership, his edition of the *Arabian Nights* did gain a broader audience. Knight attributed the edition's "instant popularity, as well as its permanent utility," to the collaborative efforts of Lane and the artist William Harvey.[81] "The artist worked with the assistance of the author's mind," Knight explains, "and the result was to produce an illustrated book which is almost without a rival."[88] In volume 3, Lane himself felt obliged to "acknowledge [his] obligation to Mr. Harvey, whose admirable designs have procured for [the] version a much more extensive circulation than it would otherwise have obtained" (3:747). Appealing and useful, beautiful and detailed, these illustrations seem to fit the agendas of publisher and writer perfectly—negotiating between the popular appeal desired by Knight and the kind of cultural accuracy valued by Lane.

The illustration of the *Arabian Nights* was, again, not without precedent. Illustrated English editions of Galland's translation had been available since at least 1785, when Edward Frances Burney, Henry Coulbert, and Thomas Stothard had undertaken such a project.[83] That the work should lend itself to illustration was not attributed solely to readers' cravings for cultural information about Arabs. The most persistent refrain suggests that the tales in the *Nights* offer a picture of Arab culture because they are inherently visual. For example, in the 1880s Sir Richard Burton was to preface his own annotated translation with such a claim: "Impossible even to open the pages," he writes, "without a vision starting into view; without drawing a picture from the pinacothek of the brain; without reviving a host of memories and reminiscences which are not the common property of travellers, however widely they may have travelled."[84] Likewise, Lane casts the process of reading the tales as a spectacle more revealing than the actual observations of travellers, stating that the *Nights* "occasionally exhibits remarkable customs, domestic habits, and traits of national character, which have always been veiled from the observation of the European traveller" (1:v).

In fact, both Arab literary productions and Arab culture itself were described as picturesque in English discourse. Travel accounts of Egypt drew increasingly quaint portraits of scenery, architecture, and costume as well as aestheticized visions of the people and their practices, accounts of the latter being based only on what is "actually visible . . . as a basically unintelligible spectacle."[85] As we have seen, this form of aesthetic appreciation is double-edged, born of an ambivalent relation between the bourgeois subject and the picturesque object. To frame something or someone as picturesque is to suggest a visual evocativeness, but also a degraded or rapidly disintegrating status. In the case of accounts of travel to Arab nations, this was evident in European writers' lack of perspective on what they had witnessed[86] and the implication that the Arabs lacked insight to their own actions.

While many travel writers regarded the Arabs themselves as a visual spectacle, an affinity *for* the picturesque was also frequently identified as the defining characteristic of the Arab imagination. For instance, by the turn of the twentieth century it was commonplace to state that European readers "have to reckon with [the *Arabian Nights*] as the product of a race keenly alive to the value of colour and pictorial description, but a race whose constructive imagination was feeble and diffuse, lacking almost entirely that great essential for the development of art in its finer forms—the economy of means towards ends."[87] Lane similarly regarded the discursive tradition, of which the *Nights* was a part, as richly descriptive and imaginative. Although he seemed to have had respect for the tales as art, what is most relevant in the present context is the fact that Lane regarded fantastical narratives not only as an aspect of a discursive tradition but as much a part of the reality of everyday life as costume or architecture. Considering that Lane saw this as "a point . . . of much importance to set the work in its proper light before [his English] countrymen," one must ask what is the relationship of reality to fantasy in the accompanying illustrations?

In his preface, Lane suggests that Harvey's illustrations serve much the same function as the annotations, providing English readers with accurate depictions of Egyptian manners and customs. To better serve such an end, Lane assures his readers that he has been involved in the process of illustrating the tales: "Excepting in a few cases, when I had given him such directions as I deemed necessary, [Harvey's] original designs have been submitted to me; and in suggesting any corrections, I have, as much as possible, avoided fettering his imagination" (1:xxi–xxii). To appreciate Lane's desire to work closely with his illustrator, one must consider not only Lane's concern with the cultural accuracy of the narratives but also the concern for pictorial accuracy that developed earlier in his career, before his attention had fixed on the *Arabian Nights.*

There had been a few collections of illustrations of Egypt published in England previous to Lane's initial efforts.[88] But Lane's *Description of Egypt* was unusual in that it contained not only 101 sepia drawings but also "detailed and lucidly descriptive" writing.[89] Ahmed points out that Lane's illustrations of Egypt were themselves distinguished from those previously published by the "clarity and precision of line" he achieved with the aid of the camera lucida: "Set beside the illustrations that had appeared in previous travel-works, it is as if the objects represented had at last been properly focused" (63). Lane's biographers appear to agree that in pictorial as in verbal representation he sought "perfect clearness," to be as "exact" and detailed about material objects as possible.[90] This is certainly evident in his annotations to the *Nights* and may even illuminate Lane's attraction to a work that has been characterized as "peculiarly rich in concrete images."[91]

Many of Harvey's designs, like Lane's, depict material artifacts— architecture, furnishings, or clothing—in minute detail. In Lane's engravings of Egyptian architecture, human figures dot the scene, providing the viewer with a sense of the grandeur of buildings and monuments, but little else.[92] Similarly, in many of Harvey's illustrations, structures overshadow tiny human forms (figure 14) or frame crowds of indistinguishable figures engaged in indefinable activity (figure 15).[93] Buildings are the focal points in cases such as these, and Lane informs the reader that to ensure pictorial verisimilitude Harvey studied a number of books and a "collection of drawings of a great number of the finest specimens of Arabian architecture in and around Cairo" (1:xxii). These human figures are of secondary importance and may rightly be described as "tiny, schematized Orientals, all basically interchangeable."[94]

In the numerous illustrations of Egyptian marketplaces, some architectural detail is still included, but the perspective is far more intimate (figures 16 and 17).[95] Likewise, when the reader is granted a view of the interiors of Egyptian palaces and homes—scenes "veiled from the observation of the European traveller," as Lane had promised—Harvey balances attention to human activity and dress with attention to architectural detail and interior

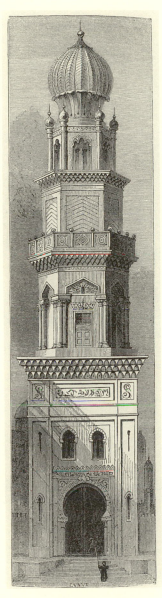

14. William Harvey (engraved by Evans), "Tower of Brass," from "The Story of the City of Brass," Edward W. Lane, *The Thousand and One Nights, Commonly Called in England The Arabian Nights' Entertainments*, vol. 3 (1841). Courtesy, The Lilly Library, Indiana University, Bloomington.

15. William Harvey (engraved by Landells), "Interior of Báb Zuweyleh," from "The Story Told by the Christian Broker," Lane's *Arabian Nights*, vol. 1 (1840). Courtesy, The Lilly Library, Indiana University, Bloomington.

decorating. For instance, Harvey illustrates a key moment in "The Story of the Fisherman." A king is exploring a mysterious black palace and follows the sound of lamentation to a chamber, hidden behind a curtain. He draws

16. William Harvey (engraved by M. Jackson), "Bázár, or Market-Street," from "The Story of the Porter and the Ladies of Baghdád," Lane's *Arabian Nights*, vol. 1 (1840). Courtesy, The Lilly Library, Indiana University, Bloomington.

17. William Harvey (engraved by T. Williams), "Khaleefeh at the Shop of the Jew," from "The Story of Khaleefeh the Fisherman," Lane's *Arabian Nights*, vol. 3 (1841). Courtesy, The Lilly Library, Indiana University, Bloomington.

this curtain back, revealing a handsome prince "sitting on a sofa" (1:105). It is this moment of suspense, as the prince is just about to lift his skirt to reveal legs turned to stone, which Harvey illustrates in figure 18. But the emphasis in this illustration is not on the unfolding drama. It is on the archway in which the two figures are situated. Likewise, the wedding of Princess Budoor, illustrated in figure 19, is nearly overpowered by the scale and detail of the chambers in which the event is imagined to take place.[96]

Lane's primary concern was a (perceived) collective cultural reality, not an idiosyncratic one, and for the most part the engravings illustrate this. Even in engravings that focus on individual figures, a degree of anonymity or interchangeability persists. There is often little or no clear indication of the point in the narrative being illustrated; the real visual interest, as in figures 20 and 21, is costume.[97] Indeed, Lane explains in his preface that authentic costuming was one of his concerns. To serve such an end, Lane provided the illustrator not with "modern dresses . . . to make his designs agree more nearly with the costumes, &c., of the times which the tales generally illustrate" (1:xxi). In such pictures, centuries are collapsed as the medieval and the modern blend, and the human figure is made a static material spectacle.

This attention to material detail—what Ahmed called an irrevocable binding to reality—forms the basis for only a portion of the work's visual vocabulary. In many other instances, Harvey chose to illustrate the more wondrous dimensions of the tales, sacrificing realistic detail to varying degrees. For example, magical characters may look and dress much like mortals, as does the "damsel" depicted in figure 22.[98] But here it is primarily the magical aspect of the damsel's appearance, hovering above the cooking fire, and not, for instance, the layout of an Arab kitchen that is of central visual interest. In other depictions of interaction between mortals and supernatural creatures, Harvey sacrifices mundane details, as evinced by the only vaguely Arab garb of the human characters in figures 23 and 24.[99] Likewise, the cultural and natural setting of the tales is frequently obscured to create an imaginatively evocative visual setting, as in the case of the mysterious and imposing mountains of figure 25.[100] Here, suspense and fear shape the landscape more than a sense of cultural and topographical accuracy.

Sometimes the architecture and natural landscape that Harvey so often details are used as pictorial indices of the fantastic, as in figure 26.[101] Harvey has chosen to illustrate a "paradise," described in the translation as "a garden . . . watered by copious streams" within a magical closet (1:190). As Harvey portrays it, however, this paradise looks much like an ordinary domestic interior with a central fountain, as illustrated at various other points in the

18. William Harvey (engraved by Orrin Smith), "The Sultán Discovering the Young King of the Black Islands," from "The Story of the Fisherman," Lane's *Arabian Nights*, vol. 1 (1840). Courtesy, The Lilly Library, Indiana University, Bloomington.

text. What makes this space unusual is that natural elements like plants and wildlife are incorporated into what has been established as a highly domestic setting. By means of minute description and pictorial detailing, even the most ordinary elements of Egyptian life are made extraordinary to the English

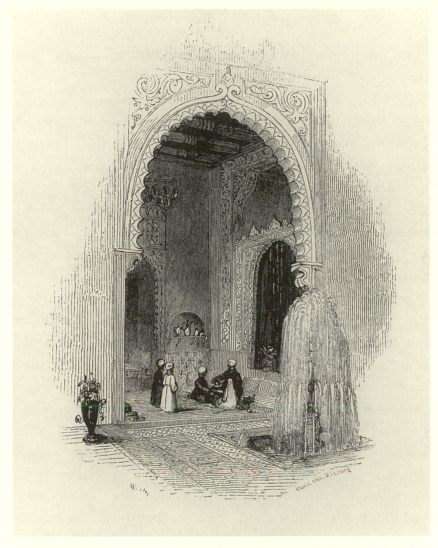

19. William Harvey (engraved by Miss Williams), "Marriage of Jubeyr and the Lady Budoor," from "The Story of Ibn Mansoor and the Lady Budoor," Lane's *Arabian Nights*, vol. 2 (1840). Courtesy, The Lilly Library, Indiana University, Bloomington.

reader/viewer. In this way an unusual grouping of man-made and natural objects comes to represent an otherworldly paradise.

20. William Harvey (engraved by Slader), "The Jeweller Finding the Letter," from "The Story of 'Alee the Son of Bekkár, and Shems En-Nahár," Lane's *Arabian Nights*, vol. 2 (1840). Courtesy, The Lilly Library, Indiana University, Bloomington.

21. William Harvey (engraved by Feldwick), "The King's Daughter," from "The Story of Joodar," Lane's *Arabian Nights*, vol. 3 (1841). Courtesy, The Lilly Library, Indiana University, Bloomington.

22. William Harvey (engraved by Kirchner), "The Cook-Maid Dressing the Fish," from "The Story of the Fisherman," Lane's *Arabian Nights*, vol. 1 (1840). Courtesy, The Lilly Library, Indiana University, Bloomington.

23. William Harvey (engraved by T. Williams), "Efreet and Lady," from
"Introduction" (the "frame story"), Lane's *Arabian Nights*, vol. 1 (1840). Courtesy,
The Lilly Library, Indiana University, Bloomington.

24. William Harvey (engraved by Thompson), "Second Prince Carried Off by the 'Efreet," from "The Story of the Second Royal Mendicant," Lane's *Arabian Nights*, vol. 1 (1840). Courtesy, The Lilly Library, Indiana University, Bloomington.

25. William Harvey (engraved by Whimper), "The Wezeer Rescuing Marzawán," from "The Story of the Prince Kamar Ez-Zemán and the Princess Budoor," Lane's *Arabian Nights*, vol. 2 (1840). Courtesy, The Lilly Library, Indiana University, Bloomington.

26. William Harvey (engraved by M. Jackson), "Garden," from "The Story of the Third Royal Mendicant," Lane's *Arabian Nights*, vol. 1 (1840). Courtesy, The Lilly Library, Indiana University, Bloomington.

What role does realistic detail play in the visual aesthetic of fantasy? Terry Reece Hackford suggests that certain visual signs that viewers "automatically recognize as belonging to the world of daily reality" provide a point of departure for Victorian illustrators of the *Arabian Nights*. He concludes that "the finest fantasy art is a liberation from reality that never loses sight of its point of departure" (172). While Hackford's argument certainly appears reasonable for the artists he has chosen to study—Arthur Boyd Houghton, John D. Batten, Henry J. Ford, and Edmund Dulac—it does little to illuminate what is going on in Harvey's popular designs. Significantly, none of Hackford's four collaborated with a translator as concerned with ethnographic detail as was Lane. In Lane's edition of the *Nights*, "the world of daily reality" takes on a radically different meaning. To the English reader, the minute detailing of manners and customs offered not automatic recognition, as Hackford suggests, but a constant reminder of the otherness of the subject matter.

In the analysis of fantasy, ethnocentrism often shapes the underlying conception of the Real: Hackford suggests that in late nineteenth-century illustrations of the *Nights*, the "persuasive fantasy image . . . depends in a complex manner upon the artistic conventions and semiotic codes associated with realism. The fantasy illustrator takes the pictorial conventions of realistic portrayal and then manipulates or inverts them to create marvelous worlds for which there can be no earthly analogy" (144). Such statements highlight the fact that the category of Realism has far less to do with the real or possible than it does with the *familiar*. In this particular edition of the *Nights*, realistic detail—both written and illustrated—does *not* stand in opposition to the realm of fantasy but becomes a sign of it. That is to say, the relentless description and depiction of Egyptian manners, customs, and material culture, down to the most seemingly insignificant detail, reinforces the "otherness" of the Arab world. It is but a small leap from that otherness to an "otherworldliness." A shift in the terms of Hackford's argument thus renders it more useful. In both its written and visual texts, in its ventures into both the realms of imagination and everyday life, this edition of the *Arabian Nights* offered its readers a marvelous world for which there could be no *British* analogy.

*   *   *

Underlying the translation, annotation, and illustration of Edward W. Lane's edition of the *Arabian Nights* is a unified philosophy of textual presentation which shaped his approach to the project and also his criticism of earlier efforts to render the tales for an English audience. Lane's voice joined those of many of his contemporaries who believed that the *Nights* offered English readers "admirable pictures of the manners and customs of the Arabs."[102] Lane hoped that by means of annotation and illustration this dimension of the text could be brought to the attention and appreciation of the mass reading public.

In his attempt to make the manners, customs, and mentality of the Egyptians "intelligible and agreeable to English readers,"[103] Lane recalls Bishop Lowth's proposition that cultural and textual appreciation go hand in hand. Lowth had envisioned the gathering of such knowledge within the confines of the imagination, but Lane offered his readers the authority of firsthand observation and experience and thus a privileged perspective otherwise unavailable. Cast as central to Egyptian national character was an affinity for the picturesque and for fantasy. For the English reader, the very act of reading the *Nights* was thus transformed into one of cross-cultural discovery. What may appear to be mutually exclusive fields of interest—the fantastic tales of the *Nights* and the very real details of Egyptian daily life—are here conjoined, as Edward Lane places storytelling in a broader cultural and metadiscursive context. The effect is an exoticization of the mundane and a naturalization of the fantastic. Each custom, practice, belief, and object affirms the otherness of the subject matter, and the supernatural character of the tales is itself cast as an index of Arab cultural difference.

Chapter 5

The Dreams of the Younger Brother: *George Webbe Dasent's* Popular Tales from the Norse

[L]ike the younger brother whom we shall meet so often in these Popular Tales, [the Western Aryan] went out into the world, with nothing but his good heart and God's blessing to guide him; and now has come to all honour and fortune, and to be a king, ruling over the world.[1]

—George Webbe Dasent, 1859

From the vantage point of 1858, London *Times* editor and Cambridge professor George Webbe Dasent had a tale to tell about modern literary study:

[J]ust at the close of that great war which Western Europe waged against the genius and fortune of the first Napoleon; just as the eagle—Prometheus and the eagle in one shape—was fast fettered by sheer force and strength to his rock in the Atlantic, there arose a man in Central Germany, on the old Thuringian soil, to whom it was given to assert the dignity of vernacular literature, to throw off the yoke of classical tyranny, and to claim for all the dialects of Teutonic speech a right of ancient inheritance and perfect freedom before unsuspected and unknown.[2]

The hero of this tale is Jacob Grimm, his noble battle against neo-classicism on behalf of Western European vernacular literature embodied by the *Kinder- und Hausmärchen.*

Thirty-seven years earlier, Edgar Taylor had had a similar response to the Grimms' collection of German popular tales, although he expressed it in more modest terms. "We can see no reason," Taylor wrote in 1821, "why the Thracian or Italian traditions which Homer or Livy occasionally embody, should be valued and, as it were, consecrated in classic memory, while these relics of a corresponding aera of expiring barbarism should be neglected or despised."[3] Emphases may have shifted in the study of popular tales, from the social evolutionary formulation of Taylor to the more philologically inflected interests of Dasent, but tales themselves had not been neglected. Whether seen primarily as a window to preindustrial society, and thus to England's past, as in *German Popular Stories*; to the worldview of England's neighbors, and thus to current Irish-English relations, as in *Fairy Legends and Traditions of the South of Ireland*; to the manners, customs, and imaginations of Egyptians, and thus to the contrast of East and West, as in the *Arabian Nights*; or to national particularities within an Indo-European heritage of language and literature, as in *Popular Tales from the Norse*, folktales continued to be regarded as "intrinsically valuable"[4] to an English readership.

By the 1850s, popular tale collections were well established in the nursery and home library, but they had also come to be seen as relevant to a large-scale history, spanning centuries and continents. The proliferation of tale collecting, translation, and publishing had made comparative study and analysis of traditional narratives a reality. While the genre had its roots in romantic nationalism and the search for nationally distinctive literary heritage, the strong similarities between stories collected in disparate regions could not be ignored. The theories and methods of comparative philology, codified in the 1830s, granted popular tales a new place of significance: In Dasent's words, the popular tales of each European nation "form, along with that language, a double chain of evidence, which proves their Eastern origin" (xl). It was this story, of Eastern origin and subsequent dispersion, that most fascinated George Webbe Dasent.

The orientalist researches of the late eighteenth and early nineteenth centuries—Sir William Jones's study of ancient Persian and Sanskrit texts, Friedrich Schegel's study of Indian languages and religion, H. T. Colebrooke's study of the Vedas—had initiated vigorous debate about the relations of world languages, literatures, and cultures. The concept of an Indo-European language family, introduced in 1816, had narrowed the focus of many European scholars to a single "Aryan" heritage—which could claim as its own the philosophical sophistication of ancient "oriental" texts like the Hindu Vedas, while providing a historical rationale for contemporary political dynamics, such as the English colonization of India.[5] Dasent situates his work squarely in the midst of this philological enterprise. While there are echoes of social evolution in Dasent's essay, popular tales figure here less as keys to the progress of human society, in general, than as supporting evidence in a projected history of Indo-European languages and cultures, in which the ulti-mate fate of Western Europeans as world rulers provides contrast with the East and implicit justification for colonialism. Within this narrative of Indo-European dispersion, a culture's special affinity for fantastical story—which in connection with *Alf Layla wa Layla* had emerged as a sign of oriental difference—was explicitly linked to political and cultural subordination.

As Dasent's romanticized portrayal of Jacob Grimm suggests, there is a second heritage of concern in the introductory essay: the historiography of the scientific study of the folktale. Situated at a pivotal moment in the his-tory of folktale collecting and publishing, *Popular Tales from the Norse* repre-sents a significant contribution to that history and to the establishment of precedents for the presentation and interpretation of oral traditions in print.

To begin with, *Popular Tales from the Norse* is characterized by a level of stylistic and structural uniformity unseen in earlier collections. Dasent trans-lated his stories in a consistent, colloquial, domesticated style that has proved enduringly popular, especially in children's publishing. In addition to intro-ducing such tales as "The Three Billy Goats Gruff" to English readers, inspir-ing innumerable retellings and illustrated editions in the twentieth century and beyond, lesser known stories from the collection have also taken picture book form.[6] *Popular Tales from the Norse* has never been out of print, and it is currently available in both facsimile and illustrated, selective editions.[7]

Dasent's project was also distinguished from the work of Taylor, Croker, and Lane because it offered examples of the comparative method celebrated in the introduction to *Popular Tales from the Norse.* Dasent himself experi-mented with the processes of collection and transcription, producing a small collection of West Indian tales that appeared as an appendix to the second edition of *Popular Tales from the Norse,* published in March 1859. The "af-finity" of these West Indian tales "with the stories of other races" is, Dasent suggests, "self-evident" (420). These materials quietly problematize the mas-ter narrative of Indo-Europeanism and resonate with the ethnological and comparative philological debates about "race" and the history of mankind that were gaining momentum in 1858.

Finally, Dasent's introduction may be the earliest example of an English editor/translator moving beyond explanation of his project's scope and de-sign to a survey of the emergent history of modern folktale study and the precedents already in place for collection, presentation, and interpretation. Dasent's introductory narrative foreshadows what has come to be common in such historiographical accounts. He asserts that the publishing history of the Grimms' *Kinder- und Hausmärchen,* from its initial appearance in

1812–14 through the reissuing of the second edition in 1856, "formed an era in popular literature, and has been adopted as a model by all true collectors ever since."[8] The Grimms themselves, Dasent asserts, "have thrown a flood of light on the early history of all branches of our race, and have raised what had come to be looked on as mere nursery fictions and old wives' fables— to a study fit for the energies of grown men, and all the dignity of a science" (xviii).

Dasent contrasts his own work with those tale collections available to English common readers of the eighteenth century—"the uncritical age" whose "spirit breathed hot and cold, east and west, from all quarters of the globe at once, confusing the traditions and tales of all times and countries into one incongruous mass of fable" (xvi)—"in which the popular tale appears to as much disadvantage as an artless country girl in the stifling atmosphere of a London theatre" (xv). In the movement from unreflective recitation among women and children, to the carelessness of eighteenth-century publication, to the scientific studies of nineteenth-century men, Dasent suggests, the popular tale had finally come of age.

In its "mature" form, the tale collection was considered a contribution to a growing body of scholarship—for instance, ethnologist E. B. Tylor praised and quoted from the "highly useful and philosophical remarks"[9] Dasent made in his introductory essay—but Dasent described his own work as "popular and readable, rather than learned and lengthy" (xlix). Dasent's vision of the popular is indebted to the philanthropic spirit of people like Lord Brougham, who had sought to bring literary "riches" and scientific discoveries, in undiluted and self-improving form, to a mass readership. Once again one finds that what would seem to be diametric oppositions between the popular and the scholarly, the imaginative and the scientific, the feminine and the masculine, the child and the adult, the East and the West, the savage and the civilized, and so forth, belie more complicated textual realities. Perhaps nowhere more than in George Webbe Dasent's *Popular Tales from the Norse* is it so apparent that even as these domains are constructed and delineated, they blur and intersect—that, for instance, the scholarly activities of folklore study themselves have tremendous imaginative appeal; that the most scientific of treatises can successfully mobilize the themes and motifs of traditional narrative; and that within an emergent model of the popular tale as "national dream," the ideal of cultural and textual accuracy and that of readability were not at odds with one another in the folklore text.

Coming of Age

George Webbe Dasent was born in 1817, far from Norway, far from England, far from any point in the projected history of the Indo-Europeans, on the West Indian island of St. Vincent. Son of that island's attorney general, George was descended from some of the earliest British settlers and administrators in St. Vincent, St. Christopher, Nevis, and Antigua. He was educated in England and received his undergraduate and graduate degrees from Oxford.

Dasent's interest in Scandinavian language and literature dates from 1840, when he began a four-year term as secretary to the British envoy in Stockholm. In 1842 he published a translation of the Prose Edda, followed in 1843 by his translation of Erasmus Rask's *Grammar of the Icelandic or Old-Norse Tongue*. When Dasent returned to England, he became an assistant editor of the *Times*. Called to the bar in 1852, Dasent accepted the post of professor of English literature and modern history at King's College in 1853.[10]

By the time *Popular Tales from the Norse* was published in 1859,[11] Dasent was able to demonstrate in a 160-page introductory essay that "Popular Tales have a literature of their own," ranging from the late seventeenth-century French courtly writers, through various European editions of the *Pantcha-Tantra* and the *Pentamerone*, to the publication of the *Kinder- und Hausmärchen* and subsequent collections from Sweden, Norway, Denmark, and Scotland, inspired by the Grimms' work.[12] In fact, *Popular Tales* is itself a translation of a collection strongly influenced by the *KHM*: Asbjørnsen and Moe's *Norske Folkeeventyr*.

Asbjørnsen and Moe published their first pamphlet of collected tales—without title, author, or introduction—in 1841, and it was followed by three more over the next three years. Taken together, these four pamphlets constitute the first edition of the *Norske Folkeeventyr*.[13] In 1851, Asbjørnsen and Moe published a second, enlarged edition, which included a lengthy introduction by Moe and a 115-page appendix of comparative notes. This is the edition on which Dasent based his 1858 English translation.[14]

Reflecting on the appeal of *Popular Tales from the Norse*, one reviewer wrote that "one hardly knew whether to admire most the raciness and vigour with which the Tales were translated, or the mingled learning and eloquence of the Introductory Essay on Popular Tales in general."[15] Dasent's enormous introductory essay establishes a framing voice and theoretical perspective to an extent unrivaled by Taylor or Croker, comparable to Lane's annotational writings in its coherence. But the tales themselves also achieve a level of

formal and stylistic homogeneity unparalleled in *German Popular Stories,
Fairy Legends and Traditions of the South of Ireland,* or the *Arabian Nights.*

Unlike these earlier collections, the stories in *Popular Tales* begin
identically[16]—"Once on a time" (the English counterpart to Asbjørnsen and
Moe's "Der var engang"), followed by the Propp-er introduction of the
dramatis personae and initial situation. For example:

Once on a time there was a Princess who was so proud and pert that no suitor was
good enough for her. She made game of them all, and sent them about their business,
one after the other; but though she was so proud, still new suitors kept on coming to
the palace, for she was a beauty, the wicked hussey! ("Hacon Grizzlebeard," 45)

Once on a time there was an old wife who sat and baked. Now you must know that
this old wife had a little son, who was so plump and fat, and so fond of good things,
that they called him Buttercup; and she had a dog, too, whose name was Goldtooth,
and as she was baking, all at once Goldtooth began to bark. ("Buttercup," 142)

Once on a time a poor couple lived far, far away in a great wood. The wife was
brought to bed, and had a pretty girl, but they were so poor they did not know how
to get the babe christened, for they had no money to pay the parson's fees. ("The
Lassie and Her Godmother," 216)

Once on a time there was a poor, poor widow, who had an only son. She dragged on
with the boy till he had been confirmed, and then she said she couldn't feed him any
longer, he must just go out and earn his own bread. ("The Widow's Son," 358)

Of the works considered in earlier chapters, only Edgar Taylor's *German Popular Stories* employs opening formulae with any kind of regularity—eleven
of the thirty-one tales begin with variations on "Once upon a time"[17]—but
nothing comparable to the formal predictability of the opening lines of these
Norse tales.

The consistency of the tales' beginnings helps to establish the collection's formal coherence, but these formulaic openings frequently serve another function: Jumping quickly into first-person narration, they unify the
narrative voice of the collection. For instance:

Once on a time there was a king who had several sons—I don't know how many
there were. ("The Mastermaid," 81)

Once on a time there was a man who had a meadow, which lay high up on the hill-
side, and in the meadow was a barn, which he built to keep hay in. Now, I must tell

you there hadn't been much in the barn for the last year or two. ("Princess on the Glass Hill," 92)

Once upon a time there was a poor cottager who had three sons. . . . I have never heard tell what became of the two elder; but as for the youngest, he went both far and long, as you shall hear. ("The Master Thief," 232)

Once on a time there was a poor couple who lived in a wretched hut, far far away in the wood. How they lived I can't tell you. ("The Seven Foals," 348)

Such uses of the first person in the opening formula foreground orality and aurality: "I can't tell you," "I have never heard tell," "you shall hear." The reader is thrust into a world of telling and hearing. Unlike Croker's use of the first person, here there are no references to or comparisons with the world of reading and publishing.

The concluding lines of the tales are not nearly as predictable as the openings: in contrast with Taylor's stubbornly upbeat *German Popular Stories*, there is not a "happily ever after" to be found.[18] Nevertheless, Dasent's use of the first person again provides a degree of intertextual continuity and establishes a pervasive storytelling voice:

Oh! If one only knew where the trap-door was, I'll be bound there's a whole heap of gold and silver down there still! ("The Old Dame and Her Hen," 24)

. . . and all I can say is, if they haven't left off their merry-making yet, why, they're still at it. ("Princess on the Glass Hill," 118)

. . . and if the Smith didn't get in then, when the door was ajar, why I don't know what has become of him. ("The Master-Smith," 129)

Then they made ready for the wedding, and you may fancy what a grand one it was, when I tell you that the fame of it was noised abroad over seven kingdoms. ("Short-shanks," 171)

One type of formulaic conclusion that makes use of the first person playfully erases the gap between the narrator and her characters. The narrator adopts the authoritative perspective of firsthand experience:

[S]o there was a wedding that lasted eight whole days, and a feast besides, and after it was over I stayed no longer with Lord Peter and his lovely queen, and so I can't say anything more about them. ("Lord Peter," 347)

[T]here was mirth and fun at that wedding. I was there, too; but there was no one to care for poor me; and so I got nothing but a bit of bread and butter, and I laid it down on the stove, and the bread was burnt and the butter ran, and so I didn't get even the smallest crumb. Wasn't that a great shame? ("The Seven Foals," 357)

Toying with generic convention, teasing the audience, these narrative techniques establish a distinctive voice that is maintained throughout.

Dasent acknowledges that "the language and tone" found in *Popular Tales from the Norse* "are perhaps rather lower" than those of other tale collections, and he explains that this is attributable to their origins in Norwegian folk culture: "It must be remembered that these are the tales of 'hempen homespuns,' of Norse yeomen, of *Norske Bönder*, who call a spade a spade, and who burn tallow, not wax" (clii). To convey this characteristic style, Dasent domesticates the language of the tales, making extensive use of English colloquialisms, both in the first-person narration of the stories and in quoted speech:

Next morning the Giant got up cruelly early, and strode off to the wood; but was hardly out of the house before Boots and the Princess set to work to look under the door-sill for his heart; but the more they dug, and the more they hunted, the more they couldn't find it.

"He has baulked us this time," said the Princess, "but we'll try him once more." ("The Giant Who Had No Heart in His Body," 74)

Well, the Mastermaid asked him, as she had the Constable, if he had a good lot of money? And the Attorney said he wasn't so badly off; and as a proof he went home to fetch his money. So at even he came back with a great fat sack of money—I think it was a whole bushel sack—and set it down on the bench; and the long and the short of the matter was, that he was to have her, and they went to bed. ("The Mastermaid," 96–97)

"Oh!" said his old dame, "I don't care a farthing about such a pack of rubbish; if they don't like it they may lump it, and be off; but just do come and look at this lad out in the yard, so handsome a fellow I never saw in all my born days; and if you'll do as I wish, we'll ask him to step in and treat him a little, for, poor lad, he seems to have had a hard fight of it."

"Have you lost the little brains you had, Goody?" ("The Best Wish," 291)

The reader of *Popular Tales* quickly learns to recognize the characteristic style of the collection, that energetic narration and sly wit which Dasent describes as "bold, outspoken, and humourous" (cl).

Asbjørnsen and Moe had inherited the Grimms' "principle of faithfully collecting these traditions from the mouths of the people, without adding one jot or tittle, or in any way interfering with them, except to select this or that variation as most apt or beautiful,"[19] as well as the rhetorical and practical complexities attendant to the application of that principle. Although they "proposed to improve upon the Grimms' methods, feeling that the brothers had taken too many liberties in rewriting oral texts," Asbjørnsen and Moe took liberties of their own, following a vision of appropriateness and beauty.[20] In an effort "to capture the narrative style of the people," they avoided literary language in favor of "provincialisms and popular idioms," and with the result that in Norway "purists were repelled by what they considered the barbarisms in the stories."[21] In marked contrast, the language and tone of Dasent's collection—predictable, consistent, distinctive, and highly colloquial—were deemed "infinitely better" than those of its predecessors.[22]

In addition to seeking stylistic equivalencies in his translation, Dasent adopted traditional English character designations—such as "Goody" for the farmwoman or housewife who figures in so many of the tales. But there is one character who has a special hold on Dasent's imagination: the brave or clever youngest brother, "the man whom Heaven helps, because he can help himself," who "after his brothers try and fail . . . can watch in the barn, and tame the steed, and ride up the glass hill, and gain the Princess and half the kingdom" (cliv).

"Of particular characters," Dasent explains, "one occurs repeatedly. This is that which we have ventured, for want of a better word, to call 'Boots,' from that widely-spread tradition in English families, that the youngest brother is bound to do all the hard work his brothers set him, and which has also dignified him with the term here used." He continues,

In Norse he is called *"Askefis,"* or *"Espen Askefjis."* By M. Moe he is called *"Askepot,"* a Danish word which the readers of Grimms' Tales will see at once is the brother to *Aschenpüttel* . . . and in Norway, according to M. Moe, the term is almost universally applied to the youngest son of the family. (cliii)

Boots may be Cinderella's brother, but according to Dasent he has no true female counterpart (cliv). In fact, *Popular Tales from the Norse* presents a number of strong and admirable heroines: Katie Woodencloak and the equally brave and clever youngest daughters from such tales as "The Old Dame and Her Hen" and "East o' the Sun and West o' the Moon." Nevertheless, Dasent insists—as Jørgen Moe had before him—that the stories are primarily concerned with the triumph of the youngest male: "These tales," he explains, "are uttered with a manly mouth" (clv).

Dasent's invocation of this image may reflect his anxiety about the genre's traditional association with women and children and his wish to demonstrate its scientific and therefore "manly" status. But despite Dasent's rhetorical masculinization of both the style and worldview of the Norse tales, the storytelling mouth quickly changes gender. Dasent imagines the unified narrative voice as distinctly female. Again citing Moe, he suggests that popular tales should be read "as if we sat and listened to some elderly woman of the middle class, who recites them with a clear, full, deep voice" (cxlv). Moe's quotation would seem to suggest that the authenticity of such written texts is reflected by a book's ability to convey its oral origins—to create a unified storytelling voice, to create a reading experience akin to the field encounter. As we have seen, Dasent utilizes a number of narrative techniques to support this.

The "I" of this collection is generalized and anonymous. No actual elderly woman of the middle class is described or named, but both Asbjørnsen and Dasent experimented with fictionalized frames that gave form to the narrating voice. In the late 1840s, Asbjørnsen published a tale collection on his own in which he "introduced the fictional device of a frame setting with an imaginary village narrator relating the olden stories."[23] Similarly, when some of Dasent's first attempts at translating Asbjørnsen and Moe's work were published in *Once a Week*, they were set "in a frame formed by the imaginary adventures of English sportsmen on the Fjeld or Fells in Norway." As he continued the project of translation, Dasent dropped this frame story, growing "weary of the setting and framework, [so that] when about a third of the volume had been thus framed he resolved to let the Tales speak for themselves."[24]

Once collected and documented, tales would seem to speak for themselves. The peasant storyteller becomes dispensable, although as "source" she continues to fuel the imagination. As Dasent turned to discussion of the collection process in his introductory essay, it was the well-established and powerful image of the woman storyteller, evocative of fictional figures like Mother Goose, Mother Bunch, Gammer Grethel, and Shahrazád as well as the Grimms' mythologized informant, Dorothea Viehmann, that shaped his portrait. It was from such women, Dasent suggests, that the "collector" extracts his material, like a honeybee gathering pollen:

It is hard to make old and feeble women, who generally are the depositaries of these national treasures, believe that the inquirer can have any real interest in the matter. They fear that the question is put to turn them to ridicule; for the popular mind is a sensitive plant; it becomes coy, and closes its leaves at the first rude touch; and once shut, it is hard to make these aged lips reveal the secrets of the memory. (clviii–clix)

The feminized, ruralized, often infantilized images of the narrators of popular tales provide striking contrast with the rhetoric that is mobilized to characterize the study of popular tales—the voices that describe and compare, which dignify folklore with their attention, and which are clearly imagined by Dasent to be male.

And yet, despite the apparent clarity of this distinction between the (female, folk) narrative voice and the (male scholarly) critical voice, there remains some ambiguity. The elevation of popular tales to the object of scientific research did not, for Dasent, entail the abandonment of a child audience. Like Edgar Taylor before him, Dasent states explicitly his intention to publish popular tales for both adults and children.[25] Like Edward Lane, Dasent acknowledges potential points of conflict between his material and English notions of propriety, particularly in works for a readership that included women and children. Unlike Taylor and Lane, however, Dasent does not mark points of editorial intervention in annotation—of which there is none in *Popular Tales from the Norse*. Instead, Dasent issues an initial prohibition to young readers and draws on the characters and plot of the Norwegian tale "The Lassie and her Godmother" to do so.

In his preface to the second edition of *Popular Tales from the Norse*, issued just two months after the first, in March 1859, Dasent writes:

[B]efore the Translator takes leave of his readers for the second time, he will follow the lead of the good godmother in one of these Tales, and forbid all good children to read the two which stand last in the book. There is this difference between him and the godmother. She found her foster-daughter out as soon as she came back. He will never know it, if any bad child has broken his behest. . . . If, after this warning, they peep in, they may perhaps see something that will shock them.

"Why print them at all?" some grown reader asks. Because this volume is meant for you as well as for children, and if you have gone ever so little into the world with open eyes, you must have seen, yes, every day, things much more shocking. Because there is nothing immoral in their spirit. (vi–vii)

It is not only Dasent's relationship to his child readers but also the process of reading the collection that is transposed to fairyland:

If the reader will only bear in mind that this, too, is an enchanted garden, in which whoever dares to pluck a flower, does it at the peril of his head; and if he will then read the book in a merciful and tender spirit, he will prove himself what the Translator most longs to find, 'a gentle reader,' and both will part on the best terms. (x)

Borrowing fairy-tale motifs, casting himself as godmother and his master work as an enchanted garden, Dasent's own identity as objective translator, heir to the dignified and mature science of grown men, becomes slightly less clear. Similarly, as the focus of Dasent's historiographical survey narrows and the theorizing intensifies, Dasent's rhetoric becomes increasingly fanciful and impressionistic.

All in the Family

At the center of Dasent's introductory essay is the comparativist perspective of Indo-Europeanist philology, which figures here not only as the predominant model for literary historical study but also as a field with which every learned nineteenth-century man must be acquainted:

The affinity, which exists in a mythological and philological point of view, between the Aryan or Indo-European languages on the one hand, and the Sanscrit on the other, is now the first article of a literary creed. . . . The science of comparative philology—the inquiry, not into one isolated language—for now-a-days it may fairly be said of a man who knows only one language that he knows none—but into all the languages of one family, and thus to reduce them to a common centre, from which they spread like the rays of the sun. (xix–xx)

Similarities in narrative traditions, Dasent summarizes, provide clues to the historical relations of various nations: "The groundwork or plot of many of these tales is common to all the nations of Europe, is more important, and of greater scientific interest, than at first might appear. They form, in fact, another link in the chain of evidence of a common origin between East and West" (xxxi).

To appreciate the Indo-Europeanist heritage of popular tales, Dasent asserts, is to discover a history directly relevant to English people: the basis of a new and important form of transcultural literacy. Linking "all the nations of Europe," Indo-Europeanist philology provides a framework for the appreciation of national tale collections beyond their borders. As important links between nations, and even between the East and the West, the popular tales of Norway are thus framed as keys to England's own history and present status as a world power.

Dasent proceeds to construct a narrative of emigration and settlement, from which Englishmen and Norwegians alike are descended:

We all came, Greek, Latin, Celt, Teuton, Slavonian, from the East, as kith and kin, leaving kith and kin behind us; and after thousands of years, the language and traditions of those who went East, and those who went West, bear such an affinity to each other, as to have established, beyond discussion or dispute, the fact of their descent from a common stock. (xxx)

As the quotation with which I began indicates, Dasent draws on traditional motifs to construct this story of Indo-European dispersion, casting the western-traveling Aryan as the younger brother of his tale, destined for greatness. "Of those who went west," he writes "we have only to enumerate the names under which they appear in history—Celts, Greeks, Romans, Teutons, Slavonians—to see and to know at once that the stream of this migration has borne on its waves all that has become most precious to man" (xxiii–xxiv).

From here, Dasent turns his eye eastward to examine the fate of the remainder of the Aryan race:

Let us now see what became of the elder brother, who stayed at home some time after his brother went out, and then only made a short journey. Having driven out the few aboriginal inhabitants of India with little effort, and following the course of the great rivers, the Eastern Aryans gradually established themselves all over the peninsula; and then, in calm possession of a world of their own, undisturbed by conquest from without, and accepting with apathy any change of dynasty among their rulers, ignorant of the past and careless of the future, they sat down once for all and *thought*— thought not of what they had to do here, that stern lesson of every-day life from which neither men nor nations can escape if they are to live with their fellows, but how they could abstract themselves entirely from their present existence, and immerse themselves wholly in dreamy speculations on the future. (xxv)

Reminiscent of Edward Lane's characterization of Egyptians as having a special affinity for the unreal, the eastern Aryans are the "dreamers" of Dasent's tale.

The intellectual exercises in which these elder brothers engage are contrasted with the readiness to learn which, Dasent suggests, has distinguished western peoples and led eventually to their cultural, commercial, and spiritual prominence. This triumvirate of power bases emerges as Dasent quotes Max Müller: "In continual struggle with each other, and with Semitic and Mongolian races, these Aryan nations have become the rulers of history, and it seems to be their mission to link all parts of the world together by the chains of civilization, commerce, and religion" (xxiv). The noble line of descent in which Norway and England alike are seen to be situated is "distinguished from all other nations, and particularly from their elder brothers whom they left behind, by their common sense"; more specifically, "they have been teachable, ready to receive impressions from without, and, when received, to develope them" (xxiv). Directed toward a general readership engaged in a process of cross-cultural discovery—and in a popular form so frequently cast as instructive—this self-characterization is particularly resonant.

The master narrative of Indo-Europeanism may dominate the introductory essay, but the English reader should pause, Dasent suggests, to glance beyond local preoccupations and concerns: "Let us lift our eyes and see if something more is not to be discerned on the wide horizon now open on our view." Specifically, Dasent directs our gaze to the "most interesting problem for man to solve": "the origin of his race" (xlix). Contemporaneous with the publication of Darwin's *Origin of Species*, in the midst of heated debates between the defenders of monogenism and those of polygenism,[26] Dasent makes his own stance clear:

Of late years comparative philology, having accomplished her task in proving the affinity of language between Europe and the East, and so taken a mighty first step towards fixing the first seat of the greatest—greatest in wit and wisdom, if not actual numbers—portion of the human race, has pursued her enquiries into the languages of the Turanian, the Semitic, and the Chamitic or African races, with more or less successful results. In a few more years, when the African languages are better known, and the roots of Egyptian and Chinese words are more accurately detected, Science will be better able to speak to the common affinity of all tribes that throng the earth. (xlix)

The linguistic categories named by Dasent are those established in Christian Bunsen's influential *Outlines of the Philosophy of Universal History, Applied to Language and Religion* (1854). Despite the faith Dasent places in the methods of comparative linguistics, in this new and ambitious sphere of inquiry he suggests that "the testimony of tradition and popular tales" (xlix) is currently the most compelling evidence of "common affinity."

Dasent proceeds to compare, briefly, European, African, Middle Eastern, and Asian variants, suggesting that such parallels represent more than

natural resemblances, parallelisms suggested to the senses of each race by natural objects and every-day events . . . [that] might spring up spontaneously all over the earth as home growths, neither derived by imitation from other tribes, nor from seeds of common tradition shed from a common stock. (1)

Faced with such striking similarities, filial relations are again invoked:

Then arises a like impression on the mind, if we find the same tradition in two tribes at the opposite ends of the earth, as is produced by meeting twin brothers, one in Africa and the other in Asia; we say at once, "I know you are so and so's brother, you are so like him." (1)

Like Bunsen and his student Friedrich Max Müller, Dasent predicts that further folkloristic inquiry would reveal that all are "children of the same father—whatever their country, their colour, their language, and their faith,"[27] Englishmen and Norwegians are likewise brothers to Africans and Asians.

Dasent has an opportunity for a more detailed consideration of "common affinity" in the appendix of West Indian Anánsi tales[28] included in the second edition of *Popular Tales from the Norse*. Dasent explains that these stories are such as he recalled from his own "early childhood . . . in those islands," where they had been told by "his nurse, who was African born" (483). Because "the rich store which she possessed has altogether escaped his memory," Dasent collected these thirteen stories "from the mouth of a West Indian nurse in his sister's house" (483–84).

Dasent makes a point of establishing that his informant was "born and bred" in his sister's household and was "rather regarded as a member of the family than as a servant." Like the Grimms, Dasent claims that the tales "are printed just as [the female informant] told them" (484). Dasent's desire to establish, however loosely, the connection of this West Indian nursemaid and his own family echoes the familial metaphors of the introductory essay; at the same time, it marks Dasent's departure from the rhetorical strategies established by the Grimms, who had made every effort to downplay or erase their own informants' connections to bourgeois society.

Dasent introduces these stories to the English reader of *Popular Tales from the Norse* by pointing out motifs common to Norwegian, German, Hindu, and West African narrative traditions, and by casting the central figure of Anánsi himself as a mixture of the Norwegian Master-thief and of Boots (485). The perceived status of these collected tales as variants of widespread types is reinforced formally: More than half of them begin with "There once was" or a subtle variation thereof. Dasent calls one story that lacks this opening formula "*imperfect* at the beginning."[29]

Dasent indicates that these stories of the hearth and nursery—used by

West Indian women to entertain the English children in their care—were formerly a male domain, associated with the most solemn of rites:

The Negroes in the West Indies still retain the tales and traditions which their fathers and grandfathers brought with them from Africa. Some thirty years back these "Ananzi Stories," as they are called, were invariably told at the Negro wakes, which lasted for nine successive nights. The reciters were always men. In those days when the slaves were still half heathen, and when the awful *Obeah* was universally believed in, such of the Negroes as attended church or chapel kept their children away from those funeral gatherings. The wakes are now, it is believed, almost entirely discontinued, and with them have gone the stories. The Negroes are very shy of telling them, and both the clergymen of the Church of England, and the Dissenting Minister set their faces against them, and call them foolishness. (483)

Like the Norwegian tale—manly in character, but located in the memories of women—Dasent asserts that the West Indian story, in its purest state, is both culturally significant and masculine.

Dasent attributes the decline of West Indian customs to the English presence in the islands, while allowing for the possibility that storytelling and other customary practices may yet continue, both inside and outside the English nursery. Moreover, Dasent invites his English readers to take seriously those very traditions deemed foolish by religious authorities—and which may ultimately prove storyteller and reader, nursemaid and child to be of one family.

The "Character of the Race" and the Character of the Text

If popular tales ultimately demonstrated common affinity—a "common stock" of narrative, language, and bloodline—what, if anything, was nationally distinctive about them? Peter Asbjørnsen and Jørgen Moe did not extend their theorizing to the "ends of the earth," but the interrelatedness of Indo-European traditions forced them to contemplate this question as well. The issue posed an ideological problem for them, but the resolution they reached addressed a secondary problem: the ongoing tension between authenticity and readability in the folklore book.

In a prospectus for their project, Asbjørnsen and Moe categorized their work as "scientific," aligning their efforts with those of the Grimms.[30] In the late 1840s, Moe wrote to Jacob Grimm about the difficulties he and Asbjørnsen had faced as scholars with interests in Norwegian folktales:

Last year I applied for and received such a stipend in order to study our folk poetry in relationship to that of related races. It was only with great difficulties that the scholarship came through, not because those in charge were in doubt of my competence but because this subject could not be brought under any academic discipline. Consequently many of our highly learned people were very much in doubt about the scientific value of such studies.[31]

Moe requested Jacob Grimm's support of the ongoing project, citing their shared interest in "comparative studies of folk poetry" and the "awakening nationalistic strivings" that were making "the particular poetic creations by the folk everywhere . . . more and more the subject for attention and careful collecting."[32]

When the Norwegians sought funding for a definitive edition of the popular tales in 1844, Moe proposed a lengthy introduction in which he would investigate "the relationship of the native folklore to corresponding stories among other peoples, and . . . the Norwegian folk tale's uniqueness."[33] As their fieldwork concluded and writing of his essay began, Moe ran into difficulty accommodating his nationalist impulses with the results of the comparative method, as Oscar Falnes has summarized:

In common with the students of his day, Moe accepted the Aryan hypothesis, but its acceptance for a time left him in "doubt and perplexity" since the comparative method which figured so prominently in the formulation of the hypothesis seemed to point to a common Aryan folklore. This in turn suggested that the rich traditions which Asbjørnsen and he had gathered really were part of a common Aryan possession so that Norwegian tales were really not distinctive. In his dilemma Moe came to doubt if a folk tale could be peculiarly national; everything seemed to indicate that the stories he had helped to collect were common and not distinctive, European or even Eurasian, not national. (227)

Moe emerged from this crisis with a model that accommodated both the transnationalism of Indo-Europeanist philology and the romantic nationalism that had inspired the Norwegians' project. He concluded that similarities in general plot structures may point to common origins but that national distinctiveness is located in minor variations in plot and especially in style—which are not attributable to the Indo-European heritage but "grown organically and from within" each nation.[34]

Dasent likewise cites tales from various nations "told in all with such variations of character and detail, and such adaptations to time and place, as evidently show the original working of the national consciousness upon a stock of tradition common to all the race, but belonging to no tribe of that

race in particular" (xxxiii). Despite Dasent's foregrounding of the philological tradition and the sustained attention he grants to the subject of common
stock, the Norse popular tales are not treated with scientific detachment as
clues to the historical relations between nations. And despite his adoption of
Moe's organicist model of national distinctiveness, Dasent makes no effort to
identify constellations of formal features or characteristic adaptations of plot
that might distinguish one national corpus of tales from another.

"The tales of all races," Dasent summarizes, "have a character and manner of their own" (cxliv), in spite of their shared heritage. The image Dasent
invokes to reinforce this point is again familial, although in contrast with his
earlier personification of eastern and western Aryans, national corpora of
tales within the Indo-European tradition are here imagined not as brothers
but as sisters:

They are like as sisters of one house are like. They have what would be called a strong
family likeness; but besides this likeness, which they owe to father or mother, as the
case may be, they have each their peculiarities of form, and eye, and face, and still
more, their differences of mind and intellect. (xl)

Dasent highlights mental and intellectual distinctiveness in this simile. In
fact, it is not biology but psychology that provides him with his favored
metaphor: "Shall we take another likeness," he proposes, "and say that [popu-
lar tales] are national dreams; that they are like the sleeping thoughts of
many men upon one and the same thing" (xli).

The metaphor of the "national dream" proves good to think with.
Through it, Dasent addresses two questions fundamental to the folkloristics
of his time: How can popular tales reflect national character? And if the
Indo-European heritage is unified, how can a nation's repertoire of tales be
seen as distinctive?

He continues:

There is, indeed, a greater truth in this likeness than may at first sight appear. In
the popular tale, properly so called, the national mind dreams all its history over again;
in its half conscious state it takes this trait and that trait, this feature and that feature, of
times and ages long past. It snatches up bits of its old beliefs, and fears, and griefs, and
glory, and pieces them together with something that happened yesterday, and then
holds up the distorted reflection in all its inconsequence, just as it has passed before
that magic glass, as though it were genuine history, and matter for pure belief. (xli–xlii)

Born of the half-conscious workings of the collective "national mind," popular tales appear here as a patchwork of belief, memory, and emotion, em-

braced uncritically by the nation that produces them. The particular shape these "distorted reflections" of empirical truth take is unique:

> Suppose a hundred men to have been eye-witnesses of some event on the same day, and then to have slept and dreamt of it; we should have as many distinct representations of that event, all turning upon it and bound up with it in some way, but each preserving the personality of the sleeper, and working up the common stuff in a higher or lower degree, just as the fancy and the intellect of the sleeper was at a higher or lower level of perfection. (xli)

The histories of the Indo-European nations may overlap and merge, but the popular tales they produce are distinctive and of varying degrees of sophistication.

For Dasent, the project of translation extends beyond the linguistic level, which in and of itself fails to convey accurately the textual character of the tales and the national character of the "race."[35] An accurate text, in Dasent's view, will not necessarily resemble verbatim transcription or literal translation—which may not capture what is distinctive about the tales. Instead, "accuracy" stands as the ability to convey the workings of the national mind. It is not idiosyncratic realities and perspectives, not individual artistry and creativity, that are valued here. Unity of voice, homogeneity of style and worldview—that is, the very qualities that render a tale collection highly coherent and readable—mark strivings for "accuracy" within this model.

In fact, Dasent suggests that the shaping effects of a national consciousness on the common stock of popular tales may be beyond description. Firsthand experience emerges once again as the key to true transnational literary appreciation:

> [T]o those who have never been in [Norway] . . . and who are not familiar with that hearty simple people, no words can tell the freshness and truth of the originals. It is not that the idioms of the two languages are different, for they are more nearly allied, both in vocabulary and construction, than any other two tongues, but it is the face of nature herself, and the character of the race that looks up to her, that fail to the mind's eye. (clx)

Thus, although Dasent sought English equivalencies in his translation of the Norwegian tales, he also acknowledges the limitations of that process to convey "the character of the race" across national boundaries.

Despite the proclaimed inadequacy of descriptive language to capture national character, Dasent's introduction is a showpiece of highly romantic rhetoric, as popular tales inspire him to poetical characterization of place, people, and tradition. For instance, of the popular tale in India—the jewel of the philological tradition—Dasent writes that "the straight stem of the story is overhung with a network of imagery which reminds one of the parasitic growth of a tropical forest"; in the Middle East, "the tale is more elegant, pointed with a moral, and adorned with tropes and episodes"; in Italy "it is bright, light, dazzling, and swift"; in France "we have passed from the woods, and fields, and hills, to my lady's *boudoir*,—rose-pink is the prevailing colour, and the air is loaded with patchouli and *mille fleurs*." Dasent clearly has his own preferences: "We miss the song of birds, the modest odour of wild-flowers, and the balmy fragrance of the pine forest" (cxliv–cxlv).[36]

Not surprisingly, Norway receives flattering treatment as Dasent continues his northwestward march, emerging as manly, rustic, independent, strong:

When in the midst of all this natural scenery we find an honest manly race, not the race of the towns and cities, but of the dales and fells, free and unsubdued, holding its own in a country where there are neither lords nor ladies, but simple men and women, who cling to the traditions of their forefathers, and whose memory reflects as from the faithful mirror of their native steel the whole history and progress of their race—when all these natural features, and such a manly race meet; then we have the stuff out of which these tales are made, the living rock out of which these sharp-cut national forms are hewn. (clxi–clxii)

The Norse popular tales, he suggests, are born of a mixture of natural and cultural circumstances: Rural landscape, preindustrial and nonhierarchical social conditions, and long-standing traditions combine to give the tales their distinctive shape.

While Norway and England may be united by a shared Indo-European heritage and, more specifically, a shared descent from the "younger brother" of the Aryan family, the portrait that Dasent draws of contemporary Norway stands in marked contrast to that of England. Dasent locates the interest of the Norse tales in both their rugged, northern character and their rootedness in a peasant culture as yet untouched by modernity:

They came from the East, and brought that common stock of tradition with them. Settled in the Scandinavian peninsula, they developed themselves through Heathenism, Romanism, and Lutheranism, in a locality little exposed to foreign influence, so that even now the Daleman in Norway or Sweden may be reckoned among the most primitive examples left of peasant life. We should expect, then, that these Popular Tales, which, for the sake of those ignorant in such matters, it may be remarked, had never been collected or reduced to writing till within the last few years, would present a faithful picture of the national consciousness, or, perhaps, to speak more correctly, of that half consciousness out of which the heart of any people speaks in its abundance. (lxxxvi–lxxxvii)

The Norwegian peasantry is held up as exemplary, marking points in the great Indo-European pilgrimage westward and also the progress of social organization. It is precisely the lack of the conditions that here characterize Norwegian history—isolation, nonindustrialized labor, tradition sustained in memory—that Dasent identifies as the reasons for the disappearance of the English popular tale.

Dasent's account begins and concludes with reflections not on Norse but on English narrative traditions. From the start, readers are reminded that "the voice of the English reciter . . . was hushed in England more than a century ago." As the introductory essay progresses, it seems that the storyteller's voice was suffocated by the classic harbingers of progress. Nursery tales, he writes, have "faded away before the light of gas and the power of steam" (xv). Invoking an admixture of technology and mythology, the printing press rounds out the cast in this story of the tale's demise:

It may, indeed, be dreaded lest the time for collecting such English traditions is not past and gone; whether the steam-engine and printing-press have not played their great work of enlightenment too well; and whether the popular tales, of which, no doubt, the land was once full, have not faded away before those great inventions, as the race of Giants waned before the might of Odin and the Aesir. (clviii)

As he moves toward conclusion, Dasent expresses his hope that English voices can join the emergent discourse on the popular tale not only as outsiders but with a national corpus of their own. "[L]et us hope," he writes, that "an English Grimm may yet arise who may . . . discover in the mouth of an Anglo-Saxon Gammer Grethel, some, at least, of those popular tales which England once had in common with all the Aryan race" (clx). Emerging triumphant in the great tales of social evolution and Indo-European migration, Dasent still yearns for an English variant of his favored tale type: *Woman Tells Stories While Man Takes Notes.*

Chapter 6
Conclusion: Dreams

The road to truth is, like the road to fairyland, fraught with perils and requires an innocent suspension of disbelief in the self and what it creates. By translating the work, one translates oneself; the little Arab boy who listened to the Thousand and One Nights *has become the English storyteller. . . . What does it matter, so long as he has dreamed, in one Baghdad or another, a dream in the lap of a fairy queen.[1]*
—Husain Haddawy, 1990

The truth lies not in one but in many dreams.[2]
—Pier Paolo Pasolini, 1974

English readers of the early to mid-nineteenth century provided a warm reception for collections of foreign folktales. In the case of *German Popular Stories*, the English enthusiasm for the Grimms' tales outdid that of German readers and left Jacob and Wilhelm searching for Edgar Taylor's magic formula. Although *Fairy Legends and Traditions of the South of Ireland* was translated into German, it was found most resonant by nineteenth-century English readers. The *Arabian Nights* may have found its first European home in France, but it was nineteenth-century Englishmen who most vigorously debated its proper form and the nature of its cultural indexicality. Finally, *Popular Tales from the Norse* found its most welcoming foreign reception not in Germany—the birthplace of the folktale collection—but in England.

Awestruck, Peter Asbjørnsen wrote to Jacob Grimm on the subject:

Our Norwegian folktales seem to be much more appealing to the English than to the Germans. At Christmas a new translation was published in Edinburgh and London with, according to the reviews, a new and enlarged introduction which received fine reviews in the *Times*, the *Athenaeum*, the *Saturday Review*, and many other English papers and magazines. Already in March another and much larger edition was issued, from which it is indicated that the book will become very popular in England. In Germany, on the other hand, there still exists only the Bresemann translation from 1847 in the first edition.[3]

The nation that had repeatedly decried the exile of the fairies and the silencing of the storyteller thus provided fairy-tale books with their greatest market. This fascination with foreign folktales may have some resonance with Victorian occultism, as Carole G. Silver has recently implied. But writers like Taylor, Croker, Lane, and Dasent were not at all concerned with the "actuality of the elfin people." Theirs was less a "quest for fairies"[4] than it was a quest for oral traditionality and, by extension, the terms in which to articulate and sometimes critique their own literate modernity.

The volumes of "popular tales" produced for an English readership set precedents for the presentation and framing of such material, which can still be seen at work today. To begin with, the books I have considered here established a model for the publication of corpora of tales nationally defined and presented to readers as sources of cultural insight, indicative of foreign national character and worldview. Works like *German Popular Stories* and *Popular Tales from the Norse* had direct links to the national frame of reference, being English translations of collections which were motivated by nationalist impulses. Edgar Taylor and George Webbe Dasent reinforced this frame by presenting their collections as the popular tales of Germany and of Norway, respectively. In Taylor's case, this required not a translation of the Grimms' title but creation of a new one that highlighted the tales' national origins. Renaming along comparable lines had occurred in the European publishing history of *Alf Layla wa Layla* as well, where similar liberties were taken to locate the text in a geographic and cultural—if not strictly national—setting. Examples of this general tendency range from Antoine Galland's creation of the subtitle *Contes Arabes*, through the eighteenth-century English convention of referring to the text as *The Arabian Nights' Entertainments*. For Edward Lane, the *Arabian Nights* provided "most admirable pictures" of Arabian manners and customs, but more specifically "those of the Egyptians."[5] Like T. Crofton Croker, Lane drew on firsthand experience—fieldwork—to position this imaginative narrative tradition in a broader cultural reality and to argue that popular tales provided a key to national character.

The national frame of reference has since become so well established that it is rarely questioned, and other modes of categorization are exceptional.

As Kimberly J. Lau has noted, this frame is still at work in the marketing and packaging of folktales.[6] The organization of the two most prominent contemporary series of folktale books stand as sufficient demonstration of this fact: the Folktales of the World series by the University of Chicago Press and Pantheon's Fairy Tale and Folklore Library, which have filled American bookstore shelves with such volumes as *Folktales of Norway, Folktales of India, Japanese Tales,* and *Italian Folktales.*[7] However, the "serial logic" Lau has so convincingly problematized is not only a matter of packaging, nor is it simply a product of late twentieth-century multiculturalism. Its roots lie in the "popular tale" collections of the early to mid-nineteenth century, where the transnational frame—the positioning of the book as a new kind of English writing, its contents as an ancient kind of foreign oral tradition—shaped elements of style, form, and content.

Why attempt to address issues of cultural and national identity in the context of such storybooks? The reasons given in this formative period were varied. For Taylor, German popular stories deserved the attention of English readers because they illuminated earlier points in social and literary evolution. Taylor argued that the range of literary forms extant in Germany, from the nursery tale to the novel, was unique to that nation, and provided keys to national history and progress. Croker suggested that fairy legends mirrored the worldview, specifically the superstitiousness, of the Irish peasantry and were therefore key to an English understanding of Irish character and behavior. Lane adopted the Lowthian proposition that detailed cultural information could enable readers to cross the boundaries of time and space, to penetrate foreign texts. Furthermore, Lane proposed that proclivities for fantasy and storytelling were of such central importance to Egyptian national character that the complex and fantastic tales of *Alf Layla wa Layla* were themselves key ethnographic artifacts. Finally, Dasent argued that tales which can be linked in a comparativist framework due to their similarities in plot were distinctive in their minor variations, style, and implicit worldview—indelibly stamped with the character of the "national mind" that produced them.

Echoes of such formulations resound in twentieth-century writings. For example, historian Robert Darnton's influential study of French folktales, "Peasants Tell Tales," begins with an attempt to bridge "the distance between our mental world and that of our ancestors" by providing contemporary American readers with a brief overview of peasant life and customs in Old Regime France.[8] Later in that essay, Darnton ventures a comparative analysis in order to isolate and identify the "distinct cultural style" that constitutes the tales' "Frenchness." They convey, Darnton suggests, a particular view of the world—a sense that life is hard, that you had better not have any illusions about selflessness in your fellow men, that clear-headedness and quick wit are necessary to protect what little you can extract from your surroundings, and that moral nicety will get you nowhere. (61)

In addition to providing a characteristic perspective on life, Darnton continues, French folktales have a "peculiar flavor" linked to their rootedness in particular social conditions: "They taste of salt. They smell of the earth. They take place in an intensely human world, where farting, delousing, rolling in the hay, and tossing on the dung heap express the passions, values, interests, and attitudes of a peasant society that is now extinct" (52–53).

Similar assumptions about the representation (and representativeness) of national culture, character, and worldview underlie espousals of folktales' value as cross-cultural educational resources. This deserves some attention, for it is in children's literature and the elementary classroom that most Americans now encounter the genre. Folklorists Beverly Stoeltje and Nancy Worthington advise educators that the "significance of oral tradition is most readily grasped if we seek to identify the communicative purposes they serve in social relationships, whether they create hostilities, transcend differences, or disguise messages in codes."[9] But rarely is it the folktale's capacity to confront or address social issues or the teller's use of the genre as coded communication that is discussed. For many elementary educators, "folk literature" plays an important part in the effort to introduce children to reading material that "presents diverse experiences, celebrates common bonds, and introduces the wonderful variety of our world."[10] Retellings of folktales from Iraq, Siberia, Cuba, and Australia enter the classroom, in book form, in "story hours, reading units, social studies units, voluntary reading and analysis."[11] A modern form of the "popular tale" book lives on, and continues to be framed as an upbeat, celebratory, and wondrous source of cultural information and insight. Folktales may currently play such a prominent role in multicultural education because they have been rendered uncontroversial in print, and we now assume that this is their nature.

In the same year that Darnton's *Great Cat Massacre* was published, educators Jesse Goodman and Kate Melcher proposed using collections of folktales in elementary classrooms "to study cultures inaccessible to direct observation,"[12] adopting the proposition made by fellow educators that "Folklore is something called the 'mirror of a people.'"[13] Specifically, Goodman and Melcher suggest using English-language collections of Ashanti Anánsi tales to teach American school children about moral values (cooperation, selflessness) and "facts" of daily life (housing types, hunting methods, foodways) in West Africa—decidedly not modern and utterly anachronistic. The cultural distance these writers initially address is quickly transformed into a temporal one, as Goodman and Melcher shift from reference to African and American contexts to statements about childhood past and present. Folktales, they write, "*were* often used to teach children about their own heritage, values, and customs. Through an anthroliterary approach, today's children can learn in the same way children have learned for centuries—by listening to and interpreting stories" (200).

While Darnton, Goodman and Melcher, and many others have sought to penetrate the "traditional" cultures that they state or imply have vanished, they fail to recognize the centuries-old discursive tradition in which their respective arguments are entrenched and which is closer to home than either early modern France or an apparently timeless West Africa. Each of these contemporary statements about the meaning and significance of traditional narratives is itself based on published collections of tales. Notes indicate that Darnton is basing his analysis on Paul Delarue and Marie-Louise Teneze's *Le Conte populaire français* (1976),[14] and in parentheses Goodman and Melcher inform educators who wish to implement this instructional unit that they may find the tales in either Harold Courlander's *Hat Shake Dance* (1957) or Robert Rattray's *Akan-Ashanti Folk-Tales* (1969).[15] Such collections extend the nineteenth-century practice of presenting a corpus of tales as the product of a particular nation, representative of national character, unified by worldview, manners, and customs, and modified for mass consumption. Texts of this kind not only lend themselves to but precipitate the kind of analyses ventured by Darnton and Goodman and Melcher. Perhaps what these writers have discovered are not solely the secrets of other cultures but the guiding principles of our own such textual productions.

Framing, textual practice, and interpretation are inextricably linked. For instance, Taylor modified the tone and content of the *Kinder- und Hausmärchen* to produce a world of amusing and relatively harmless magic and a romanticized portrait of peasant life, reinforced in Cruikshank's illustrations. This vision of folktales and folk culture suited nineteenth-century English standards of propriety and visions of the English past, capturing the imaginations of Victorian readers like John Ruskin and Charlotte Yonge. By the time Ruskin wrote his introductory essay for the reprinting of *German Popular Stories* in the 1860s, these textual modifications could be invoked to construct a portrait of "genuine" peasant society. As Regina Bendix has summarized, "Authenticity came to be associated with materialized texts, while those harboring the texts remained largely anonymous and were increasingly projected into a more appealing past."[16] The interrelatedness of frame, text, and authenticity becomes especially clear in Ruskin's essay. "For every fairy tale *worth recording at all*," he writes, "is the remnant of a tradition possessing true historical value;—historical, at least so far as it has naturally arisen out of the mind of a people under special circumstances."[17] The potential of an orally told tale to support a social evolutionary model and a particular vision of folk society thus emerges as not only proof of its authenticity but the very reason for its entextualization in written form.

Writing a year later, Yonge attributed the return to England of "the true unadulterated fairy tale" to Taylor's *German Popular Stories*, which was itself exemplary of "the genuine—we had almost said authentic—fairy tale . . . that is the true delight of childhood."[18] Yonge's hesitancy to apply the term *authentic* to fantastical narratives reveals her rationalist bent, but she defines a category of "genuine" tales, nonetheless. The content of tales may be unreal, but as written texts they can truthfully represent a particular narrative tradition.

Of course, a contrasting conception of what constituted and characterized the "true" folk fairy tale could have quite different textual ramifications. For instance, Ruth Bottigheimer has demonstrated that Wilhelm Grimm's revisions of the *Kinder- und Hausmärchen* (following its initial publication in 1812) produced increasingly isolated and endangered heroines and increasingly brutal punishments, accentuating exactly the same elements that Taylor chose to modify or eliminate.[19] Wilhelm Grimm located the true home of the German *Märchen* in "the rude cottage and the bawdy marketplace,"[20] while Taylor situated the tales in a quaint and rustic environment, mellowing the threats to characters' happiness and well-being, frequently imbuing supernatural agents with comic appeal, and substituting forgiveness for bloody retribution.

Like Taylor, Lane sought to adapt a text in translation to suit English readers' sensibilities, but his own conception of the *Nights'* cultural indexicality and his vision of Egyptian culture itself had equal impact on his textual practices. Appealing to his status as a cultural authority, Lane sometimes modified the *Nights* to make it correspond with his Egyptian experience. In an equally circular fashion, Dasent offered his sustained account of the historiography of the popular tale, its meaning and significance, and also produced a collection of such formal and stylistic regularity that it indeed appears to be the product of a single (national) mind and voice. In short, conceptions of the nature of popular tales and assumptions regarding the socio cultural environments in which they arise have shaped the destiny of the tales as written texts;

equally, the form they have been given on the page leans toward particular modes of analysis, as Darnton, Goodman and Melcher have recently demonstrated. The form, function, and meaning of such tale collections are so intertwined that to discuss the "significance" of fairy tales without discussing the ideological and methodological dimensions of their entextualization in print form is moot.

The very existence of such books—traditional narratives produced by foreign national minds, in written form for an English nation of readers—stood as evidence of English mass literacy and modernity, and continues to be invoked as a central point of contrast between traditional and modern cultures. For example, in Yonge's discussion of fairy tales, it goes without saying that the English narrative tradition to which she refers is a commodified one: "A real traditional fairy tale," she writes, "is a possession" (306). A century later, Katharine Briggs wrote that there were "few civilized nurseries into which 'The Nursery and Household Tales' did not make their entry."[21] The implied contrast between the traditional or folk nursery in which tales are narrated orally and the modern or "civilized" nursery in which *books* of tales have a place may be seen at work in Goodman and Melcher's essay as well: These educators assume as much about the nature of contemporary American childhood and enculturation as they do West African. Repeatedly, studies of the folktale as a source of cultural insight, as mirrors of otherness, reflect and construct dreams of the self.

Examining popular tales as indexically related to premodern social formations and as historically related to an Indo-European heritage of language and literature, English writers of the early to mid-nineteenth century developed their own very powerful and enduring tales. In the narrativization of both paradigms—social evolution and comparative philology—modern England would seem to emerge heroic. Yet if foreign folk traditions offered a flattering mirror image of England's own mass literacy and industrial capitalism, they also afforded opportunities for critical self-reflection.

This critical impulse can be seen at work throughout the history of the literary fairy tale—from the revolt against neo-classicism in the late seventeenth-century tales of Charles Perrault and Madame d'Aulnoy, to the reimagining of sexual politics in the late twentieth-century stories of Angela Carter and Emma Donoghue.[22] In nineteenth-century England, the study of foreign folktales would inspire reconsideration of the long-standing assumption that England was bereft of oral traditions. From the 1860s through the early twentieth century, an increasing number of English enthusiasts entered the field to make collections of their own, and many started by looking in

England. In 1890, the methods of domestic field collection were codified in both Charlotte Burne's "Collection of English Folk-Lore in England" and George Laurence Gomme's *Handbook of Folklore*.[23]

If foreign and domestic folklore could offer windows to the past, such material also inspired critiques of the modern, industrial present, and thus provided the imaginative foundations for visions of England's future. For example, folk traditions inspired not only John Ruskin's commentary on Grimms' fairytales but also William Morris's artistic and political writings and practices and Ruskin's own influential reflections on Gothic art, architecture, and society.

In the popular tale collection, English people found opportunities to dream their own history over again, and if Dasent's trope can be applied to folk and editorial narrators alike, it is equally applicable to historiographers. In the master narrative of the history of English children's literature, the early to mid-nineteenth century stands as a watershed, the period in which "delight" triumphed over "instruction."[24] The works I have considered here figure prominently in this story of the transformation of children's books, paving the way for the golden age of imaginative literature for children in the late nineteenth and early twentieth centuries.[25] Ill at ease with visions of children's literature as inherently political or openly didactic, we tend to value books for children according to the degree to which they camouflage or erase their ideological foundations. Serving as supernatural helpers in this pervasive historiographical tale of children's search for imaginative freedom, the popular tale collection is, I suggest, too easily divorced from its political and ideological underpinnings.[26]

Thirty years ago, in *The British Folklorists*, Richard Dorson wrote passionately about the British folklore movement, which had reached its pinnacle in the nineteenth century. As a "story that began with Camden's history of Britannia and reached its apogee at the outbreak of the Great War," unified by a "firm thread" that binds from "Camden to Lang," we can recognize in Dorson's account the search of the academic folklorist for a distinguished scholarly heritage in which he could position himself and his beloved discipline.

Dreaming his field's intellectual history over again, Dorson pieced together selectively, granting little consideration to the books I have examined here. Dorson gives sustained attention only to Croker's *Fairy Legends and Traditions of the South of Ireland* (44–51); he mentions Taylor only as the inspiration for William John Thoms's complaint that *German Popular Stories* was "too free, omitting homely expressions and repetitions." (78); Lane is not mentioned at all, and despite Dorson's claim that *Popular Tales from the Norse* gained "a public favour surpassed only by the Grimms' *Household Tales*," Dasent figures only as the source of inspiration for John Francis Campbell's 1860 *Popular Tales of the West Highlands, Orally Collected* (393). Reflecting his own conception of folkloristics, Dorson was most interested in writers like Croker or Campbell who had themselves engaged in fieldwork which was, by the mid-twentieth century, the hallmark of serious academic folklore study. In fact, such works were anomalies. For instance, Campbell's was a highly idiosyncratic collection of narratives, relatively inaccessible to general readers, and difficult to read aloud *because* of the features that Dorson would have prized in the tale texts (instances of dialect and colloquialisms, wide variations in narrative style, and plot inconsistencies, all interpreted as indications of unretouched transcription) and the editorial notes (extensive details about location and date of each field encounter and the identity and occupation of each storyteller). Extending from his own retrospective preferences and biases, Dorson sometimes overlooked writers whose textual treatment and interpretive framing of tales in translation helped establish the enduring popularity of the genre, setting precedents for later collections of tales and perspectives on their significance. Dorson wished to downplay the degree to which proto-folklorists had catered to popular reading tastes and a broad-based audience.

The roots of the discourse and discipline of Folklore are undeniably bound up with their popular appeal. Jacob and Wilhelm Grimm understood this, expressing their wish both to contribute to an emergent history of German poetry and to entertain readers everywhere. Taylor's publisher, Charles Baldwyn, sensed immediately that an English translation of the *Kinder- und Hausmärchen* had as much imaginative as intellectual appeal, recognizing the tales' illustratability and commissioning George Cruikshank for the job. Croker's desired audience was also a mass English readership: His primary objective was to reveal through story and description the worldview and character of the Irish, and this mission was best served in a book with popular appeal. Lane had scholarly aspirations of his own, despite his lack of formal training; nonetheless, he found a degree of success as a writer only when his publisher, Charles Knight, recognized the potential of massively revised versions of Lane's work to fit the ideals and objectives of the Society for the Diffusion of Useful Knowledge, specifically their Library of Entertaining Knowledge series. Dasent drew on models established in the preceding few decades, gearing his own work toward a general readership that included children and adults, and addressing both the appeal of the tales and their sociohistorical significance.

From the Grimms, to Taylor, to Croker, to Lane, to Dasent, we witness popularity as a driving force in the textual history of tale collections. The processes of revision and modification applied by the Grimms to the *Kinder- und Hausmärchen*, driven by the warm reception the tales received as literature for children, have been well documented—and variously evaluated. But regardless of how one assesses the textual practices of the Grimms, the impact of real and perceived reader response on the history of the *KHM* is unquestionable.

The ramifications of real or perceived reader response on textual form and purpose is equally clear in Lane's *Arabian Nights*. Lane regarded his introduction, translation, annotations, and William Harvey's illustrations as extensions of a unified vision of cultural and textual character—and as means toward the common end of representing the manners, customs, and imaginative proclivities of Egyptians. But Knight found the book's appeal was divided between readers who were drawn to the fantastical tales and the detailed illustrations and those who were interested in Egyptian culture and the detailed annotations. Accordingly, the future of Lane's work on the *Nights* took divergent paths. His notes were eventually divorced from the text they had been intended to illuminate and published as *Arabian Society in the Middle Ages* while his translation of *Alf Layla wa Layla* was claimed as a "classic," unencumbered by editorial commentary.[27]

Most fundamentally, the commercial success of popular tale collections resulted in the production of more text. One of the most appealing and fanciful images of readers' hunger for more stories comes from the publishing history of the *Nights*: A legend grew around Antoine Galland's popularity in which members of his enthusiastic readership appeared at his bedroom window, echoing Dunyázád's plea to her sister Shahrazád for just one more delightful tale.[28] Taylor may not have received midnight pleas for additional fairy tales, but the popularity of *German Popular Stories* in 1823 not only encouraged reprints in 1824 and 1825 but also inspired him to move beyond the selections from the *Kinder- und Hausmärchen* made initially with David Jardine, and produce a second volume of *German Popular Stories* in 1826. Similarly, within a year of the initial appearance of *Fairy Legends and Traditions of the South of Ireland* in 1825, publisher John Murray had reprinted the work and sent Croker back into the field to find material for two additional volumes of tales. The commercial success of Lane's *Modern Egyptians* was what made the project of retranslating, annotating, and illustrating the *Arabian Nights* a viable one. Even Dasent's thick *Popular Tales from the Norse* was expanded from its initial 1858 format to include thirteen additional tales translated from Asbjørnsen and Moe's collection as well as the appendix of thirteen West Indian "Ananzi stories," collected by the translator himself and offered as a further point of cultural comparison.

In his 1960 study of the oral epic, Albert Lord drew attention to the role of the audience in the creative moment of performance, highlighting the adjustments made by the "singer of tales" according to audience response. Over a hundred years earlier, Croker took note of folk wisdom on the subject: From Peggy Barrett we learn that "all experienced story-tellers" adapt their tales "both in length and subject, to the audience and the occasion."[29] The world of the writers of tales is similar, despite our tendency—experiencing these books only as static and sometimes dusty objects on library shelves—to read them as de facto manifestations of writers' unified and unmediated intentions. Particularly in the case of popular editions of popular tales, publishing history is not simply an interesting but expendable bit of context; relocating these books in the communicative circuit within which they originally emerged is absolutely essential. I have endeavored to demonstrate how the facts of publishing history enliven our understanding of how these objects came to be, the various forms they took, and the ways we make sense of them in the present.

I have suggested that there are factors that lie beyond the immediate intellectual and ideological concerns of individual writers that cannot be overlooked: Publishers wanted to attract as large a readership as possible, and the imaginative appeal of written popular tales had been well established in the previous century. Philanthropic societies interested in edifying and, to a certain extent, monitoring the growing body of readers hoped that entertainment and instruction would combine happily in the study of foreign manner, custom, and story. Undeniably, one outcome of this dual emphasis was the discovery that the "scientific" study of such matters—what would after 1846 be known as "Folk-lore"—itself possessed great imaginative appeal. Armchair scholars pored over the innumerable tale texts; the new breed of field-based scholars took the place of "the listening child and the untutored peasant"[30] at hearthside and listened to stories. It was not at all difficult to recast oneself fancifully as a field collector (as did Taylor in later editions of *German Popular Stories*), or as a fairy-tale godmother (as did Dasent in the introduction to *Popular Tales from the Norse*), or as a fictionalized *raconteuse extraordinaire*. As Husain Haddawy's romantic articulation of his own scholarly enterprise of translation makes clear, these processes can still be experienced as magical, and "serious" engagement with such texts can still be cast as dreamlike.

One problem with applying Dasent's trope of the "national dream" to the English context is that the politics of literary culture are not nearly as democratic as the workings of the unconscious. In *Fairy Tales and the Art of Subversion,* Jack Zipes reminds us that access to these sorts of "dreams" was limited to the literate:

Reading of printed fairytales in the 19th century was a socially exclusive process: it was conducted mainly in bourgeois circles and nurseries, and members of the lower classes who learned how to read were not only acquiring a skill, they were acquiring a value system and social status depending on their conformity to norms controlled by bourgeois interests. (54–55)

In fact, we may now have caught glimpses of the various forces that shaped these texts and the images of self and Other embedded within them, but we don't know how the resultant books were read. If we are to resist what Jonathan Rose calls the "receptive fallacy," the assumption that "whatever the author put into a text—or whatever the critic chooses to read into that text—is the message that the common reader receives,"[31] then certain questions remain. Did English common readers attend to the interpretive frames laid out for them? Did they recognize themselves in the books' implied portraits of national character? We can analyze these texts to see how they construct foreignness and, in effect, Englishness. Following Louis Althusser, we can examine how modes of address produced a readership for the popular tale collection, creating the possibility of subjectivity for a diverse range of English readers. But there is a danger in adopting the Althusserian position in all its apparent determinism, as many critics have noted. The reader always has the option of ignoring or subverting the "interpellation"[32] and modes of address directed at her: In Michel de Certeau's terms, there is always the possibility of oppositional "misreading."[33] Zipes steers us toward the liberating potentialities of our familiar trope. "In some respects," he continues, "reading can function explosively like a dream and serve to challenge socialization and constraints. . . . it is practically impossible to determine what direct effect a fairy tale will have upon an *individual* reader in terms of validating his or her own existence" (55). Many minds, as Dasent proposes, may dream on one thing, but the contours of those dreams remain both individual and unpredictable.

Notes

Chapter 1

1. Edgar Taylor, "German Popular and Traditionary Literature," *New Monthly Magazine and Literary Journal* 2 (1821): 146.

2. Charlotte Yonge uses the term "class literature" extensively in her three-part series, "Children's Literature of the Last Century"; see, e.g., *Macmillan's Magazine* 20 (1869): 229.

3. Peter Burke, "The 'Discovery' of Popular Culture," in Raphael Samuel, ed., *People's History and Socialist Theory* (London: Routledge and Kegan Paul, 1981), 216.

4. The Grimms stand as forefathers of modern, field-based folklore study. For example, see Linda Dégh, "Folk Narrative," in Richard M. Dorson, ed., *Folklore and Folklife: An Introduction,* (Chicago: University of Chicago Press, 1972), 54; Dan Ben-Amos, "Folktale," in Richard Bauman, ed., *Folklore, Cultural Performances, and Popular Entertainments: A Communications-Centered Handbook* (New York: Oxford University Press, 1992), 106; Robert A. Georges and Michael Owen Jones, *Folkloristics: An Introduction* (Bloomington: Indiana University Press, 1995), 37–38. This convention was firmly in place by 1858, when Dasent penned his introductory essay for *Popular Tales from the Norse.*

5. The legacy of the Grimms has recently been explored by a number of folklorists. See Roger D. Abrahams, "Phantoms of Romantic Nationalism in Folkloristics," *Journal of American Folklore* 106 (1993): 3–37; Regina Bendix, "Diverging Paths in the Scientific Search for Authenticity," *Journal of Folklore Research* 29, no. 2 (1992): 103–32, and *In Search of Authenticity: The Formation of Folklore Studies* (Madison: University of Wisconsin Press, 1997); and Charles Briggs, "Metadiscursive Practices and Scholarly Authority in Folkloristics," *Journal of American Folklore* 106 (1993): 387–434.

6. Collections inspired by the Grimms' example include Asbjørnsen and Moe's *Norske Folkeeventyr* (1842), translated by George Webbe Dasent as *Popular Tales from the Norse* (discussed in chapter 5); Sutermeister's *Kinder- und Hausmärchen aus der Schweiz* (1869); and Afanasév's *Narodnye Russkie Skaski* (1855–63). In his 1946 study, *The Folktale*, Stith Thompson provides an appendix, "Principal Collections of Folktales," organized by nation. It is remarkable how many of the key European collections were made concurrently, in the mid- to late nineteenth century. See Thompson's *Folktale* (Berkeley: University of California Press, 1977), 467–79.

7. Jacqueline Simpson and Steve Roud, introduction to *A Dictionary of English Folklore* (New York: Oxford University Press, 2000), i. E. J. Hobsbawm cites the

establishment of England's Folklore Society in 1878 as "proof" that there is "no necessary connection" between nationalism and folklore study. See Hobsbawm, *Nations and Nationalism since 1780: Programme, Myth, Reality*, rev. ed. (New York: Cambridge University Press, 1990), 104.

8. Michael Herzfeld, *Ours Once More: Folklore, Ideology, and the Making of Modern Greece* (Austin: University of Texas Press, 1982); William A. Wilson, *Folklore and Nationalism in Modern Finland* (Bloomington: Indiana University Press, 1976); Christa Kamenetsky, "Folklore as a Political Tool in Nazi Germany," *Journal of American Folklore* 85 (1972): 221–35.

9. Antoine Berman uses the term *foreignizing* to describe the approach to translation advocated by Friedrich Schleiermacher in his 1813 essay "Über die verschiedenen Methoden des Uebersetzens." For a discussion of how translation figures in German romantic nationalism, see Berman, *The Experience of the Foreign: Culture and Translation in Romantic Germany*, trans. S. Heyvaert (Albany: State University of New York Press, 1992).

10. Linda Colley, *Britons: Forging the Nation, 1707–1837* (New Haven, Conn.: Yale University Press, 1992), 6. See also Colley, "Britishness and Otherness: An Argument," *Journal of British Studies* 31 (1992): 309–29, and Peter Sahlins, *Boundaries: The Making of France and Spain in the Pyrenees* (Berkeley: University of California Press, 1989).

11. Richard Bauman, "The Nationalization and Internationalization of Folklore: The Case of Schoolcraft's 'Gitshee Gauzinee,' " *Western Folklore* 52 (April 1993): 247–69.

12. Richard M. Dorson, *The British Folklorists: A History* (Chicago: University of Chicago Press, 1968), 1.

13. Dorson, *British Folklorists,* 202.

14. On the role of print culture in the formation of national identity, see Benedict Anderson's *Imagined Communities: On the Rise and Spread of Nationalism*, rev. ed. (London: Verso, 1991); the essays collected in Homi K. Bhabha, ed., *Nation and Narration* (London: Routledge, 1990); Simon Gikandi, *Maps of Englishness: Writing Identity in the Culture of Colonialism* (New York: Columbia University Press, 1996); Nancy Armstrong and Leonard Tennenhouse, "A Novel Nation; or, How to Rethink Modern England as an Emergent Culture," in Marshall Brown, ed., *Eighteenth-Century Literary History: An MLQ Reader* (Durham N.C.: Duke University Press, 1999), 9–26.

15. Anderson, 37.

16. Among the many national collections that entered the English literary marketplace during the later nineteenth century are Nikolay Vasilyevich Gogol's collection, translated by George Tolstoy as *Cossack Tales* (1860), Henry Callaway's *Nursery Tales, Traditions, and Histories of the Zulus in Their Own Words* (1868), and Susan Ballard's *Fairy Tales from Far Japan* (1898). See Dorson's selective bibliography (442–60).

17. John Aubrey, "Remaines of Gentilisme and Judaisme," qtd. in Oliver L. Dick, *Aubrey's Brief Lives* (London: Secker and Warburg, 1950), xxxiii.

18. Elizabeth L. Eisenstein, *The Printing Press as an Agent of Change* (Cambridge: Cambridge University Press, 1979).

19. Francis Grose, *A Provincial Glossary*, 2d ed. (London: S. Hooper, 1790), vii–viii.

20. Richard D. Altick, *The English Common Reader: A Social History of the Mass Reading Public, 1800–1900* (Chicago: University of Chicago Press, 1957), 4.

21. Ruth Finnegan, *Literacy and Orality: Studies in the Technology of Communication* (New York: Basil Blackwell, 1988), 140.

22. Finnegan, 140–41.

23. The dichotomization of orality and literacy has been problematized by the ethnographic studies of the contributors to Jonathan Boyarin, ed., *The Ethnography of Reading* (Berkeley: University of California Press, 1993), and David R. Olson and Nancy Torrance, eds., *Literacy and Orality* (Cambridge: Cambridge University Press, 1991), Shirley Brice Heath, *Ways with Words: Language, Life, and Work in Communities and Classrooms* (New York: Cambridge University Press, 1983), and numerous others. For an overview, see James Collins, "Literacy and Literacies," *Annual Review of Anthropology* 24 (1995): 75–93.

This binary has also been deconstructed by postcolonial critics: see, e.g., Ian Adam, "Oracy and Literacy: A Post-Colonial Dilemma?" *Journal of Commonwealth Literature* 31, no. 1 (1996): 97–109, and Maria de la Caridad Casas, "Orality and Literacy in a Postcolonial World," *Social Semiotics* 8, no. 1 (1998): 5–24.

24. Wolfgang Iser suggests that a crucial shift in historical thought occurs in *Parallèle des Anciens et des Modernes* (1688–97), Charles Perrault's contribution to the Querelle des anciens et des modernes, which immediately precedes the publication of his famous fairy-tale book, *Histoires, ou Contes du Temps Passé* (1697). See Iser, "The Emergence of a Cross-Cultural Discourse: Thomas Carlyle's *Sartor Resartus*," in Sanford Burdick and Wolfgang Iser, eds., *The Translatability of Cultures: Figurations of the Space Between* (Stanford, Calif.: Stanford University Press, 1996), 246.

25. For a discussion of "classical" or "sociocultural evolutionism" as it emerged in the 1850s and was codified as the basis of a comparative method, see George W. Stocking Jr., *Victorian Anthropology* (New York: Free Press, 1987), 169–85.

26. The most famous example is the title-page illustration to Charles Perrault's *Histoires, ou Contes du Temps Passé* (1697), reproduced in Robert Samber's 1729 translation, which depicts such a storyteller at fireside, narrating to an audience of young aristocrats.

27. Lawrence Stone quantifies the growth in literacy during this period. He estimates that by 1840, approximately 95 percent of the middle class and 60 percent of the "labouring poor" could read and write. See "Literacy and Education in England, 1640–1900," *Past and Present* 42 (February 1969): 109–12.

28. For a discussion of the sales of *Rights of Man*, see Altick, 67–77.

29. On the perceived neutrality of the chapbook fairy tale as popular reading material, see Alan Richardson, "Wordsworth, Fairy Tales, and the Politics of Children's Reading," in James Holt McGavran Jr., ed., *Romanticism and Children's Literature in Nineteenth-Century England* (Athens: University of Georgia Press, 1991), 40.

30. Francis Cohen, "Antiquities of Nursery Literature: Review of *Fairy Tales, or the Lilliputian Cabinet, Containing Twenty-four Choice Pieces of Fancy and Fiction,* collected by Benjamin Tabart," *Quarterly Review* 21, no. 41 (January 1819): 91.

31. George Lillie Craik, *The Pursuit of Knowledge under Difficulties* (London: Charles Knight, 1830), 3.

32. Yonge, 306.

33. Yonge, 306.

34. Peter Hunt, *Children's Literature: An Illustrated History* (New York: Oxford University Press, 1995), 86.

35. Jacqueline Rose, *The Case of Peter Pan; or, The Impossibility of Children's Fiction*, rev. ed. (London: Macmillan, 1994), 56.

36. Jack Zipes has lamented and addressed the lack of a social "history of the fairy tale for children." *Fairy Tales and the Art of Subversion* (New York: Methuen, 1988), 1. For examples of the directions this line of inquiry has taken, see the essays in Ruth B. Bottigheimer, ed., *Fairy Tales and Society: Illusion, Allusion, and Paradigm*, (Philadelphia: University of Pennsylvania Press, 1986). The hegemonic and potentially counterhegemonic functions of fairy tales—particularly in terms of gender and sex role stereotyping—are explored in such studies as Cristina Bacchilega's *Postmodern Fairy Tales* (Philadelphia: University of Pennsylvania Press, 1998) and Marina Warner's *From the Beast to the Blonde: On Fairy Tales and Their Tellers* (New York: Noonday Press, 1994).

37. Klaus Roth, "Crossing Boundaries: The Translation and Cultural Adaptation of Folk Narratives," *Fabula* 39, nos. 3–4 (1998): 243–55. The issue of who "owns" transcribed or otherwise recorded folklore has been a persistent question—philosophical, ethical, and *legal*. See Margaret Mills, "Cultural Properties, Cultural Documents, and Cultural Effects: An Ethics Discussion for ISFNR," *Fabula* 40, nos. 1–2 (1999): 1–16. For discussion of contemporary issues in the transnationalizing of folk musics, see the special issue of *The World of Music* 35, no. 2 (1993), especially Veit Erlmann, "The Politics and Aesthetics of Transnational Musics" (3–15) and Reebee Garofalo, "Whose World, What Beat? The Transnational Music Industry, Identity, and Cultural Imperialism" (16–32).

38. Dorson, *British Folklorists*, 440.

39. For Dorson, Campbell stands as the British "counterpart to the brothers Grimm" (393); Dorson provides an extended discussion of Campbell's contributions to the field (393–402).

40. Dorson, "Fakelore," *Zeitschrift für Volkskunde* 65 (1969): 56–64.

41. The quote is from Amy Shuman and Charles Briggs, introduction to "Theorizing Folklore: Towards New Perspectives on the Politics of Culture," *Western Folklore* 52, nos. 2–4 (1993): 111; the essays in that special issue of *Western Folklore* reflect on Folklore's recent past and projected future. Other key critical reassessments of the discipline include Barbara Kirshenblatt-Gimblett's "Mistaken Dichotomies," in Robert Baron and Nicholas Spitzer, eds., *Public Folklore* (Washington, D.C.: Smithsonian Institute Press, 1992), 29–48; Bendix, "From Fakelore to the Politics of Culture: The Changing Contours of American Folkloristics," in *In Search of Authenticity*, 188–218. For multiple perspectives on the future of folklore as an academic discipline, also see the contributions to the *Journal of American Folklore* 111 (1998).

42. This subject has been touched upon in other historiographies of the discipline—e.g., Simon Bronner's *American Folklore Studies: An Intellectual History* (Lawrence: University of Kansas Press, 1986) or Giuseppe Cocchiara's *History of Folklore in Europe* (Philadelphia: ISHI, 1981)—but has not received sustained attention there.

43. Susan Stewart, *Crimes of Writing: Problems in the Containment of Representation* (New York: Oxford University Press, 1991), 104; Bendix, *In Search of Authenticity*, 8–9, and "Diverging Paths in the Scientific Search for Authenticity," 111.

44. See, e.g., Elizabeth C. Fine, *The Folklore Text: From Performance to Print* (Bloomington: Indiana University Press, 1984); Richard Bauman, "The Nationalization and Internationalization of Folklore: The Case of Schoolcraft's 'Gitshee Gauzinee,'" *Western Folklore* 52 (April 1993): 247–69; Charles Briggs, "Metadiscursive Practices and Scholarly Authority in Folkloristics," *Journal of American Folklore* 106 (1993): 387–434.

45. Robert Darnton, *The Kiss of Lamourette: Reflections in Cultural History* (New York: W. W. Norton, 1990), 111. As Darnton points out, even the relationship of reader to writer is a dynamic one, since the reader "influences the author both before and after the act of composition. Authors are readers themselves. By reading and associating with other readers and writers, they form notions of genre and style and a general sense of the literary enterprise, which affects their texts" (111).

46. Richardson, 34–53.

47. See Scott Lash, *Reflexive Modernization: Politics, Tradition, and Aesthetics in the Modern Social Order* (Cambridge: Polity Press, 1994), 111–13.

Chapter 2

1. John Rowe Townsend, *Written for Children: An Outline of English-Language Children's Literature*, 3d ed. (London: Penguin, 1987), 127.

2. F. J. Harvey Darton, *Children's Books in England: Five Centuries of Social Life*, 3d ed., rev. by Brian Alderson (New York: Cambridge University Press, 1982), 98, 215.

3. Michael Patrick Hearne, *The Victorian Fairy Tale Book* (New York: Pantheon, 1988), xix.

4. Jack Zipes, *Victorian Fairy Tales: The Revolt of the Fairies and Elves* (New York: Methuen, 1987), xviii.

5. Edgar Taylor, "German Popular and Traditionary Literature, Part I," *New Monthly magazine and Literary Journal* 2 (1821): 148.

6. Sam Smiles, "Dressed to Till: Representational Strategies in the Depiction of Rural Labor, c. 1790–1830," in Michael Rosenthal, Christina Payne, and Scott Wilcox, eds., *Prospects for the Nation: Recent Essays in British Landscape, 1750–1880*, ed. (New Haven, Conn.: Yale University Press, 1997), 84.

7. *Dictionary of National Biography* (1949–50) 19:407

8. Edgar Taylor's series "German Popular and Traditionary Literature" was issued in four parts—the first three published in volume 2 of *New Monthly Magazine and Literary Journal* (146–52, 329–36, and 537–44); the fourth in volume 4 (289–96).

9. Qtd. in Ruth Michaelis-Jena, *The Brothers Grimm* (New York: Praeger, 1970), 176. To date, the most complete narrative of the making of *GPS* has been made by Robert Patten, "George Cruikshank's Grimm Humor," in Joachim Möller, ed., *Imagination on a Long Rein: English Literature Illustrated*, (Marburg, Germany: Jonas, 1988), 13–18. Patten also cites the passage from Taylor's initial correspondence with

the Grimms to understand how the former initially encountered the *KHM*. Patten extrapolates what I think is an overly imaginative narrative: "The story begins with a certain Mr. Jardine, who while a student at the University of Göttingen happened across a copy of the Grimm brothers' tales. He brought it back to England, and showed it to his friend, Edgar Taylor, a successful London lawyer who belonged to a large family originating in Norwich" (14). In fact, there seems to be no indication that Jardine stumbled across the work while a student in Germany. The reference to Jardine's studies at Göttingen appears instead to be an attempt to establish the credibility of the translators. No evidence is offered to support the assertion that Jardine was the one to introduce the *KHM* to Taylor.

Christa Kamenetsky suggests that the antiquary Francis Cohen, better known after a change of name as Sir Francis Palgrave, was Taylor's anonymous collaborator on *German Popular Stories*. See *The Brothers Grimm and Their Critics: Folktales and the Quest for Meaning* (Athens: Ohio University Press, 1992), 198; hers is a lone voice.

10. *Dictionary of National Biography* 19:407.

11. The nature of Taylor and Jardine's collaboration remains ambiguous (Taylor's letter to Jacob Grimm and the use of plural pronouns in the preface to the first, anonymous edition of *German Popular Stories* are the clearest indications of collaborative authorship), and is limited to the first volume of *German Popular Stories*. Taylor adopted the role of spokesperson for the project, and was the sole author of a second volume and a second, revised edition of the collection. Reprints of *German Popular Stories* are credited to Taylor alone, and throughout this chapter I will follow suit, attributing to Taylor the anonymous statements of purpose found in the preface to volume 1.

12. Vincent Crapanzano, "'Self'-Centering Narratives," in Michael Silverstein and Greg Urban, eds., *Natural Histories of Discourse* (Chicago: University of Chicago Press, 1996), 112.

13. Charlotte Yonge, "Children's Literature of the Last Century," *Macmillan's Magazine* 20 (1869): 302.

14. William John Thoms, *Lays and Legends of Spain* (London: George Cowie, 1834), 54 n; cited in Richard Dorson, *The British Folklorists* (Chicago: University of Chicago Press, 1968), 78.

15. The impact of the work of the Grimms on English scholarship has been explored by Katharine M. Briggs, "The Influence of the Brothers Grimm in England," *Brüder Grimm Gedenken* 1 (1963): 511–24, and by David Blamires, "The Early Reception of the Grimms' *Kinder- und Hausmärchen* in England," *Bulletin of the John Rylands Library* 71, no. 3 [1989]: 63–76.

16. Although Blamires cites reprints in 1823, 1824, and 1825 (53), I have been unable to find other references to an 1823 reprint. Nonetheless, the frequency with which *German Popular Stories* was reissued is striking, including editions by London publishers Robins (1825, 1826, 1827), Hotten (1826, 1868), Cundall (1846), Bohn (1851), Bell and Daldy (1869), and Chatto and Windus (1875). Among the early American editions of *GPS* are the editions published by Monroe (1840), Crosby and Nichols (1862), and Porter and Coates (1873).

Only a year after the publication of the second volume of *German Popular Sto-*

ries, Taylor became seriously ill, and by 1832 he had retired from legal practice. A revised edition of the collection was published in 1839 under the title *German Popular Stories and Fairy Tales as told by Gammer Grethel* (usually referred to simply as *Gammer Grethel*), and Taylor died the same year.

17. Thus, contemporary readers' experiences of these tales in book form are likely to reflect Taylor and Cruikshank's legacy, whether the beloved volume reproduces the text of *German Popular Stories* or not.

The widely available Puffin Classics edition of *Grimms' Fairy Tales* is a reproduction of the work of Taylor and Cruikshank. Although this fact is briefly acknowledged, readers are given no indication that the book they hold in their hands is far removed from the words the Grimms put to paper. See Jacob and Wilhelm Grimm, *Grimms' Fairy Tales* (London: Puffin, 1994).

18. Letter to Arnim, qtd. in Michaelis-Jena, 51.

19. Yonge, 229.

20. "Antiquities of Nursery Literature: Review of *Fairy Tales, or the Lilliputian Cabinet, Containing Twenty-four Choice Pieces of Fancy and Fiction,* Collected by Benjamin Tabart," *Quarterly Review* 21, no. 41 (January 1819): 95. The anonymous author of this review has been identified as Francis Cohen (Sir Francis Palgrave); see Kamenetsky, *The Brothers Grimm*, 195; and Brian Alderson, "The Spoken and the Read: *German Popular Stories* and English Popular Diction," in Donald Haase, ed., *The Reception of Grimms' Fairy Tales: Responses, Reactions, Revisions* (Detroit: Wayne State University Press, 1993), 62.

21. Cohen, 95.

22. Qtd. in Maria Tatar, *The Hard Facts of the Grimms' Fairy Tales* (Princeton, N.J.: Princeton University Press, 1987), 206.

23. Tatar, 204.

24. J. A. MacCulloch, *The Childhood of Fiction: A Study of Folk Tales and Primitive Thought* (London: John Murray, 1905).

25. Taylor, *German Popular Stories* (London: Baldwyn, 1823), viii. All references to *German Popular Stories* are from this edition, unless otherwise noted.

26. Taylor, "German Popular and Traditionary Literature, Part I," 147.

27. Taylor, *German Popular Stories*, iii. Emphasis added.

28. Taylor, "German Popular and Traditionary Literature, Part I," 147.

29. Sidney Oldall Addy, *Household Tales and Other Traditional Remains* (London: D. Nutt, 1895), 9.

30. See Blamires, 63–65. Maria Tatar concurs: "Several of the Grimms' contemporaries had already registered respectable successes with collections of stories for children, and the appearance of the *Nursery and Household Tales* coincided to some extent with a developing market for collections of fairy tales" (11).

31. Qtd. in Tatar, 210. Tatar notes, "Wilhelm Grimm was responsible for the wording of the two prefaces; the spirit of what he had to say, however, reflects the shared sentiments of the two brothers on folklore and the art of collecting it" (203). I am assigning to their joint authorship claims made in the preface, as a matter of convenience.

32. The work of Heinz Rölleke has been especially important to the understanding

of the Grimms' textual practices. See Rölleke, ed., *Die älteste Märchensammlung der Brüder Grimm: Synopse der handschriftlichen Urfassung von 1810 under der Erstdrucke von 1812* (Cologne: Foundation Martin Godmer, 1975); Rölleke's edition of *KHM* (Stuttgart: Reclam, 1980); and the two English-language essays cited in my bibliography.

33. See Roger Abrahams, "Phantoms of Romantic Nationalism in Folkloristics," *Journal of American Folklore* 106 (1993): 3–37; Regina Bendix, "Diverging Paths in the Scientific Search for Authenticity," *Journal of Folklore Research* 29, no. 2 (1992): 103–32, and *In Search of Authenticity: The Formation of Folklore Studies* (Madison: University of Wisconsin Press, 1997), esp. 45–67; and Charles Briggs, "Metadiscursive Practices and Scholarly Authority in Folkloristics," *Journal of American Folklore* 106 (1993): 387–434.

34. Bendix, "Diverging Paths," 111.

35. Tatar, 11.

36. Tatar summarizes: "As Jacob Grimm pointed out during his search for a publisher, the main purpose of the proposed volume was not so much to earn royalties as to salvage what was left of the priceless national resources still in the hands of the German folk. . . . Still, the brothers expressed the hope that the volume in the offing would find friends everywhere—and that it would entertain them as well" (11).

Despite such early statements by the Grimms, the notion persists that the "brothers had originally set their sights on producing a contribution to the 'history of poetry' and had no intention of publishing an 'entertaining volume' " (Tatar, 204). It seems clear that by the time the brothers were ready to publish the *Märchen* at all, they regarded their entextualization and analysis of German oral narrative traditions as a contribution to both German literary history and German popular reading.

37. Tatar, 11.

38. Qtd. in Tatar, 211.

39. It may be precisely the coherence of the critical writings in the *KHM* that enabled both Brentano and Arnim to conceive of divorcing them from the *Märchen*.

40. Qtd. in Tatar, 214. As the preface continues, the Grimms address complaints about the versions selected for inclusion: "These different versions seem more noteworthy to us than they do to those who see in them nothing more than variants or corrupt forms of a once archetypal form. For us they are more likely attempts to capture through numerous approaches an inexhaustibly rich ideal type" (214–15).

41. Charles Briggs elaborates on the Grimms' methods of creating cohesive written narratives from their researches (392–404). On the nature of the Grimms' conception of "authenticity" see Bendix, "Diverging Paths," and Bendix, *In Search of Authenticity*, 45–67.

42. Qtd. in Kamenetsky, *The Brothers Grimm*, 187.

43. Michaelis-Jena, 47–48.

44. Qtd. in T. F. Crane, "The External History of the *Kinder- und Hausmärchen* of the Brothers Grimm," *Modern Philology* 14, no. 10 (February 1917): 151–52.

45. Crane, 156.

46. Michaelis-Jena, 53. Ludwig Grimm did provide an illustration for the frontispiece of the second edition of 1819.

47. Qtd. in Michaelis-Jena, 53–54.

48. Jacob argued that "all children should read the entire folktale collection and be left to themselves in this process. What is the difference if there are some incomprehensible elements in the language and narrative of the folktales, such as in the Low German tales? One can always skip those things and even be glad if something is left for the future. Anyhow, you won't ever be able to give a book to children that is perfectly comprehensible to them" (qtd. in Tatar, 214).

49. Qtd. in Tatar, 214. Jacob's writings confirm that he regarded the collection as operating on different levels—including the philological ones that intrigued him most—and did not present the collection's perceived multifunctionality as problematic:

> My old principle, [which] I have already defended earlier, has always been that one should write to please oneself rather than to give in to external pressures.
>
> Therefore, this book of folktales has not been written for children at all, but it makes me very glad that they do like it. I would not have worked on it with such pleasure if I had not believed that with respect to poetry, mythology, and history it would have appeared just as important to the more serious and older adults as it has to me. (Qtd. in Kamenetsky, 193)

It is interesting to note that the "pleasure" of the text is here extended from the domain of children to that of the scholar.

50. Tatar, 217.

51. For a discussion of the Grimms' sources, see Heinz Rölleke, "The 'Utterly Hessian' Fairy Tales by 'Old Marie': The End of a Myth," in Ruth B. Bottigheimer, ed., *Fairy Tales and Society: Illusion, Allusion, and Paradigm* (Philadelphia: University of Pennsylvania Press, 1986), 287–300.

52. Michaelis-Jena, 92–93.

53. Ruth B. Bottigheimer, "The Publishing History of Grimms' Tales: Reception at the Cash Register," in Donald Haase, ed., *The Reception of Grimms' Fairy Tales: Responses, Reactions, Revisions* (Detroit: Wayne State University Press, 1993), 83.

54. Some information on the making of *German Popular Stories* is included in the preface to a reprint of the work (London: Hotten, 1868), iii–iv. Written by a publisher not involved in the initial development of the project, nearly fifty years after the fact, I don't consider this the most reliable source of data. Patten offers an overview of Baldwyn's life and dealings with *German Popular Stories* in *George Cruikshank: Life, Times, and Art* (New Brunswick, N.J.: Rutgers University Press, 1992), 2:238–40, 247–55. Patten depends on Hotten and "an album about the book and its reprint compiled in 1881 by Charles Augustus Howell"—John Ruskin's secretary, who was involved in negotiations with Cruikshank and Hotten to create the 1868 edition (455 n. 33). No further bibliographic information is given. Howell's reliability as a source cannot be assessed, although it must be noted that this work also dates from many decades after the initial publication of *GPS*.

55. Cohen, 95.

56. See Richard D. Altick, *The English Common Reader: A Social History of the Mass Reading Public, 1800–1900* (Chicago: University of Chicago Press, 1957), 263.

57. See Patten, *George Cruikshank,* 1:240.

58. *Points of Humour* (priced at 8s. plain and 12s. 6d. colored) sold well, and the advertisement following the stories announced the first, anonymous edition of *GPS,* "To Be Continued Occasionally." See Patten, *George Cruikshank,* 1:242–43.

59. Before his death, Baldwyn had been discussing a second volume of tales with Taylor. As the deceased publisher's list was picked up by various other houses, *GPS* fell into the hands of James Robins, who published a second volume in 1826. The translations this time were by Edgar Taylor alone, again published anonymously, and once more Cruikshank was commissioned to provide the illustrations. See Patten, *George Cruikshank,* 1:241.

60. Christian Emmrich, "Niemals ohne Beziehung auf das Leben: Zur Märchen-rezeption der Bruder Grimm," *Beiträge zur Kinder- und Jugendliteratur* 83 (1987): 15; qtd. in Bottigheimer, *Fairy Tales and Society,* 84.

61. Qtd. in Kamenetsky, 199.

62. Bottigheimer, *Fairy Tales and Society,* 84.

63. Tatar, 19. Bottigheimer argues strongly and persuasively against such "mythologized" accounts of the publishing history of the *KHM* (84).

64. See Bottigheimer, 86–95. The collection eventually became canonical in Germany, being used in schools by the 1870s and becoming "second only to the Bible as a best-seller in Germany" at the turn of the twentieth century (Zipes, *Victorian Fairy Tales,* 15).

65. See Betsy Hearne, "Booking the Brothers Grimm: Art, Adaptations, and Economics," in James M. McGlathery, ed., *The Brothers Grimm and Folktale* (Urbana: University of Illinois Press, 1991), 220–33.

66. See Ralph Manheim, ed. and trans., *Grimms' Tales for Young and Old* (New York: Doubleday, 1983), and Jack Zipes, *The Complete Fairy Tales of the Brothers Grimm* (New York: Bantam, 1992).

67. Marisa Bulzone and Stefan Matzig, eds., *Grimm's Grimmest* (San Francisco: Chronicle Books, 1997).

68. For summaries of the publishing history of the *KHM,* see Crane, 129–30, and Tatar, esp. 11–38. For information on the abridged or "Small" edition of the *KHM,* see Tatar, 19–20, and Jack Zipes's *Brothers Grimm: From Enchanted Forests to the Modern World* (New York: Routledge, 1988), 15.

69. See, e.g., Jack Zipes, *Fairy Tales and the Art of Subversion: The Classical Genre for Children and the Process of Civilization* (New York: Methuen, 1988), 45–70; Tatar, 3–38; and John Ellis's controversial positioning of the Grimms' *KHM* as a kind of literary hoax in *One Fairy Story Too Many: The Brothers Grimm and Their Tales* (Chicago: University of Chicago Press, 1983). Christa Kamenetsky suggests that persistent "myths" about the Grimms' methodological and theoretical claims (which Ellis sought to debunk) are principally the result of nineteenth-century English misreadings (195–202). Resolution of this issue is beyond the bounds of this study and beyond my linguistic capabilities. English readers can judge the Grimms' prefatory claims for themselves in the translations offered by Tatar, 203–22.

70. It is tempting to hold up the more accurate translation made by Margaret Hunt in 1884 for comparison with Edgar Taylor's. But here it must be noted that

whereas *GPS* was a selective translation of the 1819 edition of *KHM*, Hunt worked from the 1857 ("final") edition. Manheim has recently published a translation of what he assumed to be the 1819 edition, but Maria Tatar warns that Manheim's is actually yet another translation of the 1857 edition (which included a reprint of the preface to the 1819 edition; see Tatar, xxii). In short, no complete English translation of the second edition of *KHM* exists with which to compare *German Popular Stories*.

71. Outside sources account for an additional four tales in volume 2 of *German Popular Stories* (see Blamires, 70). Taylor took liberties with these tales as well: for instance, he explains that "The Elfin Grove" is "an abridgement of a story in Tieck's *Phantasus*, founded on an old and well-known tradition, but considerably amplified by him. We have reduced it nearer to its primitive elements." Although Taylor notes that it "does not pretend to that authenticity of popular currency which is claimed for the other stories," the reader would only realize this if the notes were read (*GPS* [1868], 329–30).

72. See Blamires, 70; *German Popular Stories*, 230, 236.

73. For some comparisons of the 1819 *KHM* and *GPS*, see Blamires, 70–73.

74. Taylor, *German Popular Stories*, 230.

75. Blamires notes that all forms of explicitly religious reference are avoided by Taylor (70). For example, the overreaching desires of the fisherman's wife culminate in a wish not to be God but rather "to be lord of the sun and moon"; the notes explain that the translators "have softened the boldness of the lady's ambition" (37–38, 217). Interestingly, the transformation of religious themes into "supernatural phantasies" is named by Ruskin as a characteristic not of Taylor's treatment of the *KHM* but of genuine oral tradition: "The good spirit descends gradually from an angel into a fairy, and the demon shrinks into a playful grotesque of diminutive malevolence, while yet both keep an accredited and vital influence upon the character and mind." "Introduction," in *German Popular Stories* (London: Hotten, 1868), xii.

76. Taylor, *German Popular Stories* (1868), 332.

77. Blamires, 69.

78. *Grimm-Nachlass* no. 1700. Staatsbibliothek Preussischer Kulturbesitz Handschriftenabteilung, Berlin-Dahlem; qtd. in Michaelis-Jena, 176.

In the preface to *German Popular Stories*, the translators explain that they "can do little more than direct the attention of the curious reader to the source whence they have selected their materials. The nature and immediate design of the present publication exclude the introduction of some of those stories which would, in a literary point of view, be most curious" (xi).

79. Alderson, 67.

80. Lawrence Venuti provides an extended analysis of the strategy of fluency in English translation history. See *The Translator's Invisibility: A History of Translation* (New York: Routledge, 1995), 43–98.

81. Venuti, 61. Venuti's discussion here concerns Denham's 1656 translation of Virgil, but he goes on to demonstrate that by the early nineteenth century, the "fluent strategy" exemplified by Denham "was firmly entrenched as a canon in English-language translation" (77, 76).

82. Venuti, 110.

83. André Lefevere, ed. and trans., *Translating Literature: The German Tradition from Luther to Rosenzweig* (Assen: Van Gorcum, 1977), 80; discussed by Venuti, 110.

84. Taylor, *German Popular Stories,* xi.

85. Michaelis-Jena, 54.

86. Donald Ward, "New Misconceptions about Old Folktales: The Brothers Grimm," in James M. McGlathery, ed., *The Brothers Grimm and Folktale* (Urbana: University of Illinois Press, 1991), 95.

87. Yonge, 302.

88. Patten, *George Cruikshank,* 1:248.

89. Later in his career, Cruikshank wanted to return to the genre with which he had had so much success. Lacking a collaborator like Taylor, Cruikshank provided himself with texts to illustrate, writing new versions of traditional tales to reflect his own teetotalism. See Patten, *George Cruikshank,* 1:247; and Zipes, *Victorian Fairy Tales,* 37–38.

90. Ann Bermingham, *Landscape and Ideology: The English Rustic Tradition, 1740–1860* (Berkeley: University of California Press, 1986), 66. Bermingham provides a discussion of "the cult of the picturesque," beginning with William Gilpin's seminal essays of the 1780s; see 57–85.

91. Uvedale Price, *An Essay on the Picturesque as Compared with the Sublime and the Beautiful* (London, 1842), 87; qtd. in Bermingham, 68.

92. C. Gray describing the work of William Henry Pyne, qtd. in Smiles, 81.

93. Qtd. in Bermingham, 69.

94. The umlaut on *Märchen* is missing on volume 1 (see figure 1).

95. For a discussion of the prevalence of the spinning woman in fairy-tale illustration, see Tatar, 106–33; Marina Warner, *From the Beast to the Blonde: On Fairy Tales and Their Tellers* (New York: Noonday Press, 1999), esp. 12–25; more generally, see Marta Weigle, *Spiders and Spinsters: Women and Mythology* (Albuquerque: University of New Mexico Press, 1982).

96. Karen E. Rowe, "To Spin a Yarn: The Female Voice in Folklore and Fairy Tales," in Ruth B. Bottigheimer, ed., *Fairy Tales and Society: Illusion, Allusion, and Paradigm* (Philadelphia: University of Pennsylvania Press, 1986), 62–63. Also see Warner, 111–28, and Tatar, 133.

97. From at least the fourth century onward, wool had represented a significant part of England's economic base and was closely associated with England's emergence as a world power. Wool had formed the basis of international trade, was the subject of the first customs duty in the thirteenth century, and thus emerged as a commodity to be controlled for political purposes. As Asa Briggs has noted, "Judges and the Lord Chancellor in the Great Council sat on a wool sack"—and not simply for the sake of comfort. See Briggs, *A Social History of England* (London: Weidenfield and Nicolson, 1994), 77.

98. In this modern industrial age, one railway "pioneer" recommended that the Lord Chancellor "ought rather to sit on a bag of coals." George Stephenson, qtd. in Briggs, 206–7.

99. For a more literalist "reading" of these visual images as accurate representations of "typical" storytelling scenarios, see Warner, esp. 21–23.

100. *Gammer Grethel* was reissued at least twice in the Victorian period: by Cundall (1846) and Bell (1901). Subsequent references are from the 1901 reprint.

101. For a discussion of the "mythologizing" of Frau Viehmann by the Grimms, see Heinz Rölleke, "The 'Utterly Hessian' Fairy Tales," and "New Results of Research on *Grimms' Fairy Tales*," in James M. McGlathery, ed., *The Brothers Grimm and Folktale* (Urbana: University of Illinois Press, 1991), 104. Ellis's *One Fairy Story Too Many* drew attention to inconsistencies in the Grimms' methods and claims, including their portrayal of Viehmann as a German peasant woman; for a response to Ellis, see Ward, 91–100.

102. See Patten, *George Cruikshank*, 2:429–39.

103. Ruskin, "Introduction," xiv.

104. See Patten, *George Cruikshank*, 2:431.

105. Yonge, 306.

Chapter 3

1. T. Crofton Croker, *Fairy Legends and Traditions of the South of Ireland*, 2d ed. (London: John Murray, 1826), iv–v.

2. Review of *Fairy Legends and Traditions of the South of Ireland*, *Quarterly Review* 32 (1825): 198. Emphasis in original.

3. Review, 197.

4. Thomas Wright, preface to *Fairy Legends and Traditions of the South of Ireland, a New and Complete Edition* (London: William Tegg, 1862), ii.

5. Charlotte Yonge, "Children's Literature of the Last Century," *Macmillan's Magazine* 20 (1869): 306.

6. For an example of how Croker's work continues to be framed as children's literature, see *Irish Folk Stories for Children* (Dublin: Mercier, 1983), in which seven of Croker's legends, unabridged, are presented with new illustrations by Frances Boland.

7. See Hultin and Ober's introduction to their facsimile edition of Croker's *Fairy Legends of the South of Ireland* (Delmar, N.Y.: Scholars' Facsimiles and Reprints, 1983), xxxiii.

8. Richard M. Dorson, *The British Folklorists: A History* (Chicago: University of Chicago Press, 1968), 45. See also Henry Glassie, *Irish Folk Tales* (New York: Pantheon, 1985), 11; Eileen Fitzsimons, "Jacob and Wilhelm Grimm's *Irische Elfenmärchen*, a Comparison of the Translation with the English Original: *Fairy Legends and Traditions of the South of Ireland*," diss., University of Chicago, 1978, 14; and Francesca Diano's introduction to the most recent facsimile edition of Croker's *Fairy Legends and Traditions of the South of Ireland* (Cork: Collins, 1998), xxiii.

9. Review, 198.

10. See Américo Paredes and Richard Bauman, eds., *Toward New Perspectives in Folklore* (Austin: University of Texas Press, 1972).

11. Both the Grimms and Dorson reached this conclusion. See Fitzsimons, 185–86, and Dorson, *British Folklorists*, 45.

12. Review of *Fairy Legends, Quarterly Review* 32 (1825): 198.

13. Two quotes from "Legends and Traditions of the South of Ireland," *Blackwood's Magazine* 18 (1825): 55.

14. Croker, *Fairy Legends and Traditions of the South of Ireland* (London: John Murray, 1825), frontispiece. All references to *Fairy Legends* are from this edition, unless otherwise indicated.

15. In later decades, writers would turn their attention to the "English peasantry," the agricultural workers of England who were faring poorly by the 1870s. See, e.g., Francis George Heath, *The English Peasantry* (London: F. Warne, 1874). Croker uses the term *peasant* to designate both rural laborers and landholders, thereby encompassing a more economically diverse population than might be assumed.

16. "Legends and Traditions," *Blackwood's Magazine* 18 (1825): 55. Emphasis added.

17. See Marie Niedzielska, "The Intellectual Property Aspects of Folklore Protection," *Copyright* 16 (1980), 339–46. For an overview of more recent developments, see Joseph Wambugu Githaiga, "Intellectual Property Law and the Protection of Indigenous Folklore and Knowledge," *E Law: Murdoch University Electronic Journal of Law* 5, no. 2 (June 1998), http://www.murdoch.edu.au/ elaw/issues/v5n2/githaiga52_body.html.

18. Michel Foucault, "What Is an Author?" in his *Language, Counter-Memory, Practice: Selected Essays and Interviews*, trans. Donald F. Bouchard and Sherry Simon (Ithaca, N.Y.: Cornell University Press, 1977), 115.

19. On the emergence of the public domain and the development of a national literary canon, see Trevor Ross, "Copyright and the Invention of Tradition," *Eighteenth-Century Studies* 26, no. 1 (fall 1992): 1–27; on the contrasting models of collectivity and individual authorship, see Martha Woodmansee, "On the Author Effect: Recovering Collectivity," in Martha Woodmansee and Peter Jaszi, eds., *The Construction of Authorship: Textual Appropriation in Law and Literature* (Durham, N.C.: Duke University Press, 1994), 5–28.

20. M. M. Bakhtin, *The Dialogic Imagination: Four Essays*, ed. Michael Holquist (Austin: University of Texas Press, 1981), 324.

21. Clifford Geertz, *Works and Lives: The Anthropologist as Author* (Stanford: Stanford University Press, 1988).

22. See Homi K. Bhabha, "Of Mimicry and Man: The Ambivalence of Colonialist Discourse," in *The Location of Culture* (New York: Routledge, 1994), 85–92.

23. Jacqueline Rose, *The Case of Peter Pan; or, The Impossibility of Children's Fiction*, rev. ed. (London: Macmillan, 1994).

24. Bhabha encourages reading against colonialist texts: "The discourse of post-Enlightenment English colonialism often speaks in a tongue that is forked, not false. If colonialism takes power in the name of history, it repeatedly exercises its authority through the figures of farce. For the epic intention of the civilizing mission . . . often produces a text rich in the traditions of *trompe-l'oeil*, irony, mimicry and repetition" (85).

25. Fiona Giles, " 'The Softest Disorder': Representing Cultural Indeterminacy," in Chris Tiffin and Alan Lawson, eds., *De-Scribing Empire: Post-coloniality and Textuality* (New York: Routledge, 1994), 141.

26. Obituary of Thomas Crofton Croker, *Gentleman's Magazine* n.s. 42 (October 1854): 397.

27. Robert Kee, *Ireland: A History*, rev. ed. (London: Abacus, 1995), 30.

28. Nicholas Canny, "Early Modern Ireland c. 1500–1700," in R. F. Foster, ed., *Oxford Illustrated History of Ireland* (New York: Oxford University Press, 1989), 127.

29. Of the early modern period in Irish history, Canny writes,

Assault was always a possibility. The [English] settler population had originally been established in Ireland in the wake of a partial military conquest of Ireland, and memories of the original conflict were still vividly remembered on both sides. Recollections of lost greatness had encouraged successive generations of Gaelic chieftains to launch attacks upon the settler community"(104).

30. Hultin and Ober, xiii.

31. See obituary of Thomas Crofton Croker, 397–98, and T. F. Dillon Croker, "Memoir of the Author," in *Fairy Legends and Traditions of the South of Ireland, a New and Complete Edition* (London: William Tegg, 1862), iv–v.

32. Obituary of Thomas Crofton Croker, 398.

33. David Fitzpatrick, "'A Peculiar Tramping People': The Irish in Britain, 1801–70," in W.E. Vaughan, ed., *A New History of Ireland*, vol. 5 (Oxford: Clarendon, 1989), 623.

34. "Ireland," *Blackwood's Magazine* 15 (1824): 269.

35. "Ireland," 272.

36. "Works on Ireland: Memoirs of Captain Rock; Croker's South of Ireland," *Blackwood's Magazine* 15 (1824): 555.

37. John Murray's letter to Croker is reproduced by Dillon Croker, vi.

38. Dillon Croker, vi.

39. Obituary of Thomas Crofton Croker, 398.

40. Thomas Keightley, *Tales and Popular Fictions* (London: Whittaker, 1834), 180.

41. Hultin and Ober, xxiv.

42. Hultin and Ober, xv.

43. This sentiment is echoed by one of Croker's reviewers: "The superstitions described in this volume are not generally different from those of the English peasantry in the days of Elizabeth or of the Scotch in a considerably later period; and therefore, though the particular facts given in illustration are new, yet the effect is not of novelty." *Blackwood's Magazine* 15 (1824): 555.

44. The years 1840 to 1870 are known as the golden age of fairy painting in England. For an overview, see Jeremy Maas, "Victorian Fairy Painting," in Jane Martineau, ed., *Victorian Fairy Painting* (London: Royal Academy of Arts, 1997), 11–21.

45. See *Gentleman's Magazine* n.s. 42 (1854): 453; cited in Dillon Croker's *Memoir of the Author*, ix. Pamela White Trimpe names Maclise as the new contributor; see "Victorian Fairy Book Illustration," in Jane Martineau, ed., *Victorian Fairy Painting*, (London: Royal Academy of Arts, 1997), 55. Carole G. Silver cites George Cruikshank as a later illustrator of Croker's *Fairy Legends* (*Strange and Secret Peoples: Fairies and Victorian Consciousness* [New York: Oxford, 1999], 28), but I have not been able to

locate any record of this. Cruikshank did, however, create a title-page illustration for Thomas Keightley's *Fairy Mythology* (1850).

46. The review was in the January 1826 issue. See John Hennig, "The Brothers Grimm and T. C. Croker," *Modern Language Review* 41 (1946): 44–45.

47. It is generally acknowledged that Wilhelm Grimm was the primary author of the translation. See Hennig, 46–48.

48. Dorson qualified his ennobling comparison of Croker's *Fairy Legends* and the Grimms' *Kinder- und Hausmärchen* based on the generic differences of the contents of their respective works. Positing an oddly schizophrenic model of scholarly imagination, Dorson insists that it "was the Jacob Grimm of the *Deutsche Mythologie*, not of the *Kinder- und Hausmärchen*, who was fascinated by the Irish legends" (45). Although the generic distinction between *Märchen* and legend was an issue of ongoing interest to Jacob Grimm, he did not publish his *Deutsche Mythologie* until 1835. The Grimms' choice of a title for their translation of Croker's work—*Irische Elfenmärchen*—suggests more of a perceived generic affinity than Dorson allows for. Eileen Fitzsimons's close comparison of the German translation with the English original strongly supports this: The Grimms translated very freely, making stylistic choices and changes that reflect their own conceptions of *Volksliteratur* and, more specifically, of *Märchen*. See Fitzsimons, 181–87.

Tellingly, Dorson eclipses the opinions of Wilhelm Grimm, who publicly praised Croker's *Fairy Legends* for the work's formal resemblance to Edgar Taylor's *German Popular Stories*, especially in terms of illustration (Hennig, 44).

49. Croker translated these added notes and appended them to volume 3 of *Fairy Legends* (London: John Murray, 1828). The Grimms found most of Croker's own notes irrelevant and in that regard characteristically English (see Hennig, 51; Fitzsimons, 30). Dorson regards the notes to *Fairy Legends* as more pleasing to "the modern folklorist" than the "embellished texts" (46).

A correspondence developed between Croker and the Grimms following the publication of the translation, beginning with a letter sent by Croker to the Grimms through their publisher. Here Croker revealed his identity as the author of *Fairy Legends* and praised the Grimms' translation. The first of Wilhelm Grimm's letters to Croker is reproduced in Dillon Croker's "Memoir of the Author," vii–ix.

50. Hultin and Ober, xi.

Chapter 4

1. Anonymous review of *The Thousand and One Nights*, *Foreign Quarterly Review*, July 1838, 255.

2. For an overview of the work's history in manuscript form, see Husain Haddawy, introduction to *The Arabian Nights* (New York: W. W. Norton, 1990), xi–xiii.

3. English transliteration of characters' names varies. For the sake of clarity and convenience, I will use Lane's spellings throughout.

4. Edward W. Lane, ed. and trans., *The Thousand and One Nights, Commonly Called in England The Arabian Nights' Entertainments*, 3 vols. (London: Charles

Knight, 1839–41), 1:xviii. All references to the *Arabian Nights* are to this edition, unless otherwise indicated.

5. Stanley Lane-Poole, ed. and trans., preface to *Stories from the Thousand and One Nights (The Arabian Nights' Entertainments)* Harvard Classics no. 16 (New York: Collier, 1909), 4.

6. *Gentleman's Magazine* 76 (1794): 783.

7. The publication dates of Payne and Burton's editions for their respective sub-scribers are taken from the extensive bibliography provided by Muhsin Jassim Ali, *Scheherazade in England: A Study of Nineteenth-Century English Criticism of the Ara-bian Nights* (Washington, D.C.: Three Continents Press, 1981), 147–88.

8. The second edition of Lane's *Nights* (London: J. Murray, 1847) made the in-tended readership explicit, including in its subtitle: "translated and arranged for family reading, with explanatory notes."

In various forms, Lane's versions of tales have been reissued in every decade from the 1840s through the 1950s, and William Harvey's illustrations currently appear alongside N. J. Dawood's retellings of selected tales in the Puffin Classics books, *Aladdin and Other Tales from the Arabian Nights* and *Sindbad the Sailor and Other Tales from the Arabian Nights*. Lane's edition continues to earn mention in histories of children's literature, such as John Rowe Townsend's *Written for Children: An Outline of English-Language Children's Literature,* 3d ed. (London: Penguin Books, 1987), 38.

9. As the list of illustrations that begins each volume suggests, the engravings were executed by a number of individuals, although the designs were Harvey's.

10. Haddawy, *Arabian Nights,* 1:viii.

11. The quote is from Sandra Naddaff, *Arabesque: Narrative Structure and the Aesthetics of Repetition in* 1001 Nights (Evanston, Ill.: Northwestern University Press, 1991), 14, but the examples of this critical trend are numerous. For discussion, see Fedwa Malti-Douglas, *Woman's Body, Woman's Word: Gender and Discourse in Arabo-Islamic Writing* (Princeton, N.J.: Princeton University Press, 1991), esp. 11–28.

12. Hasan M. El-Shamy, ed., *Folktales of Egypt* (Chicago: University of Chicago Press, 1980), xlviii–xlix.

13. A few key examples are the studies of Malti-Douglas; Naddaff; Mia I. Ger-hardt, *The Art of Storytelling: A Literary Study of* The Thousand and One Nights (Lei-den: E. J. Brill, 1963); David Pinault, *Story-Telling Techniques in the* Arabian Nights (Leiden: E. J. Brill, 1992); and Robert Irwin, *The Arabian Nights: A Companion* (New York: Penguin Books, 1994), 103–19.

14. For example, see Rana Kabbani, *Europe's Myth of the Orient* (Bloomington: Indiana University Press, 1986), 37, and Ali, 96.

15. Kabbani, 37.

16. Edward W. Said, *Orientalism* (New York: Vintage, 1979), 164.

17. Kabbani, 43.

18. Said, 177.

19. V. G. Kiernan, *The Lords of Human Kind: Black Man, Yellow Man, and White Man in an Age of Empire* (Boston: Little, Brown, 1969), 131.

20. Kabbani, 36.

21. Irwin, 2.

22. Lane, 1:xiii–xiv.

23. Fedwa Malti-Douglas has noted that the scholarship surrounding it is hardly less daunting (11). For a recent overview of the known textual history of the *Nights* and its introduction to European readers, see Haddawy's introduction to *Arabian Nights*.

24. Gerhardt dates the publication of Galland's volumes to the period 1703–13. However, 1704–17 is cited by Ali, Haddawy, and Duncan B. McDonald ("A Bibliographical and Literary Study of the First Appearance of the *Arabian Nights* in Europe," *Library Quarterly* 2, no. 4 [1932]: 387–420).

25. McDonald, 393.

26. McDonald, 394. See also Gerhardt, 67, 71–74; and James Holly Hanford, "Open Sesame: Notes on the *Arabian Nights* in English," *Princeton University Library Chronicle* 26, no. 1 (1964): 48–49.

27. McDonald, 394–95; Haddawy, *Arabian Nights,* xiii; Jack Zipes, ed., introduction to *Spells of Enchantment: The Wondrous Fairy Tales of Western Culture* (New York: Penguin, 1991), xx–xxi.

28. As Haddawy has detailed, the European popularity of such stories as these resulted in their subsequent appearance in Arabic manuscript form. After the publication of Galland's edition, the "mania for collecting more stories and 'completing' the work led some . . . to resort even to forgery" (*Arabian Nights,* xiii).

29. Among these were several versions and excerpts published in installments, as Lane's version was later to be issued. The *Churchman's Last Shift* published "The Voyage of Sindbad the Sailor" and other tales from the *Nights* in weekly installments in 1720; the *London News* published a version with episodes appearing three times a week, beginning in 1723 and continuing for three years; and late in the eighteenth century, selections from the *Nights* appeared in the *General Magazine* (see Ali, 11–12).

30. Peter Caracciolo, *The* Arabian Nights *in English Literature: Studies in the Reception of* The Thousand and One Nights *into British Culture* (New York: Macmillan, 1988), 6.

31. *Gentleman's Magazine* 64 (September 1794): 783.

32. *Gentleman's Magazine* 68 (September 1798): 757.

33. Leila Ahmed, *Edward W. Lane* (London: Longman, 1978), 155, 128.

34. Henry Weber, *Tales of the East* (1802; Edinburgh: James Ballantyne, 1812), 1:ii.

35. Ahmed, 154–56.

36. *Foreign Quarterly Review,* July 1838, 255.

37. Lane-Poole, *Life of Edward William Lane* (London: Williams and Norgate, 1877) 11–12. Little is known about Lane's life prior to his first voyage to Egypt. Lane's father, who died when Lane was a child, had been a Prebendary of Hereford Cathedral, and Lane's mother, Sophia, is often noted simply as a "niece of [the painter] Gainsborough." See Ahmed, vii; Lane-Poole, *Life,* 10.

38. Lane-Poole, *Life of Lane,* 13–14; Ahmed, 1–2.

39. Lane-Poole, *Life of Lane,* 17–18.

40. Ahmed, 23.

41. As I write, Lane's *Description of Egypt* is scheduled to be published for the

first time, edited by Jason Thompson (Cairo: American University in Cairo Press, 2000).

42. Lane-Poole, *Life of Lane*, 36.

43. See Ahmed, 34–37; Lane-Poole, *Life of Lane*, 34–38; Anthony Sattin, *Lifting the Veil: British Society in Egypt, 1768–1956* (London: J. M. Dent, 1988), 70.

44. Henry Curwen, *A History of Booksellers: The Old and the New* (London: Chatto and Windus, 1873), 258.

45. John Murray, publisher of Croker's *Fairy Legends,* was originally slotted for the SDUK's projects.

46. Quoted by Curwen, 258–59.

47. Curwen, 235. On the SDUK's Library of Entertaining Knowledge, of which Lane's works were part, see Richard D. Altick, *The English Common Reader: A Social History of the Mass Reading Public, 1800–1900* (Chicago: University of Chicago Press, 1957), 270.

48. Charles Knight, *Passages of a Working Life, during Half a Century with a Prelude of Early Reminiscences,* vol. 2 [1864–65] (Shannon: Irish University Press, 1971), 68–69. Emphasis in original.

49. Lane-Poole, *Life of Lane*, 85. The 1917 edition of the *Dictionary of National Biography* attests to the durability of Lane's reputation: "The value of the 'Modern Egyptians' lies . . . chiefly in its microscopic accuracy of detail, which is so complete and final that no important additions have been made to its picture of the life and customs of the Muslims of modern Egypt, in spite of the researches of numerous travellers and scholars" (11:513–14).

50. Edward W. Lane, *An Account of the Manners and Customs of the Modern Egyptians* (1835; London: J. M. Dent, 1963), xxiii; referred to hereafter simply as *Modern Egyptians.*

51. For details regarding Lane's *Selections from the Kur-án* and his *Arabic-English Lexicon,* see Ahmed, 178–97.

52. Ahmed, 38.

53. To the frustration of his biographers, Edward Lane left little behind in the way of diaries or letters. As Lane-Poole describes, "Mr. Lane had a deeply rooted objection to the publication of letters meant only for private friends, and he unfortunately took care to have all his own letters from Egypt destroyed; whilst after his return to England he hardly ever wrote one except on questions of scholarship which he was asked to decide" (*Life of Lane,* v–vi).

54. Lane-Poole, *Life of Lane,* 34.

55. Lane, *Arabian Nights,* 1:viii.

56. Johann Gottfried Herder, "On the German-Oriental Poets," in Ernest A. Menze and Karl Menges, eds., *Johann Gottfried Herder: Selected Early Works, 1764–67,* (University Park: Pennsylvania State University Press, 1992), 187.

57. Robert Lowth, *Lectures on the Sacred Poetry of the Hebrews* (1787; Hildesheim: Georg Olms, 1969), 1:113.

58. Lowth exemplifies this approach as he turns his attention to scriptural references to "the infernal regions and the state of the dead" (156). Beginning with an

architectural description of the "sepulchres of the Hebrews," Lowth moves from a description of the structure and its barricaded entranceway, to a call for readers to imagine themselves within "a vast, dreary, dark, sepulchral cavern" (165). This imaginative process was seen as key to modern readers' comprehension of biblical imagery related to death, dying, and the afterlife.

59. Samuel Burder, *Oriental Customs; or, An Illustration of the Sacred Scriptures,* 6th ed. (London: Longman, 1822), 1:xvi.

60. Johannes Fabian, *Time and the Other: How Anthropology Makes Its Object* (New York: Columbia University Press, 1983).

61. Lane argues that the world described in the tales most resembles Cairo, and that Cairo, in turn, is exemplary among the modern Arab cities: "Cairo is the city in which Arabian manners now exist is the most refined state; and such I believe to have been the case when the present work was composed" (*Modern Egyptians,* 1:ix). The matter of Cairo's representativeness as an Arab city is never fully addressed, and although Lane offers a very brief historical perspective, he appears to rely more on personal experience and observation than anything else.

62. *Foreign Quarterly Review,* July 1838, 255.

63. I use Haddawy's translation as a point of comparison. It is based on Muhsin Mahdi's "definitive edition" of a fourteenth-century manuscript believed to be the most reliable of available versions. Lane, on the other hand, based his translation on three late manuscripts, known in *Nights* scholarship as the Bulaq (what Lane calls the Cairo edition), the first Calcutta, and the Breslau. (A brief summary of this history is offered by Haddaway, *Arabian Nights,* xiii–xvi.)

Comparison of Lane's treatment of particular episodes with Haddawy's does not, therefore, reveal precisely the inaccuracies of Lane's translation; this method does, however, expose the general principles to which Lane adhered.

64. Husain Haddawy, trans., *Arabian Nights* (New York: W. W. Norton, 1990), 4, 5.

65. Haddawy, *Arabian Nights,* 66–74.

66. "I here deviate a little from the Cairo edition," Lane writes, "in which the cateress is described as having drunk three cups of wine successively before she handed any to her sisters" (*Arabian Nights,* 1:214).

67. Kabbani, Ali, and others have explored the narrative cohesiveness of Lane's annotations, epitomized by their separate publication (*sans nuits!*) as *Arabian Society in the Middle Ages* (London: Chatto and Windus, 1883). In his introduction to this work, Lane's grandnephew and future editor, Stanley Lane-Poole, suggested that the notes are a reflection of Lane's scholarly ambition and that they have an authoritativeness that extended beyond the general reader:

[Lane] was not content with producing a mere rendering of the Arabic text: he saw that the manners and ideas there described required a commentary if they were to become intelligible to the learned reader. . . . These notes have long been recognized by Orientalists as the most complete picture in existence of Arabian society. (vii–viii)

68. For Lane-Poole these notes represent "monographs on the various details of Arabian life" (*Life of Lane,* 93), which were inconveniently appended to a narrative text (*Arabian Society in the Middle Ages,* vii–viii).

69. Not surprisingly, one single-volume reprint of Lane's translation that includes his notes does so by placing them at the back of the book, as an "appendix" to the tales: *The Arabian Nights' Entertainments; or, The Thousand and One Nights* (New York: Tudor, 1927). Collections of selected tales from the *Nights*, such as Lane-Poole's in the Harvard Classics series, make use of Lane's translations but exclude the notes altogether.

70. Lane, *Arabian Nights*, 1:309. Of the approximately 550 pages in volume 1, almost 130 are notes of this kind; of the 488 pages in volume 2, 147 are of the small print variety, but the majority of these are "abstracts" of tales cut from the main body of the translation; and of the 714 pages in volume 3, 138 fall after the close of the chapters proper, and the majority of these are abstracts.

71. Ahmed, 141.

72. Knight, 258.

73. Lane-Poole, *Life of Lane*, 96.

74. Kabbani, 43.

75. Similarly, there were those readers of Sir Richard Burton's edition who objected to editorial commentary. Upon the publication of Burton's 1887 translation, an anonymous writer in the *Saturday Review* comments that "unfortunately [Burton] must needs bespatter the whole with comments and notes which would have been better omitted. There are many matters concerning public morals the discussion of which is out of place, to say the least of it, in the translation of a great literary work" (April 30, 1887, 633). In this case, protest against ethnographic commentary is on both moral and aesthetic grounds: It is the status of the *Nights* as "Literature," and not simply readers' inconvenience, that makes such annotation undesirable.

76. It is interesting to recall that the demands of a reading public and publisher had had an enormous influence on the edition of the *Nights* Lane most detested: the early eighteenth-century French translation by Antoine Galland. As mentioned earlier, it was the very popularity of the tales that drove Galland's publisher to forgery (presenting as "translation" original work by another author) and Galland to deviation from Arabic manuscripts (McDonald, 394; Hanford, 48–49).

77. Lane-Poole, *Arabian Society in the Middle Ages*, vii.

78. As one considers the content of the annotations, it is striking to note the breadth of subject matter Lane attempted to cover. Although the scope of the present project does not allow for thorough study of them all, certain "clusters" of subject matter do emerge as one peruses the three volumes. The subjects covered by Lane may be roughly divided into those "philological" in nature (dealing with matters such as transliteration, translation, the variant manuscripts, the publishing history of the *Nights* and related works, etc.), and those which may be generally characterized as "ethnographic."

79. Immediately prior to the publication of Lane's *Arabian Nights*, Charles Knight and the Society for the Diffusion of Useful Knowledge had been engaged in the production of a project which similarly involved the illustration and annotation of a translated text for a popular audience: *The Pictorial Bible* of 1836–38. Inspired in part by an edition of the Bible being published in inexpensive installments by a German firm, Knight's vision here was of a "publication in which Art should be

employed to delight the young, and learning should not be wanting" (Knight, 252). The comparability of such an approach to the Bible with Edward Lane's treatment of the *Nights* was not lost on the publisher. In his memoirs, Knight recalls Lane's "bold and simple rendering of Eastern modes of expression," which was found to be reminiscent of "our translation of the Bible" (258). The success of this earlier publication, in which the dividing line between "delight" and "learning" was purposefully blurred, may very well have shaped the form Lane's work was to take—or rather, the form in which Knight was to publish it.

Prefiguring the approach to be taken with *Nights*, this edition of the Bible included "ample commentary on such passages as are connected with the History, Geography, Natural History, and Antiquities of the Sacred Scriptures," and the illustrations were intended to highlight "landscape scenes . . . costume . . . zoology and botany . . . [and] the remains of ancient architecture" (Knight, 252–53). Issues of belief, credulity, and fantasy—which figure powerfully in Lane's notes—are not treated in any depth by Knight's annotated *Pictorial Bible*.

80. For a direct translation of this episode from "The Adventures of Qamar al-Zaman's Two Sons, Amjad and As'ad," see Haddawy, *The Arabian Nights II: Sinbad and Other Popular Stories* (New York: W. W. Norton, 1995), 222–26.

81. Perhaps ironically, the illustrations were dubbed by Lane's grandnephew "the least excellent part of the book," were apparently considered superfluous by Lane (see Lane-Poole, *Life of Lane*, 95–96), and are always granted secondary importance in critical writings about the edition.

82. Knight, 258–59.

83. Christopher M. Murphy, "A Brief Look at Illustrated Translations of the *Arabian Nights*," in Kay Haroly Campbell, ed., *The 1001 Nights: Critical Essays and Annotated Bibliography* (Cambridge, Mass.: Dar Mahjar, 1985), 88.

84. Richard F. Burton, *The Book of the Thousand Nights and a Night: A Plain and Literal Translation of the Arabian Nights' Entertainments* (London: Kamashastra Society, 1885), 1:vii.

85. Ahmed, 68–69.

86. Ahmed also points out that many were quick to analyze situations, feeling themselves familiar with the Arab world by way of the Bible and the *Arabian Nights*: "They were more apt to assume that they were quite capable of construing the significance of native forms of behaviour than they might have been in a country less familiar to their imagination" (69).

87. Laurence Housman, preface to *Stories from the Arabian Nights* (London: Hodder and Stoughton, 1907), ix. Such a claim justified both Housman's disregard for cultural detail in the tales and the generalized oriental character of Edmund Dulac's accompanying illustrations, by suggesting that the tales themselves lacked internal coherence and accuracy.

88. Ahmed cites Luigi Mayer's *Views in Egypt*; Henry Salt's *Views in St. Helena . . . and Egypt*; and Belzoni's *Plates Illustrative of Researches and Operations* as English works predating Lane's efforts at depicting Egypt. See Ahmed, 63.

89. Ahmed, 63–64. See also Lane-Poole, *Life of Lane*, 35–36.

90. Lane-Poole, *Life of Lane*, 35–36.

91. Ahmed, 12.

92. Examples of Lane's sepia drawings from the unpublished manuscript of "Description of Egypt" are reproduced by Ahmed, 62, 65.

93. Lane, *Arabian Nights*, 3:140 and 1:344, respectively.

94. Terry Reece Hackford, "Fantastic Visions: Illustration of the *Arabian Nights*," in Roger C. Schlobin, ed., *The Aesthetics of Fantasy Literature and Art* (Notre Dame, Ind.: University of Notre Dame, 1982), 145.

95. Lane, *Arabian Nights*, 1:204 and 3:535, respectively.

96. Lane, *Arabian Nights*, 2:492.

97. Lane, *Arabian Nights*, 2:25 and 3:228, respectively.

98. Lane, *Arabian Nights*, 1:101.

99. Lane, *Arabian Nights*, 1:9 and 1:164, respectively.

100. Lane, *Arabian Nights*, 2:117.

101. Lane, *Arabian Nights*, 1:190.

102. Lane, *Modern Egyptians*, xxiv.

103. Lane, *Arabian Nights*, 1:xviii.

Chapter 5

1. George Webbe Dasent, *Popular Tales from the Norse*, 2d ed. (Edinburgh: Edmonston and Douglas, 1859), xxv. All subsequent references to *Popular Tales from the Norse* are drawn from this edition, unless otherwise indicated.

2. Dasent, *Popular Tales from the Norse*, xvii.

3. Edgar Taylor, "German Popular and Traditionary Literature," *New Monthly Magazine and Literary Journal* 2 (1821): 152.

4. Dasent, *Popular Tales from the Norse*, vii.

5. George W. Stocking Jr. provides an overview of comparative philology's orientalist roots in *Victorian Anthropology* (New York: Free Press, 1987), 20–25.

6. A notable example is *The Cat on the Dovrefell: A Christmas Tale* (New York: Putnam, 1979), which reproduces Dasent's treatment of this brief and odd tale verbatim—brought to life by Tomie de Paola's illustrations of the rowdy pack of trolls who are outwitted by a traveling man and his bear.

7. Facsimile editions include a reprint of the third edition (1888) of *Popular Tales from the Norse*, issued by Dover in 1970 (and still in print as of 2001). Renamed *East o' the Sun and West o' the Moon*, the volume is a complete facsimile in terms of the Norwegian tale texts, but leaves out both Dasent's introductory essay and his appendix of West Indian tales. In 1996, Dover published an abridged selection of Dasent's tale translations as *East o' the Sun and West o' the Moon and Other Fairy Tales*, illustrated by Marty Noble.

Like Dasent and his English-language heirs, Peter Christian Asbjørnsen and Jørgen Moe recognized the appeal of their work as a form of children's literature. Asbjørnsen was a driving force behind the production of illustrated editions of the tale collection, much as Wilhelm Grimm had been for the *Kinder- und Hausmärchen*. The first illustrated edition of *Norske Folkeeventyr* appeared in 1879, featuring the work of several Norwegian painters. Erik Werenskiold and Theodor Kittelsen provided art-work for the second illustrated edition (1881). This edition "quickly established [it-self] as a national treasure"; see Pat Shaw Iversen, *Norwegian Folk Tales* (New York: Viking, 1960), 8. It has also provided English editors and publishers with images and inspiration for their own illustrated editions of the Norwegian tales. For example, Iversen and Carl Norman illustrated their translation of Asbjørnsen and Moe's col-lection with Werenskiold and Kittelsen's drawings; and Dover's 1970 *East o' the Sun and West o' the Moon* includes seventy-seven illustrations by Werenskiold, Kittelsen, and others, as they appeared in *Samlede Eventyr* (Oslo: Glydenal Norsk, 1936).

8. Dasent, *Popular Tales from the Norse*, cli, n. Writing in 1858, Dasent seems to be unaware of the so-called final edition of the *Kinder- und Hausmärchen*, published in 1857.

9. Edward Burnett Tylor, *Anahuac; or, Mexico and the Mexicans, Ancient and Modern* (London: Longman, 1861), 339.

10. For a summary of biographical information, see *Dictionary of National Bi-ography* (New York: Oxford University Press, 1949–50), 22:536–37. See also Arthur Ir-win Dasent, "Memoir of Sir George Webbe Dasent, D.C.L.," in *Popular Tales from the Norse* (Edinburgh: David Douglas, 1903), xvii–xli.

11. Dasent's "Notice to the First Edition" is dated December 12, 1858; the book was published in January 1859. The first of Dasent's translations of Norwegian folk-tales appeared in *Blackwood's Magazine* (November 1851).

12. See Dasent, *Popular Tales from the Norse*, cxlv–clii n.

13. Richard M. Dorson, foreword to Reidar Christiansen, ed., *Folktales of Nor-way* (Chicago: University of Chicago Press, 1964), vii.

14. Dorson, foreword, xi.

15. David Masson, "Gaelic and Norse Popular Tales: An Apology for the Celt," *Macmillan's Magazine* 3 (1861): 213.

16. Of the fifty-four tales, there are only three exceptions: "Why the Bear Is Stumpy-Tailed" (197), "One's Own Children Are Always the Prettiest" (206), and "Bruin and Reynard" (472–74).

17. There are eight occurrences of "There was once." See Edgar Taylor, *German Popular Stories* (London: Baldwyn, 1823), 27, 57, 75, 81, 96, 140, 184, 195. "Once upon a time" occurs thrice: see 51, 86, 106.

18. At least twelve of Taylor's translations end with variations on "happily ever after": see 16, 38, 57, 75, 81, 118, 139, 143, 163, 183, 195, 210.

19. Dasent, *Popular Tales from the Norse*, cli n. Moe concludes the prospectus for the project (1840): "Our plan coincides with that of the Grimms in their excellent *Kinder- und Hausmärchen*"; qtd. in Oscar J. Falnes, *National Romanticism in Norway* (New York: Columbia University Press, 1933), 215.

20. See Dorson, foreword, ix.

21. Falnes, 217.

22. Charlotte Yonge, "Children's Literature of the Last Century," *Macmillan's Magazine* 20 (1869): 306.

23. Dorson, foreword, viii. See also Falnes, 219–20. The Grimms' translation of Croker's *Fairy Legends* has been credited as the inspiration for this experiment (see

Falnes, 220 n.), although the fictionalized settings and narrators of Taylor's *Gammer Grethel* seems a far better point of comparison.

24. See Dasent, *Tales from the Fjeld* (1874; London: Gibbings, 1896), vi–vii.

25. As noted earlier, *Popular Tales from the Norse* earns honorable mention in Charlotte Yonge's 1869 overview of children's literature (306).

26. See Stocking, esp. 62–69.

27. Friedrich Max Müller, "Presidential Address to Section H," *Report of the British Association of Advanced Science* 61 (1891): 786–87; qtd. in Stocking, 59.

28. Although Dasent initially entitled his appendix "Ananzi Stories," he added a note on West African traditions and acknowledged that "the true spelling of the word should be Anánsi" (487).

29. Dasent, *Popular Tales from the Norse*, 493. Emphasis added.

30. Falnes, 215.

31. See letter to Jacob Grimm, October 12, 1849, qtd. in Dorson, foreword, vii.

32. Qtd. in Dorson, foreword, vii–viii.

33. Falnes, 224.

34. Qtd. in Falnes, 228.

35. Dasent here seems to inherit the ideological and rhetorical legacy of Anglo-Saxon racialism, linking climate, mentality, physique, behavior, and morality in his characterizations. For a discussion of national identities constructed through a racialist lens, see Stocking, 62–63.

36. This kind of impressionistic, sensual characterization of national popular tale traditions is not unique to Dasent's writing. For instance, when comparing John Francis Campbell's 1860 *Popular Tales of the West Highlands* to the work that inspired it, *Popular Tales from the Norse*, one reviewer wrote that Campbell's tales "are, as nearly as possible, the Gaelic counterparts of Dr. Dasent's Norse translations." He explains that they are

> exactly the same kinds of stories about kings' sons and daughters, younger and elder brothers, giants, fairies, enchantments, magic horses, talking beasts and birds, miraculous swords, golden apples, &c., as compose Dr. Dasent's volume; with this difference, that there the manner of thinking, the tone, the colour, the whole air and scenery are Norse, whereas here they are Gaelic. . . . The Gaelic tales want the breadth, the hearty humour, the open freshness of their Norse counterparts; in reading which we seem to be among the fair-haired Scandinavians, free and ruddy under their cold, blue skies. These are more narrow, concentrated, sly, and sombre, as of a people living in glens, and by the lips of dark deep lochs, though with woods and mountains of heather and fair green spots all round and at hand. (Qtd. in Masson, 223)

Chapter 6

1. Husain Haddawy, introduction to *The Arabian Nights* (New York: W. W. Norton, 1990), xxix.

2. Translation of the words that open Pier Paolo Pasolini's film *Il Fiore delle Mille et una Notte* (1974).

3. Letter dated May 6, 1859, qtd. in Richard M. Dorson, *The British Folklorists: A History* (Chicago: University of Chicago Press, 1968), xi–xii.

4. Carole G. Silver, *Strange and Secret Peoples: Fairies and Victorian Consciousness* (New York: Oxford University Press, 1999), 31.

5. Edward W. Lane, *An Account of the Manners and Customs of the Modern Egyptians* (1835; London: J. M. Dent, 1963), xxiv–xxv.

6. Kimberly J. Lau, "Serial Logic: Folklore and Difference in the Age of Feel-Good Multiculturalism," *Journal of American Folklore* 113 (winter 2000): 70–82.

7. Reidar Christiansen, ed., and Pat Shaw Iversen, trans., *Folktales of Norway* (London: Routledge, 1964); Brenda E. F. Beck et al., eds., *Folktales of India* (Chicago: University of Chicago Press, 1987); Royall Tyler, ed. and trans., *Japanese Tales* (New York: Pantheon, 1987); Italo Calvino, ed., and George Martin, trans., *Italian Folktales* (New York: Pantheon, 1980).

8. Robert Darnton, *The Great Cat Massacre and Other Episodes in French Cultural History* (New York: Vintage, 1984), 13.

9. Beverly J. Stoeltje and Nancy Worthington, "Multiculturalism and Oral Traditions," in John Miles Foley, ed., *Teaching Oral Traditions* (New York: Modern Language Association of America, 1998), 427.

10. Rebecca L. Thomas, *Connecting Cultures: A Guide to Multicultural Literature for Children* (New Providence, N.J.: R. R. Bowker, 1996), x.

11. Elsie B. Ziegler, *Folklore: An Annotated Bibliography and Index to Single Editions* (Westwood. Mass.: F. W. Faxon, 1973), ix.

12. Jesse Goodman and Kate Melcher, "Culture at a Distance: An Anthro-Literary Approach to Cross-Cultural Education," *Journal of Reading* 28, no. 3 (December 1984): 200.

13. Mary Hill Arbuthnot and Zena Sutherland, *Children and Books* (Glenview, Ill.: Scott, Foresman, 1972), 138, qtd. in Goodman and Melcher, 201.

14. See Darnton, 265.

15. See Goodman and Melcher, 204.

16. Regina Bendix, *In Search of Authenticity: The Formation of Folklore Studies* (Madison: University of Wisconsin Press, 1997), 48.

17. John Ruskin, introduction to *German Popular Stories* (London: Hotten, 1868), ix. Emphasis added.

18. Charlotte Yonge, "Children's Literature of the Last Century," *Macmillan's Magazine* 20 (1869): 306.

19. Bottigheimer identifies "a dynamic cultural process" in which the Grimms' work reflected and contributed to social, cultural, and historical shifts—particularly a shift in the expectations for bourgeois women. See Ruth B. Bottigheimer, "From Gold to Guilt: The Forces Which Reshaped *Grimms' Tales*," in James M. McGlathery, ed., *The Brothers Grimm and Folktale* (Urbana: University of Illinois Press, 1988), 192–204.

20. Bottigheimer, "From Gold to Guilt," 196.

21. Katharine M. Briggs, "The Influence of the Brothers Grimm in England," *Brüder Grimm Gedenken* 1 (1963): 512.

22. As demonstrated by Cristina Bacchilega in *Postmodern Fairy Tales: Gender*

and Narrative Strategies (Philadelphia: University of Pennsylvania Press, 1997), Jack Zipes in *Fairy Tales and the Art of Subversion: The Classical Genre for Children and the Process of Civilization* (New York: Methuen, 1988) and others, the fairy tale as a form can be put in service of various ideologies and agendas—from the most hegemonic to the most subversive.

23. See Charlotte Burne, "The Collection of English Folk-Lore," *Folk-Lore* 1 (1890); George Laurence Gomme, ed., *The Handbook of Folk-Lore* (Nendeln/Liechtenstein: Kraus Reprint, 1967). Richard Dorson provides a representative bibliography of English folklore collections from this period; see *The British Folklorists*, 320.

24. This evolution inspired the title of Patricia Demers and Gordon Moyles, *From Instruction to Delight: An Anthology of Children's Literature to 1850* (Toronto: Oxford University Press, 1982).

25. Roger Lancelyn Green coined the phrase in "The Golden Age of Children's Books," *Essays and Studies* n.s. 15 (1962): 59–73, and Humphrey Carpenter enlivened study of the period in *Secret Gardens: A Study of the Golden Age of Children's Literature* (Boston: Houghton Mifflin, 1985).

As we have seen, the books I have considered here have been regarded as pivotal in the history of children's literature since at least 1869 (see chapter 1). Taylor's translation of the Grimms and the collections of imported tales that followed have maintained their status in the historiography of children's literature ever since.

26. Alan Richardson has problematized and politicized nineteenth-century debates about amusement and instruction in literature for children. See "Wordsworth, Fairy Tales, and the Politics of Children's Reading," in James Holt McGavran, Jr., ed., *Romanticism and Children's Literature in Nineteenth-Century England* (Athens: University of Georgia Press, 1991), 34–53.

27. *Arabian Society in the Middle Ages*, edited by Stanley Lane-Poole, was published in 1883. Selections from Lane's translation of the *Arabian Nights* were published without any of the corresponding annotations in the Harvard Classics series in 1909.

28. This legend is diffused by the Victorian translator of the *Nights*, Richard Burton. In the notes to his text, Burton writes:

In the Biographie Universelle of Michaud we find:—Dans les deux premiers volumes de ces contes l'exorde était toujours, "Ma chère soeur, si vous ne dormez pas, faites-nous un de ces contes vous savez." Quelques jeunes gens, ennuyés de cette plate uniformité, allerent une nuit qu'il faisait très-grand froid, frapper à la porte de l'auteur, qui courut en chemise à la fenêtre. Apres l'avoir fait morfondre quelque temps par diverses questions insignificantes, ils terminerent en lui disant, "Ah, Monsieur Galland, si vous ne dormez pas, faites-nous un de ces beaux contes que vous savez si bien."

See Richard F. Burton, *The Book of a Thousand Nights and a Night* (London: Kamashastra Society, 1885–86), 10:100.

29. T. Crofton Croker, *Fairy Legends and Traditions of the South of Ireland* (London: Murray, 1825), 296.30. Francis Cohen, "Antiquities of Nursery Literature: Review of *Fairy Tales, or the Lilliputian Cabinet, Containing Twenty-four Choice Pieces of*

Fancy and Fiction, collected by Benjamin Tabart," *Quarterly Review* 21, no. 41 (January 1819): 93.

31. Jonathan Rose, "Rereading the English Common Reader: A Preface to a History of Audiences," *Journal of the History of Ideas* 53 (1992): 49.

32. Louis Althusser, "Ideology and Ideological State Apparatuses," in *Lenin and Philosophy, and Other Essays,* trans. Ben Brewster (New York: Monthly Review Press, 1971), 127–86.

33. Michel de Certeau, *The Practice of Everyday Life,* trans. S. Randall (Berkeley: University of California Press, 1984), xiii. For discussion of oppositional interpretations of dominant cultural forms, see Nicholas Abercrombie, Stephen Hill, and Bryan S. Turner, eds., *Dominant Ideologies* (London: Unwin Hyman, 1990).

Bibliography

Abercrombie, Nicholas, Stephen Hill, and Bryan S. Turner, eds. *Dominant Ideologies*. London: Unwin Hyman, 1990.

Abrahams, Roger D. "Phantoms of Romantic Nationalism in Folkloristics." *Journal of American Folklore* 106 (1993): 3–37

Adam, Ian. "Oracy and Literacy: A Post-Colonial Dilemma?" *Journal of Commonwealth Literature* 31, no. 1 (1996): 97–109.

Addy, Sidney Oldall. *Household Tales and Other Traditional Remains*. London: D. Nutt, 1895.

Ahmed, Leila. *Edward W. Lane*. London: Longman, 1978.

Alderson, Brian. "The Spoken and the Read: *German Popular Stories* and English Popular Diction." In Donald Haase, ed., *The Reception of Grimms' Fairy Tales: Responses, Reactions, Revisions*, pp. 59–77. Detroit: Wayne State University Press, 1993.

Ali, Muhsin Jassim. *Scheherazade in England: A Study of Nineteenth-Century English Criticism of the Arabian Nights*. Washington, D.C.: Three Continents Press, 1981.

Althusser, Louis. *Lenin and Philosophy, and Other Essays*. Trans. Ben Brewster. London: Monthly Review Press, 1971.

Altick, Richard D. *The English Common Reader: A Social History of the Mass Reading Public, 1800–1900*. Chicago: University of Chicago Press, 1957.

Anderson, Benedict. *Imagined Communities: On the Rise and Spread of Nationalism*. Rev. ed. London: Verso, 1991.

Armstrong, Nancy, and Leonard Tennenhouse. "A Novel Nation; or, How to Rethink Modern England as an Emergent Culture." In Marshall Brown, ed., *Eighteenth-Century Literary History: An MLQ Reader*, pp. 9–26. Durham, N.C.: Duke University Press, 1999.

Bacchilega, Cristina. *Postmodern Fairy Tales: Gender and Narrative Strategies*. Philadelphia: University of Pennsylvania Press, 1997.

Bakhtin, M. M. *The Dialogic Imagination: Four Essays*. Ed. Michael Holquist; trans. Caryl Emerson and Michael Holquist. Austin: University of Texas Press, 1981.

Bauman, Richard. "The Nationalization and Internationalization of Folklore: The Case of Schoolcraft's 'Gitshee Gauzinee.'" *Western Folklore* 52 (April 1993): 247–69.

Beck, Brenda E. F., et al., eds. *Folktales of India*. Chicago: University of Chicago Press, 1987.

Beck, Ulrich, Anthony Giddens, and Scott Lash. *Reflexive Modernization: Politics, Tradition, and Aesthetics in the Modern Social Order*. Stanford, Calif.: Stanford University Press, 1994.

Ben-Amos, Dan. "Folktale." In Richard Bauman, ed., *Folklore, Cultural Performances, and Popular Entertainments: A Communications-Centered Handbook*, pp. 101–18. New York: Oxford University Press, 1992.

Bendix, Regina. "Diverging Paths in the Scientific Search for Authenticity." *Journal of Folklore Research* 29, no. 2 (1992): 103–32.

––––––. *In Search of Authenticity: The Formation of Folklore Studies*. Madison: University of Wisconsin Press, 1997.

Berman, Antoine. *The Experience of the Foreign: Culture and Translation in Romantic Germany*. Trans. S. Heyvaert. Albany: State University of New York Press, 1992.

Bermingham, Ann. *Landscape and Ideology: The English Rustic Tradition, 1740–1860*. Berkeley: University of California Press, 1986.

Bhabha, Homi K., *The Location of Culture*. New York: Routledge, 1994.

––––––, ed. *Nation and Narration*. London: Routledge, 1990.

Blamires, David. "The Early Reception of the Grimms' *Kinder- und Hausmärchen* in England." *Bulletin of the John Rylands Library* 71, no. 3 (1989): 63–76.

Bottigheimer, Ruth B. "From Gold to Guilt: The Forces Which Reshaped *Grimms' Tales*." In James M. McGlathery, ed., *The Brothers Grimm and Folktale*, pp. 192–204. Urbana: University of Illinois Press, 1988.

––––––. "The Publishing History of Grimms' Tales: Reception at the Cash Register." In Donald Haase, ed., *The Reception of Grimms' Fairy Tales: Responses, Reactions, Revisions*, pp. 78–101. Detroit: Wayne State University Press, 1993.

––––––, ed. *Fairy Tales and Society: Illusion, Allusion, and Paradigm*. Philadelphia: University of Pennsylvania Press, 1986.

Boyarin, Jonathan, ed. *The Ethnography of Reading*. Berkeley: University of California Press, 1993.

Briggs, Asa. *A Social History of England*. New ed. London: Weidenfield and Nicolson, 1994.

Briggs, Charles. "Metadiscursive Practices and Scholarly Authority in Folkloristics." *Journal of American Folklore* 106 (1993): 387–434.

Briggs, Katharine M. "The Influence of the Brothers Grimm in England." *Brüder Grimm Gedenken* 1 (1963): 511–24.

Bronner, Simon J. *American Folklore Studies: An Intellectual History*. Lawrence: University Press of Kansas, 1986.

Bulzone, Marisa, and Stefan Matzig, eds. *Grimm's Grimmest*. San Fransisco: Chronicle Books, 1997.

Burder, Samuel. *Oriental Customs; or, An Illustration of the Sacred Scriptures*. 6th ed. 2 vols. London: Longman, 1822.

Burke, Peter. "The 'Discovery' of Popular Culture." In Raphael Samuel, ed., *People's History and Socialist Theory*, pp. 216–26. London: Routledge and Kegan Paul, 1981.

Burne, Charlotte. "The Collection of English Folklore." *Folk-Lore* 1 (1890).

Burton, Richard F. *The Book of the Thousand Nights and a Night: A Plain and Literal Translation of the Arabian Nights' Entertainments*. 10 vols. London: Kamashastra Society, 1885–86.

Calvino, Italo, ed., and George Martin, trans. *Italian Folktales*. New York: Pantheon, 1980.

Campbell, John Francis, comp. and trans. *Popular Tales of the West Highlands*. 4 vols. Edinburgh: Edmondston and Douglas, 1860.

Canny, Nicholas. "Early Modern Ireland, c. 1500–1700." In R. F. Foster, ed., *Oxford Illustrated History of Ireland*, pp. 104–60. New York: Oxford University Press, 1989.

Caracciolo, Peter L., ed. *The Arabian Nights in English Literature: Studies in the Reception of The Thousand and One Nights into British Culture*. New York: Macmillan, 1988.

de la Caridad Casas, Maria. "Orality and Literacy in a Postcolonial World." *Social Semiotics* 8, no. 1 (1998): 5–24.

Carpenter, Humphrey. *Secret Gardens: A Study of the Golden Age of Children's Literature*. Boston: Houghton Mifflin, 1985.

Certeau, Michel de. *The Practice of Everyday Life*. Trans. Steven Rendall. Berkeley: University of California Press, 1984.

Christiansen, Reidar, ed., and Pat Shaw Iversen, trans. *Folktales of Norway*. Chicago: University of Cicago Press, 1964.

Cocchiara, Giuseppe. *The History of Folklore in Europe*. Trans. John N. McDaniel. Philadelphia: ISHI, 1981.

Cohen, Francis. "Antiquities of Nursery Literature: Review of *Fairy Tales, or the Liliputian Cabinet, Containing Twenty-four Choice Pieces of Fancy and Fiction*, collected by Benjamin Tabart." *Quarterly Review* 21, no. 41 (January 1819): 91–112.

Colley, Linda. "Britishness and Otherness: An Argument." *Journal of British Studies* 31 (1992): 309–29.

———. *Britons: Forging the Nation, 1707–1837*. New Haven, Conn.: Yale University Press, 1992.

Collins, James. "Literacy and Literacies." *Annual Review of Anthropology* 24 (1995): 75–93.

Craik, George L. *The Pursuit of Knowledge under Difficulties* London: Charles Knight, 1830.

Crane, T. F. "The External History of the *Kinder- und Hausmärchen* of the Brothers Grimm." *Modern Philology* 14, no. 10 (February 1917): 129–62.

Crapanzano, Vincent. " 'Self'-Centering Narratives." In Michael Silverstein and Greg Urban, eds., *Natural Histories of Discourse*, pp. 106–27. Chicago: University of Chicago Press, 1996.

Croker, T. Crofton. *Researches in the South of Ireland*. London: John Murray, 1824.

———. *Fairy Legends and Traditions of the South of Ireland*. London: John Murray, 1825.

———. *Fairy Legends and Traditions of the South of Ireland*. 2nd ed. London: John Murray, 1826.

———. *Fairy Legends and Traditions of the South of Ireland*. Family Library 47. London: John Murray, 1834.

———. *Fairy Legends and Traditions of the South of Ireland, a New and Complete Edition*. Ed. Thomas Wright. London: William Tegg, 1862.

———. *Fairy Legends of the South of Ireland*. Ed. Neil C. Hultin and Warren U. Ober. Delmar, N.Y.: Scholars' Facsimiles and Reprints, 1983.

———. *Irish Folk Stories for Children*. Ed. Edmund Leamy. Dublin: Mercier, 1983.

———. *Fairy Legends and Traditions of the South of Ireland*. Ed. Francesca Diano. Cork: Collins Press, 1998.

Croker, T. Crofton, Esq. F.S.A., obituary of. *Gentleman's Magazine*, n.s. 42 (October 1854): 397–401.

Croker, T. F. Dillon. "Memoir of the Author." In *Fairy Legends and Traditions of the South of Ireland, a New and Complete Edition*, pp. iv–xix. London: William Tegg, 1862.

Curwen, Henry. *A History of Booksellers: The Old and the New.* London: Chatto and Windus, 1873.

Darnton, Robert. *The Great Cat Massacre and Other Episodes in French Cultural History.* New York: Vintage, 1984.

———. *The Kiss of Lamourette: Reflections in Cultural History.* New York: W. W. Norton, 1990.

Darton, F. J. Harvey. *Children's Books in England: Five Centuries of Social Life.* 3d. ed. Revised by Brian Alderson. New York: Cambridge University Press, 1982.

Dasent, Arthur Irwin. "Memoir of Sir George Webbe Dasent, D.C.L." In George Webbe Dasent, trans., *Popular Tales from the Norse*, pp. xvii–xli. Edinburgh: David Douglas, 1903.

Dasent, George Webbe. *Popular Tales from the Norse.* 2d ed. Edinburgh: Edmonston and Douglas, 1859.

———. *Tales from the Fjeld* [1874]. London: Gibbings, 1896.

———. *East o' the Sun and West o' the Moon.* New York: Dover, 1970.

———. *The Cat on the Dovrefell: A Christmas Tale.* New York: Putnam, 1979.

Dawood, N. J. *Aladdin and Other Tales from the Arabian Nights.* New York: Puffin, 1997.

———. *Sinbad the Sailor and Other Tales from the Arabian Nights.* New York: Puffin, 1997.

Dégh, Linda. "Folk Narrative." In Richard M. Dorson, ed., *Folklore and Folklife: An Introduction*, pp. 53–83. Chicago: University of Chicago Press, 1972.

Demers, Patricia, and Gordon Moyles. *From Instruction to Delight: An Anthology of Children's Literature to 1850.* Toronto: Oxford University Press, 1982.

Dick, Oliver L. *Aubrey's Brief Lives.* 2d ed. London: Secker and Warburg, 1950.

Dorson, Richard M. Foreword to Reider Christiansen, ed., and Pat Shaw Iversen, trans., *Folktales of Norway.* Chicago: University of Chicago Press, 1964.

———. *The British Folklorists: A History.* Chicago: University of Chicago Press, 1968.

———. "Fakelore." *Zeitschrift für Volkskunde* 65 (1969): 56–64.

Eisenstein, Elizabeth L. *The Printing Press as an Agent of Change.* Cambridge: Cambridge University Press, 1979.

Ellis, John M. *One Fairy Story too Many: The Brothers Grimm and Their Tales.* Chicago: University of Chicago Press, 1983.

El-Shamy, Hasan M., ed. *Folktales of Egypt.* Chicago: University of Chicago Press, 1980.

Erlmann, Veit. "The Politics and Aesthetics of Transnational Musics." *World of Music* 35, no. 2 (1993): 3–15.

Fabian, Johannes. *Time and the Other: How Anthropology Makes Its Object.* New York: Columbia University Press, 1983.

Fairy Legends and Traditions of the South of Ireland. Review. *Quarterly Review* 32 (1825): 197–211.

Falnes, Oscar J. *National Romanticism in Norway.* New York: Columbia University Press, 1933.

Fine, Elizabeth C. *The Folklore Text: From Performance to Print.* Bloomington: Indiana University Press, 1984.

Finnegan, Ruth. *Literacy and Orality: Studies in the Technology of Communication.* New York: Basil Blackwell, 1988.

Fitzpatrick, David. " 'A Peculiar Tramping People': The Irish in Britain, 1801–70." In W. E. Vaughn, ed., *A New History of Ireland*, vol. 5, pp. 623–60. Oxford: Clarendon, 1989.

Fitzsimons, Eileen. "Jacob and Wilhelm Grimm's *Irische Elfenmärchen*, a Comparison of the Translation with the English Original: *Fairy Legends and Traditions of the South of Ireland.*" Diss., University of Chicago, 1978.

Foster, R. F., ed. *Oxford Illustrated History of Ireland.* New York: Oxford University Press, 1989.

Foucault, Michel. "What Is an Author?" In Donald F. Bouchard and Sherry Simon, trans., *Language, Counter-Memory, Practice: Selected Essays and Interviews*, ed. Donald F. Bouchard, pp. 113–38. Ithaca, N.Y.: Cornell University Press, 1977.

Garofalo, Reebee. "Whose World, What Beat: The Transnational Music Industry, Identity, and Cultural Imperialism." *World of Music* 35, no. 2 (1993): 16–32.

Geertz, Clifford. *Works and Lives: The Anthropologist as Author.* Stanford: Stanford University Press, 1988.

Georges, Robert A., and Michael Owen Jones. *Folkloristics: An Introduction.* Bloomington: Indiana University Press, 1995.

Gerhardt, Mia I. *The Art of Storytelling: A Literary Study of* The Thousand and One Nights. Leiden: E. J. Brill, 1963.

Gikandi, Simon. *Maps of Englishness: Writing Identity in the Culture of Colonialism.* New York: Columbia University Press, 1996.

Giles, Fiona. " 'The Softest Disorder': Representing Cultural Indeterminacy." In Chris Tiffin and Alan Lawson, eds., *De-Scribing Empire: Post-colonialism and Textuality*, pp. 141–51. New York: Routledge, 1994.

Githaiga, Joseph Wambugu. "Intellectual Property Law and the Protection of Indigenous Folklore and Knowledge." *E Law: Murdoch University Electronic Journal of Law* 5, no. 2 (June 1998): http://www.murdoch.edu.au/elaw/issues/v5n2/githaiga52_body.html.

Glassie, Henry, ed. *Irish Folk Tales.* New York: Pantheon, 1985.

Gomme, George Laurence, ed. *The Handbook of Folk-Lore.* Nendeln/Liechtenstein: Kraus Reprint, 1967.

Goodman, Jesse, and Kate Melcher. "Culture at a Distance: An Anthro-Literary Approach to Cross-Cultural Education." *Journal of Reading* 28, no. 3 (December 1984): 200–07.

Green, Roger Lancelyn. "The Golden Age of Children's Books." *Essays and Studies* n.s. 15 (1962): 59–73.

Grimm, Jacob, and Wilhelm Grimm. *Grimms' Fairy Tales.* London: Puffin, 1994.

Grose, Francis. *A Provincial Glossary.* 2d ed. London: S. Hooper, 1790.

Hackford, Terry Reece. "Fantastic Visions: Illustration of the *Arabian Nights.*" In Roger C. Schlobin, ed., *The Aesthetics of Fantasy Literature and Art*, pp. 143–75. Notre Dame, Ind.: University of Notre Dame, 1982.

Haddawy, Husain, trans. *The Arabian Nights.* New York: W. W. Norton, 1990.

————, trans. *The Arabian Nights II: Sinbad and Other Popular Stories.* New York: W. W. Norton, 1995.

Hanford, James Holly. "Open Sesame: Notes on the *Arabian Nights* in English." *Princeton University Library Chronicle* 26, no. 1 (1964): 48–56.

Hearne, Betsy. "Booking the Brothers Grimm: Art, Adaptations, and Economics." In James M. McGlathery, ed., *The Brothers Grimm and Folktale,* pp. 220–33. Urbana: University of Illinois Press, 1991.

Hearne, Michael Patrick, ed. *The Victorian Fairy Tale Book.* New York: Pantheon, 1988.

Heath, Francis George. *The English Peasantry.* London: F. Warne, 1874.

Heath, Shirley Brice. *Ways with Words: Language, Life, and Work in Communities and Classrooms.* New York: Cambridge University Press, 1983.

Hennig, John. "The Brothers Grimm and T. C. Croker." *Modern Language Review* 41 (1946): 44–54.

Herder, Johann Gottfried. *Johann Gottfried Herder: Selected Early Works, 1764–67.* Ed. Ernest A. Menze and Karl Menges; trans. Ernest A. Menze with Michael Palma. University Park: Pennsylvania State University Press, 1992.

Herzfeld, Michael. *Ours Once More: Folklore, Ideology, and the Making of Modern Greece.* Austin: University of Texas Press, 1982.

Hobsbawm, E. J. *Nations and Nationalism since 1780: Programme, Myth, Reality.* Rev. ed. New York: Cambridge University Press, 1990.

Housman, Laurence. *Stories from the Arabian Nights.* London: Hodder and Stoughton, 1907.

Hunt, Peter. *Children's Literature: An Illustrated History.* New York: Oxford University Press, 1995.

"The Instruction of the Irish Peasantry." *Blackwood's Magazine* 15 (May 1824): 495–508.

"Ireland," *Blackwood's Magazine* 15 (March 1824): 269–95.

Irwin, Robert. *The Arabian Nights: A Companion.* New York: Penguin Books, 1994.

Iser, Wolfgang. "The Emergence of a Cross-Cultural Discourse: Thomas Carlyle's *Sartor Resartus.*" In Sanford Burdick and Wolfgang Iser, eds., *The Translatability of Cultures: Figurations of the Space Between,* pp. 245–64. Stanford, Calif.: Stanford University Press, 1996.

Iversen, Pat Shaw. *Norwegian Folk Tales.* New York: Viking, 1960.

Kabbani, Rana. *Europe's Myth of the Orient.* Bloomington: Indiana University Press, 1986.

Kamenetsky, Christa. "Folklore as a Political Tool in Nazi Germany." *Journal of American Folklore* 85 (1972): 221–35.

————. *The Brothers Grimm and Their Critics: Folktales and the Quest for Meaning.* Athens: Ohio University Press, 1992.

Kee, Robert. *Ireland: A History.* Rev. ed. London: Abacus, 1995.

Keightley, Thomas. *Tales and Popular Fictions.* London: Whittaker, 1834.

Kiernan, V. G. *The Lords of Human Kind: Black Man, Yellow Man, and White Man in an Age of Empire.* Boston: Little, Brown, 1969.

Kirshenblatt-Gimblett, Barbara. "Mistaken Dichotomies." In Robert Baron and Nicholar Spitzer, eds., *Public Folklore,* pp. 29–48. Washington, D.C.: Smithsonian Institution Press, 1992.

Knight, Charles. *Passages of a Working Life, during Half a Century with a Prelude of Early Reminiscences.* 2 vols. Shannon: Irish University Press, 1971.

Lane, Edward W. *An Account of the Manners and Customs of the Modern Egyptians.* 1835. London: J. M. Dent, 1963.

———, ed. and trans. *The Thousand and One Nights, Commonly Called in England The Arabian Nights' Entertainments.* 3 vols. London: Charles Knight, 1839–41.

———, ed. and trans. *The Arabian Nights' Entertainment; or, The Thousand and One Nights.* New York: Tudor, 1927.

Lane-Poole, Stanley. *Life of Edward William Lane.* London: Williams and Norgate, 1877.

———, ed. *Arabian Society in the Middle Ages: Studies from the Thousand and One Nights.* London: Chatto and Windus, 1883.

———, ed. *Stories from the Thousand and One Nights (The Arabian Nights' Entertainments).* Harvard Classics. New York: Collier, 1909.

Lau, Kimberly J. "Serial Logic: Folklore and Difference in the Age of Feel-Good Multiculturalism." *Journal of American Folklore* 113 (winter 2000): 70–82.

Lefevere, André, ed. and trans. *Translating Literature: The German Tradition from Luther to Rosenzweig.* Assen: Van Gorcum, 1977.

"Legends and Traditions of the South of Ireland." *Blackwood's Magazine* 18 (July 1825): 55–61.

Lowth, Robert. *Lectures on the Sacred Poetry of the Hebrews* 1787. Hildesheim: Georg Olms, 1969.

Maas, Jeremy. "Victorian Fairy Painting." In Jane Martineau, ed., *Victorian Fairy Painting,* pp. 11–21. London: Royal Academy of Arts, 1997.

MacCulloch, J. A. *The Childhood of Fiction: A Study of Folk Tales and Primitive Thought.* London: John Murray, 1905.

Malti-Douglas, Fedwa. *Woman's Body, Woman's Word: Gender and Discourse in Arabo-Islamic Writing.* Princeton: Princeton University Press, 1991.

Manheim, Ralph, ed. and trans. *Grimms' Tales for Young and Old.* New York: Doubleday, 1983.

Masson, David. "Gaelic and Norse Popular Tales: An Apology for the Celt." *Macmillan's Magazine* 3 (1861): 213–24.

McDonald, Duncan B. "A Bibliographical and Literary Study of the First Appearance of the *Arabian Nights* in Europe." *Library Quarterly* 2, no. 4 (1932): 387–420.

Michaelis-Jena, Ruth. *The Brothers Grimm.* New York: Praeger, 1970.

Mills, Margaret. "Cultural Properties, Cultural Documents, and Cultural Effects: An Ethics Discussion for ISFNR." *Fabula* 40, nos. 1–2 (1999): 1–16.

Müller, Friedrich Max. "Presidential Address to Section H." *Report of the British Association of Advanced Science* 61 (1891): 782–96.

Murphy, Christopher M., "A Brief Look at Illustrated Translations of the *Arabian Nights.*" In Kay Hardy Campbell, ed., *The 1001 Nights: Critical Essays and Annotated Bibliography,* pp. 88–100. Cambridge, Mass.: Dar Mahjar, 1985.

Naddaff, Sandra. *Arabesque: Narrative Structure and the Aesthetics of Repetition in 1001 Nights.* Evanston, Ill.: Northwestern University Press, 1991.

Niedzielska, Marie. "The Intellectual Property Aspects of Folklore Protection." *Copyright* 16 (1980): 339–46.

Olson, David R., and Nancy Torrance, eds. *Literacy and Orality*. Cambridge: Cambridge University Press, 1991.

Paredes, Américo, and Richard Bauman, eds. *Toward New Perspectives in Folklore*. Austin: University of Texas Press, 1972.

Patten, Robert. "George Cruikshank's Grimm Humor." In Joachim Möller, ed., *Imagination on a Long Rein: English Literature Illustrated*, pp. 13–18. Marburg, Germany: Jonas, 1988.

———. *George Cruikshank: Life, Times, and Art.* 2 vols. New Brunswick, N.J.: Rutgers University Press, 1992.

Pinault, David. *Story-telling Techniques in the* Arabian Nights. Leiden: E. J. Brill, 1992.

Richardson, Alan. "Wordsworth, Fairy Tales, and the Politics of Children's Reading." In James Holt McGavran, ed., *Romanticism and Children's Literature in Nineteenth-Century England*, pp. 34–53. Athens: University of Georgia Press, 1991.

Rölleke, Heinz. "The 'Utterly Hessian' Fairy Tales by 'Old Marie': The End of a Myth." In Ruth B. Bottigheimer, ed., *Fairy Tales and Society: Illusion, Allusion, and Paradigm*, pp. 287–300. Philadelphia: University of Pennsylvania Press, 1986.

———. "New Results of Research on *Grimms' Fairy Tales.*" In James M. McGlathery, ed., *The Brothers Grimm and Folktale*, pp. 101–11. Urbana: University of Illinois Press, 1991.

———, ed. *Die älteste Märchensammlung der Brüder Grimm: Synopse der handschriftlichen Urfassung von 1810 unter der Erstdrucke von 1812.* Cologne: Foundation Martin Godmer, 1975.

———, ed. *Kinder- und Hausmärchen.* Stuttgart: Reclam, 1980.

Rose, Jacqueline. *The Case of Peter Pan; or, The Impossibility of Children's Fiction.* Rev. ed. London: Macmillan, 1994.

Rose, Jonathan. "Rereading the English Common Reader: A Preface to a History of Audiences." *Journal of the History of Ideas* 53 (1992): 47–70.

Ross, Trevor. "Copyright and the Invention of Tradition." *Eighteenth-Century Studies* 26, no. 1 (fall 1992): 1–27.

Roth, Klaus. "Crossing Boundaries: The Translation and Cultural Adaptation of Folk Narratives." *Fabula* 39, nos. 3–4 (1998): 243–55.

Rowe, Karen E. "To Spin a Yarn: The Female Voice in Folklore and Fairy Tales." In Ruth B. Bottigheimer, ed., *Fairy Tales and Society: Illusion, Allusion, and Paradigm*, pp. 53–74. Philadelphia: University of Pennsylvania Press, 1986.

Ruskin, John. "Introduction." *German Popular Stories.* Rev. ed. London: Hotten, 1868.

Sahlins, Peter. *Boundaries: The Making of France and Spain in the Pyrenees.* Berkeley: University of California Press, 1989.

Said, Edward W. *Orientalism.* New York: Vintage, 1979.

Sattin, Anthony. *Lifting the Veil: British Society in Egypt, 1768–1956.* London: J. M. Dent, 1988.

Shuman, Amy, and Charles Briggs, eds. "Theorizing Folklore: Towards New Perspectives on the Politics of Culture." Special issue of *Western Folklore* 52, nos. 2–4 (1993): 109–400.

Silver, Carole G. *Strange and Secret Peoples: Fairies and Victorian Consciousness.* New York: Oxford University Press, 1999.

Simpson, Jacqueline, and Steve Roud. Introduction to *A Dictionary of English Folklore.* New York: Oxford University Press, 2000.

Smiles, Sam. "Dressed to Till: Representational Strategies in the Depiction of Rural Labor, c. 1790–1830." In Michael Rosenthal, Christina Payne, and Scott Wilcox, eds., *Prospects for the Nation: Recent Essays in British Landscape, 1750–1880,* pp. 79–96. New Haven, Conn.: Yale University Press, 1997.

Stewart, Susan. *Crimes of Writing: Problems in the Containment of Representation.* New York: Oxford University Press, 1991.

Stocking, George W., Jr. *Victorian Anthropology.* New York: Free Press, 1987.

Stoeltje, Beverly J., and Nancy Worthington. "Multiculturalism and Oral Traditions." In John Miles Foley, ed., *Teaching Oral Traditions,* pp. 423–35. New York: Modern Language Association of America, 1998.

Stone, Lawrence. "Literacy and Education in England, 1640–1900." *Past and Present* 42 (February 1969): 69–139.

Tatar, Maria. *The Hard Facts of the Grimms' Fairy Tales.* Princeton, N.J.: Princeton University Press, 1987.

Taylor, Edgar. "German Popular and Traditionary Literature." *New Monthly Magazine and Literary Journal* 2 (1821): 146–52, 329–36, 537–44, and 4 (1823): 289–96.

———. *German Popular Stories.* London: Baldwyn, 1823.

———. *German Popular Stories and Fairy Tales as told by Gammer Grethel.* London: Robins, 1839.

———. *German Popular Stories.* Rev. ed. London: Hotten, 1868.

Thomas, Rebecca L. *Connecting Cultures: A Guide to Multicultural Literature for Children.* New Providence, N.J.: R. R. Bowker, 1996.

Thompson, Stith. *The Folktale.* 1946; Berkeley: University of California Press, 1977.

Thoms, William John. *Lays and Legends of Spain.* London: George Cowie, 1834.

The Thousand and One Nights, trans. Edward W. Lane. Review. *Foreign Quarterly Review* 42 (July 1838): 254–55.

Townsend, John Rowe. *Written for Children: An Outline of English-Language Children's Literature.* 3d ed. London: Penguin, 1987.

Trimpe, Pamela White. "Victorian Fairy Book Illustration." In Jane Martineau, ed., *Victorian Fairy Painting,* pp. 55–61. London: Royal Academy of Arts, 1997.

Tyler, Royall, ed. and trans. *Japanese Tales.* New York: Pantheon, 1987.

Tylor, Edward Burnett *Anahuac; or, Mexico and the Mexicans, Ancient and Modern.* London: Longman, 1861.

Venuti, Lawrence. *The Translator's Invisibility: A History of Translation.* New York: Routledge, 1995.

Ward, Donald. "New Misconceptions about Old Folktales: The Brothers Grimm." In James M. McGlathery, ed., *The Brothers Grimm and Folktale,* pp. 91–100. Urbana: University of Illinois Press, 1991.

Warner, Marina. *From the Beast to the Blonde: On Fairy Tales and Their Tellers.* New York: Noonday Press, 1994.

Weber, Henry. *Tales of the East.* 1802. Edinburgh: James Ballantyne, 1812.

Weigle, Marta. *Spiders and Spinsters: Women and Mythology.* Albuquerque: University of New Mexico Press, 1982.

Wilson, William A. *Folklore and Nationalism in Modern Finland.* Bloomington: Indiana University Press, 1976.

Woodmansee, Martha. "On the Author Effect: Recovering Collectivity." In Martha Woodmansee and Peter Jaszi, eds., *The Construction of Authorship: Textual Appropriation in Law and Literature,* pp. 5–28. Durham, N.C.: Duke University Press, 1994.

"Works on Ireland: *Memoirs of Captain Rock;* Croker's *South of Ireland.*" *Blackwood's Magazine* 15 (May 1824): 544–58.

Yonge, Charlotte. "Children's Literature of the Last Century." *Macmillan's Magazine* 20 (1869): 229–37, 302–10, 448–56.

Ziegler, Elsie B. *Folklore: An Annotated Bibliography and Index to Single Editions.* Westwood, Mass.: F. W. Faxon, 1973.

Zipes, Jack. *The Brothers Grimm: From Enchanted Forests to the Modern World.* New York: Routledge, 1988.

———. *Fairy Tales and the Art of Subversion: The Classical Genre for Children and the Process of Civilization.* New York: Methuen, 1988.

———, ed. *Victorian Fairy Tales: The Revolt of the Fairies and Elves.* New York: Methuen, 1987.

———, ed. *Spells of Enchantment: The Wondrous Fairy Tales of Western Culture.* New York: Penguin, 1991.

———, ed. and trans. *The Complete Fairy Tales of the Brothers Grimm.* New York: Bantam, 1992.

Index

Acknowledgments

I could not have undertaken this study if I had an aversion to libraries. In fact, this project has its origins in a moment of bibliothecal serendipity, when, as a graduate student at Indiana University, I found myself drawn to a copy of Edward Lane's nineteenth-century edition of the *Arabian Nights* perched in a Lilly library display case. Decorated with illustrations of genies and gazelles, magical transformations and bustling marketplaces, and dense with ethnographic annotation, these volumes juxtaposed fantastical elements and cultural documentation in a way I found endlessly fascinating.

Among the many teachers, friends, and students who encouraged me to investigate Lane's work further and to broaden the scope of my research, I am especially grateful to Richard Bauman, Hasan El-Shamy, Henry Glassie, Fedwa Malti-Douglas, Andrew Miller, and Gregory Schrempp for their enthusiastic and unwavering support of this project. As the manuscript developed, Dick Bauman, Henry Glassie, and Andrew Miller continued to provide me with insights and suggestions that greatly enriched my perspectives on folklore, popular print culture, and the construction of national identities. Earlier versions of Chapters 3 and 4 appeared in *The Folklore Historian* (15 [1998]: 14–30) and *Journal of American Folklore* (113 [Spring 2000]: 164–84), respectively. During the processes of writing and revision, I also received invaluable commentary and criticism from Roger Abrahams, Cristina Bacchilega, Maxine Craig, Karen Duffy, Lee Haring, and Greg Kelley. I have attempted to respond to the feedback offered by each of these scholars, and believe the manuscript to be better for it. Patricia Smith, Jerome Singerman, and Erica Ginsburg of the University of Pennsylvania Press have provided guidance throughout, and Elaine Otto gave my manuscript careful attention by means of detailed copyediting. To them I offer my sincere thanks.

My research and writing were made possible by the generous institutional support I received in the form of teaching, bibliographic, and editorial assistantships from the Folklore Institute (Indiana University), a fellowship from the College of Arts and Sciences (IU), the Research Incentive Fellowship from the University Graduate School (IU), and a summer research grant from California State University, Hayward. I also want to thank former colleagues, students, and staff in the Department of English at California State University, Hayward, particularly Eileen Barrett, Elizabeth Campos, Carol Chybowski, Jacqueline Doyle, Susan Gubernat, Dabney Lyons, E. J. Murphy, Maureen Newey, Mike Rovasio, and Marilyn Silva. They contributed more than they might realize—often by asking just the right questions at the right times.

A special acknowledgment must go to the librarians who have assisted my treasure hunts over the years. I never cease to be amazed by the skill and professionalism of the reference librarians at Indiana University and the staff of the Lilly Rare Book Library. Joel Silver and Francis Lapka of the Lilly library were especially helpful during the final stages of manuscript preparation, and many of the illustrations in this book appear with the kind permission of the Lilly library. Thanks also to Kevin Montague and Michael Cavanagh of the IU Art Museum for their assistance in reproducing the images throughout this book.

Finally, I am deeply grateful to many individuals, both family and friends, for their encouragement, patience, and good cheer: Maxine Schacker, Marjorie Schacker, Don and Ivona Schacker, Andy Mill, Miriam Davidson and Marlowe Börk, Freda Love and Jake Smith, Yvonne Bayer and Peter Sakuls, my sweet and funny children, Jackson and Chloe Mill, and most especially my father, David Schacker, whose wisdom and humor have seen me through my darkest moments and to whom I dedicate this book.